W. J. Cash and the Minds of the South

and the Minds of the South

Edited by

Paul D. Escott

LOUISIANA STATE UNIVERSITY PRESS

BATON ROUGE AND LONDON

Designer: Rebecca Lloyd Lemna
Typeface: Galliard
Typesetter: G & S Typesetters, Inc.
Printer and binder: Thomson-Shore, Inc.

Library of Congress Cataloging-in-Publication Data

W. J. Cash and the minds of the South / edited by Paul D. Escott.
        p.   cm.
     Includes bibliographical references and index.
     ISBN 0-8071-1773-0 (cloth : alk. paper)
     1. Cash, W. J. (Wilbur Joseph), 1900–1941. 2. Cash, W. J. (Wilbur
Joseph), 1900–1941. The mind of the South. 3. Southern States—
Civilization. 4. Southern States—Social conditions. I. Escott,
Paul D., 1947–
E175.5.C27W4   1992
975—dc20   92-9307
                                                                CIP

The paper in this book meets the guidelines for permanence and durability of the
Committee on Production Guidelines for Book Longevity of the Council on Library
Resources. ∞

Contents

Illustrations

Acknowledgments

Walter Beeker, a Wake Forest University alumnus of the class of 1981, first proposed the symposium from which this book developed. His knowledge of southern studies and of W. J. Cash was extremely valuable during subsequent planning, and his boundless enthusiasm pushed the expectations of everyone involved to higher and higher levels. Thomas K. Hearn, Jr., President of Wake Forest University and a perennial reader of Cash, greeted Walter Beeker's idea with enthusiasm and set it on the path to realization. Without these two individuals, there would have been no symposium and no book.

Professors J. Howell Smith and David L. Smiley of the Department of History assisted the editor in the initial planning of the symposium. Others who contributed to the work of the planning committee included Jack Fleer, Claire Hammond, Alton Pollard, Bynum Shaw, Bernie Quigley, and Ashley Hairston. Two members of the Cash family, Charles Elkins, Sr., and Charles Elkins, Jr., were extremely helpful and cooperative, and Charles Elkins, Sr., donated fascinating and valuable letters, papers, and memorabilia. I am grateful to them all.

Sandra Boyette, Vice-President for Public Affairs, was invaluable at every stage of planning and preparation, and it was always a pleasure to work with her. My gratitude, respect, and affection go out to the hardworking members of her staff, including Melody Graham, Brian Eckert, Kevin Cox, Jim Steele, Helen Moses, Eleanor Brantley, Jeanne Whitman, Cherin Poovey, and Paul Orser. The staff of the Z. Smith Reynolds Library offered valuable assistance, and I especially thank the Director, Rhoda Channing; Sharon Snow, Curator of Rare Books; and John Woodard, Director of the Baptist Collection. Kelly Greene of the *Old Gold and Black* also made a significant contribution to the symposium. Thanks to them all and to faculty and staff at Wake Forest who helped in other ways.

NOTE

All references to W. J. Cash, *The Mind of the South,* are to the Vintage paperback edition (1960) and will be given in the text.

W. J. Cash and the Minds of the South

Introduction

PAUL D. ESCOTT

Throughout the Depression years of the 1930s a troubled southerner named Wilbur J. Cash struggled to complete a book about his native region. Each page, Cash admitted, was "written in blood," wrung from his soul at considerable personal cost. Cash's work was not an academic history of the South. Rather, it was a passionate interpretation and criticism of southern society by one who simultaneously loved and loathed the character of his homeland. "Ultimately the book is one man's view," Cash observed, "a sort of personal report—which must rest in large part on the authority of my imagination and understanding at play on a pattern into which I was born and which I have lived most of my life."[1]

Despite his immersion in the South's culture, W. J. Cash had developed both insight and analytical distance on his subject. "My thesis," he told his publisher, Blanche Knopf, "is that the Southern mind represents a very definite culture, or attitude towards life, a heritage, from the old South, but greatly modified and extended by conscious and unconscious efforts over the last hundred years to protect itself from the encroachments of three hostile factors: the Yankee Mind, the Modern Mind, and the Negro."[2] At its best, the South Cash described was "proud, brave, honorable by its lights, courteous, personally generous, loyal, swift to act, often too swift, but signally effective, sometimes terrible, in its action." The South also, however, had exhibited characteristic vices throughout its history. In his unflinching indictment in *The Mind of the South,* Cash arraigned the South for its "violence, intolerance, aversion and suspicion toward new ideas, an incapacity for analy-

---

1. Quoted in Bruce Clayton, *W. J. Cash: A Life* (Baton Rouge, 1991), 162, 109.
2. *Ibid.,* 93.

1

sis, an inclination to act from feeling rather than from thought, an exaggerated individualism and a too narrow concept of social responsibility, attachment to fictions and false values, above all too great attachment to racial values and a tendency to justify cruelty and injustice in the name of those values" (*Mind*, 439–40).

Not until July of 1940 did the perpetually tardy author send his final pages of manuscript to New York City. "God be praised," exclaimed the long-suffering Alfred A. Knopf. "We can hardly believe that it is really at long last completed."[3] Knopf released *The Mind of the South* on February 10, 1941, and Wilbur Cash, recently married and now published, gained satisfaction from favorable early reviews and the award of a Guggenheim fellowship to support a year of work on a novel. Soon, however, Cash's personal triumph turned to tragedy. Depressed and overwhelmed by irrational fears, Cash hanged himself in a hotel room in Mexico City on July 1, 1941.

Most of those who knew Cash probably expected his story to end there. Despite generally positive reaction to *The Mind of the South*, sales were sluggish. The book's reception was respectable, but it did not seem destined to become a best-seller. "I think the difficulty," Alfred Knopf wrote, "is that the very nature of its subject matter simply doesn't interest enough people."[4] Seldom was the astute publisher so badly mistaken. *The Mind of the South* remained in print, and its sales and influence grew until it had earned the status of a classic. Generations of scholars and students of the South have debated Cash's work, alternately praising or assailing its bold ideas and sweeping generalizations. Criticism of the book has steadily accumulated, yet its influence, even on leading scholars, has remained potent. None other than C. Vann Woodward, the dean of southern historians and Cash's foremost critic, has written that "no other book on Southern history rivals Cash's in influence among laymen and few among professional historians."[5]

Why has the influence of this book been so profound? Why is Cash's analysis of southern history and culture so intriguing to generations of citizens, students, and scholars? On the fiftieth anniversary of

3. *Ibid.*, 162.

4. *Ibid.*, 172.

5. See Bertram Wyatt-Brown, "W. J. Cash and Southern Culture," in Brown, *Yankee Saints and Southern Sinners* (Baton Rouge, 1985), 150–53; C. Vann Woodward, "The Elusive Mind of the South," in Woodward, *American Counterpoint: Slavery and Racism in the North-South Dialogue* (1971; rpr. New York, 1983), 263.

the publication of *The Mind of the South,* Wake Forest University, W. J. Cash's alma mater, hosted a symposium to address these and related questions. The large crowds—six hundred to eight hundred people at every session—testified to the continuing importance of this book and its ideas. The varied perspectives of leading scholars, whose papers are collected here, assess both Cash's insights and errors and the new issues that must be pursued in studies of the South.[6] Together these essays direct a focused shaft of brilliant light upon the dark, intriguing history of Cash's South and upon his bold interpretation of southern culture.

The essays in this volume are grouped into three parts, which examine progressively wider issues about the South. The initial focus is on origins and influences—the origins of Wilbur Cash and his book and the influences on his thought and work. The next part examines the reevaluation of *The Mind of the South* and the criticism and assessment of some of its concepts and views on southern history. Finally, what we have learned about the South in the fifty years since Cash died is brought to bear on his interpretation of the region.

In Part I, Bruce Clayton, Raymond Gavins, and Bertram Wyatt-Brown investigate the personal history and social realities that combined to produce *The Mind of the South.* Bruce Clayton first sketches the formative influences of the southern "pattern" that W. J. Cash learned and lived. After being raised amid the racism and folk culture of piedmont towns, young "Sleepy" Cash journeyed to Wake Forest College, where he experienced intellectual emancipation and saw a courageous example of the modern mind in action in the person of President William Louis Poteat. Clayton's analysis of Cash's personal history helps us understand how this troubled man gained critical detachment from his region yet retained an emotional attachment to it.

Raymond Gavins turns his attention to the social, and particularly the racial, context of Cash's world. He traces the contours of racism in North Carolina and explores the question, To what extent would W. J. Cash see beyond the racial fictions of his time and deal with the reality of black humanity? Returning to the personal history of Wilbur Cash, Bertram Wyatt-Brown probes the nature and causes of the depression that persistently assailed Cash's mental health and eventually drove him

---

6. Only one of the essays was not originally presented at the symposium held at Wake Forest University on February 8–10, 1991. The editor invited Elizabeth Jacoway to write an essay specifically for inclusion in this volume.

to suicide. Wyatt-Brown draws on medical knowledge of depression and studies of creativity to argue, imaginatively and convincingly, that there was a connection between Cash's troubled mental state and his achievement as an analyst of the South.

Part II brings the skills of four able scholars to bear on Cash's book, *The Mind of the South,* and its major concepts. Richard King, an intellectual historian, investigates Cash's attitude toward political modernity and the dark forces of Nazism and fascism. His findings illuminate both the kind of political progress that Cash believed the South needed to make and Cash's view of history's influence on southern political culture. Nell Irvin Painter employs Freudian concepts to build a critical assessment of Cash's assumptions about race and gender. Through explication of the text and interpretation of Cash's personal life, she argues that deeply flawed maps of sexuality and power misdirected W. J. Cash's exploration of southern culture.

Continuing the theme of gender, Elizabeth Jacoway focuses her attention on Cash's analysis of the white South's cult of southern womanhood. She examines the validity of Cash's concept of "gyneolatry," its possible origins in his personal history, and the contributions of women's history to a fuller understanding of the South. David Hackett Fischer compares Cash's work with another well-known portrait of the region, James McBride Dabbs's *Who Speaks for the South?* In an essay that sparkles with insight, Fischer illuminates both books by tracing the differences of generation, social class, and southern subregion that affected their authors.

In Part III scholars from four different disciplines—political science, economics, history, and religion—evaluate *The Mind of the South* from the perspective of the vastly altered South of 1991 and the advances of scholarship in the fifty years since Cash died. Merle Black lays bare the anatomy of the modern southern political system, which differs greatly from that of Cash's time. Despite change, however, Black identifies some significant continuities and portrays a southern political temperament that W. J. Cash, were he alive today, might describe with some of the same words he used fifty years ago. Cash's emphasis on "aversion and suspicion toward new ideas, an incapacity for analysis, an inclination to act from feeling rather than from thought, [and] an exaggerated individualism and a too narrow concept of social responsibility" (439) comes readily to mind in relation to Black's analysis of southerners' reactions to symbols. Gavin Wright employs the tools of modern economics to serve a dual purpose. He analyzes and evaluates W. J. Cash's ideas about the southern economy, and he uses modern economic research to explain the history of economic development in the South. The result is a significant enhancement of purely historical insights into the region.

In a stylishly written essay, Jack Temple Kirby confronts the challenge of identifying Cash's place in and influence on modern historical scholarship. Paradoxically, although the concerns of historians have moved far beyond Cash's in many ways, his concepts continue to shape many large issues that are fundamental to the contemporary debate about the history of the South. This result, Kirby suggests, might well have pleased Wilbur Cash, himself a lover of paradox. Finally, C. Eric Lincoln blends his extensive knowledge of the South with his personal history, honestly and movingly told, to describe the black "countermind" whose existence was overlooked in the white "mind of the South" described by Cash. Lincoln's essay adds a human dimension to many of the large issues discussed by earlier essays and offers a fair-minded assessment of Cash's achievements and shortcomings.

The symposium at Wake Forest University in February, 1991, included other noted scholars, journalists, and public figures, among whom were C. Vann Woodward, George B. Tindall, Dan Carter, Samuel Hill, Pete Daniel, Thadious Davis, Hodding Carter, Howell Raines, Ed Yoder, Claude Sitton, Ed Williams, Frye Gaillard, Marilyn Milloy, Michael Riley, and former governor Gerald Baliles of Virginia.[7] Also participating were six younger scholars and journalists whose work promises to deepen our understanding of the South in the future: Pamela Grundy, Terence Finnegan, Bradley Bond, Claudia Smith Brinson, Jason DeParle, and Colin Campbell. Because many lively ideas and significant issues arose in panel discussions and other events of the symposium, this volume concludes with an essay that reflects upon the significance of these additional sessions. The editor has had to select only a few ideas from many stimulating comments and opinions, but the selection emphasizes points of consensus and major themes that developed from discussion of W. J. Cash and the history of the South.

---

7. A complete list of contributors to this volume follows the concluding essay.

PART I

Cash and His World

W. J. Cash: A Mind of the South

BRUCE CLAYTON

No one, I am sure, would be more surprised than W. J. Cash to learn that anyone, let alone academics, would gather in 1991 to say happy fiftieth birthday to *The Mind of the South*. He said so many nasty things about the region, criticizing its narrowness, sentimentality, stubborn blindness to its faults, violence, and inherent racism. Before finally finishing his book in 1940, he had been an obscure, anxiety-ridden newspaperman (with the Charlotte *News*) who had earlier published a handful of pieces in H. L. Mencken's *American Mercury*. Soon after finishing his book, he married a caring, understanding woman and won a long-desired Guggenheim fellowship to go to Mexico City and write a novel—something he had dreamed about doing for years. His book was receiving flattering reviews from an impressive array of writers and academics, but sales were modest and he was troubled by listlessness and emotional fatigue. In his darkest moments, which were often and fueled by his deeply felt anxiety and rage over Nazi aggression abroad, he fretted that a year away would do nothing to improve his life. But this he would never know. Soon after his arrival in Mexico City, his intense and complex physical and emotional problems tormented him so much that he hanged himself in a lonely hotel room. He was forty-one. In death, as in much of his life, he was a tragic figure—something of a mirror image of the South he portrayed so brilliantly.[1]

It took extraordinary courage for Wilbur Joseph Cash to write *The Mind of the South*. As an unheralded Charlotte, North Carolina, news-

---

1. Between 1929 and 1935, Cash published eight pieces in the *American Mercury*. For an incisive analysis of Cash's indebtedness to and writings for Mencken, see Fred C. Hobson, Jr., *Serpent in Eden: H. L. Mencken and the South* (1974; rpr. Baton Rouge, 1978), 111–20. For a spirited overview of Cash's life see Joseph L. Morrison, *W. J. Cash, Southern Prophet: A Biography and a Reader* (New York, 1967).

paperman making do on a paltry salary, he knew that folks in his community considered him odd and that even his friends whispered that he would probably never finish the book. It was not merely *a* book. Its scope—an exploration of the southern psyche from the emergence of the Great South down to his own time—is daunting. No one has tried it since. Who would try it today? Nor did Cash content himself with patiently explaining the thought of intellectuals or groups of writers, as academics such as Perry Miller and V. L. Parrington were beginning to do in pathbreaking books.[2]

Cash, thumbing his nose at professional assumptions, audaciously sought to get at the very essence of the collective mind. More, he boldly advanced controversial ideas at every turn. He contended that the southern psyche was an intolerant folk mind, mired in an ancient pattern of racism and violence and the prisoner of religiosity and thus an irrational, implacable foe of the modern mind, the mind of science, of rationality, of critical thought. Thus did Cash, born and bred in the South and one of its loyal sons, reject—rudely but artistically—the world of his mother and father and those who were bone of his bone and flesh of his flesh. No wonder he had trouble making himself sit down and write that book. Soon after penning his final words, he cried out that he had always approached his task with "extreme depression and dislike."[3]

Born May 2, 1900, in Gaffney, South Carolina, in the heart of the piedmont mill country, Cash knew the folk culture of the South intimately. His parents were good country people, sturdy, unassuming, uncomplaining, and hardworking. Cash's father clerked in a local textile mill and watched, admiringly, as his ambitious older brother climbed the business ladder. The Cash brothers, one or two rungs above the mill hands, did not hold with unions, abhorred strikes, and embraced the owners' oft-trumpeted assertion that they had built the mills to bring jobs to needy whites—a view seconded with numbing frequency by the town fathers. In religion, the Cashes were staunch Baptists,

2. See, for example, Perry Miller, *The New England Mind* (Cambridge, Mass., 1939); and V. L. Parrington, *Main Currents in American Thought* (3 vols.; New York, 1927–30).

3. W. J. Cash to Alfred A. Knopf, July 27, 1940, copy in Joseph L. Morrison Papers, Southern Historical Collection, University of North Carolina, Chapel Hill. The originals of this letter and all of the Cash-Knopf correspondence are in the Alfred A. Knopf Papers, Harry Ransom Humanities Research Center, University of Texas at Austin.

as were the majority of their neighbors—"fundamentalists," or "foot-washin' Baptists," as Cash called them. Mama and Daddy Cash looked with alarm at Gaffney's deserved reputation as a hard-drinking, violent town. But no more than their neighbors did they question white supremacy. Gaffney was in the center of a virulently racist culture in which segregation was the unquestioned rule and racial violence, often brutal and frequently celebrated, abounded. Gaffney's whites extolled the virtues of the "old-time" Negro and issued dire warnings against the black rapist. In this they emulated the state's race-baiting political leaders, Benjamin Tillman and Coleman Blease, two of the most notorious racists in an era honeycombed with political demagogues who pandered to whites by slandering blacks. On one occasion in Gaffney, "Coley" Blease shouted to an admiring throng that "when a nigger laid his hand upon a white woman the quicker he was placed under six feet of dirt, the better."[4]

In an atmosphere in which racist slurs slipped effortlessly but cruelly from the lips of even well-meaning whites, concepts like decency and humanity could be stretched to the limit without embarrassment. In 1906, the year Cash was six years old, a large mob in a nearby county took an accused Negro rapist from jail, tied him to a tree, and riddled his body with bullets. The local newspaper noted approvingly that only the pleas of a well-known moderate politician prevented the crowd from burning the man alive and prompted a "humane man" to pull "the doomed negro's hat over his face before the crowd started shooting." Then the victim's head "was literally shot into pulp, his brains covering his hat and face." A month later, news of race riots in Atlanta, Georgia, shocked the entire nation. For four days white mobs, inflamed by the Democratic party's successful racist election campaign made worse by lurid newspaper headlines, "looted, plundered, lynched, and murdered." White officials estimated that twenty-five blacks had been killed, but Atlanta's black leaders put the number higher.[5]

Such was Cash's boyhood world. As a scrawny, bespectacled reader with squinting eyes—called "Sleepy" by his friends—he thrilled to the racist historical novels of Thomas Dixon and fantasized, as small boys

4. Gaffney (S.C.) *Ledger,* November 21, 1911. This description of Gaffney is based on reading the Gaffney *Ledger* for the years 1900–1913.

5. *Ibid.,* August 21, 1906; C. Vann Woodward, *Origins of the New South, 1877–1913* (Baton Rouge, 1951), 350; Pete Daniel, *Standing at the Crossroads: Southern Life in the Twentieth Century* (New York, 1986), 59–60.

did in those days, about saving the day at Gettysburg. Dixon, born in nearby Shelby, North Carolina, near Boiling Springs, where Cash's family moved in 1913, was a best-selling novelist and local deity whose goings and comings and pronouncements were much commented on and complimented with sonorous amens. When in 1916 Sleepy saw the epic film *Birth of a Nation,* adapted from Dixon's *Clansman,* he shouted his "fool head off" in patriotic appreciation—a reaction common to his generation of whites. A much older, more mature southerner, President Woodrow Wilson, ecstatically greeted the film as "history written with lightning."[6]

Sleepy Cash's world was immediate and specific. Reality and art, however ugly and distorted as in Dixon's powerful but now forgotten novels, reinforced each other, drilling the lurid messages of the folk culture deeply into the psyche. Years later, Cash wrote that southerners, such as himself, had a casual, accepting attitude toward a violent world. When a lynching occurred, even children knew the lyncher's identity. Impressionable lads, Cash remembered, looked upon "such a scoundrel very much as he saw himself: as a gorgeous *beau sabreur,* hardly less splendid than the most magnificent cavalry captain" (*Mind,* 126). Is this yet another example of what some have termed Cash's "extravagant" style? Listen to his contemporary Lillian Smith remember her girlhood in the Deep South: "One day, sometime during your childhood or adolescence, a Negro was lynched in your county or the one next to yours." The murderers went free and uncondemned. "And afterward, maybe weeks or months or years afterward, you sat casually in the drugstore with one of the murderers and drank the Coke he casually paid for."[7] Youngsters such as himself, Cash would one day write, were quick "to see that the man who was pointed out as having slain five or eight or thirteen Negroes (I take the figures from actual cases) still walked about free" (126), an embarrassment to some, a hero to most.

Everyone learned the catechism of the folk culture. The conven-

6. Charlotte *News,* February 9, 1936; Ralph McGill, *The South and the Southerner* (Boston, 1963), 129; John Kneebone, *Southern Liberal Journalists and the Issue of Race, 1920–1944* (Chapel Hill, 1985), 5. For this incident in Cash's life and for an analysis of his racial thought and its context, see Bruce Clayton, "The Proto-Dorian Convention: W. J. Cash and the Race Question," in *Race, Class, and Politics in Southern History: Essays in Honor of Robert F. Durden,* ed. Jeffrey J. Crow, Paul D. Escott, and Charles L. Flynn, Jr. (Baton Rouge, 1989), 260–88.

7. Lillian Smith, *Killers of the Dream* (Rev. ed.; New York, 1978), 97.

tional wisdom was endlessly embroidered in editorials, sermons, novels, political speeches, and gossip around the courthouse square. "So we learned the dance that cripples the human spirit, step by step by step," Lillian Smith wrote of race, religion, and the interconnected but taboo subject of sex, "we who were white and we who were colored, day by day, hour by hour, year by year until the movements were reflexes and made for the rest of our life without thinking." But what if one began to think? What then?[8]

"A thinker in the South," Cash would one day write in the *American Mercury*, "is regarded quite logically as an enemy of the people, who, for the commonweal, ought to be put down summarily—for to think at all, it is necessary to repudiate the whole Southern scheme of things, to go outside God's ordered drama and contrive with Satan for the overthrow of heaven." Thinking in the South "involves unpleasant realities, unsavory conditions; and happily, there is no need for it, since, as everything is arranged by God, there is nothing to think about." When Cash wrote those words in 1929, he had been thinking for a decade, formulating the ideas he would pour into *The Mind of the South*.[9]

I doubt that Sleepy Cash had any intention of becoming a thinker and thus "an enemy of the people," to repeat Henrik Ibsen's ironic phrase, when he enrolled at Wake Forest College in 1920. Cash complained to his aloof, unyielding father that Wake Forest was just another "preacher's school," another Wofford College, where he had spent an unhappy freshman year. He yearned to go to the University of North Carolina at Chapel Hill. But Wake Forest, though a small Baptist school with its share of young men preparing for the ministry, turned out to be intellectually challenging for Sleepy Cash. Gerald W. Johnson, class of 1911, and Laurence Stallings, class of 1915, writers Cash admired, remembered that a lively atmosphere of learning and ideas permeated the campus. The tone was set by President William Louis Poteat, a biologist, who had recruited dedicated teachers and whose championing of science, even the dreaded Darwin, had made him a symbol of intellectual freedom and courage—or heresy, depending on one's point of view. Spurred on by "Dr. Billy," the campus became a lively market-

8. *Ibid.*, 96.
9. W. J. Cash, "The Mind of the South," *American Mercury*, XVII (October, 1929), 191.

place of ideas. William James, Josiah Royce, and George Santayana "were all ours for the asking on some drowsy afternoon beneath a magnolia tree," remembered Stallings. "Truly," said Cash's classmate Edwin Holman, "Wake Forest was a rare phenomenon—a small Baptist college with the liberality and the integrity of a university."[10]

Sleepy took a fairly nonchalant, he might even have said southern, attitude toward his formal courses in biology, English, philosophy, law, and political economy. Several gentleman's C's, as his generation at the all-male school put it, dot his transcript, along with several 90's in science and history courses. Predictably, his marks in gym classes were consistently low—no doubt gifts from his bemused coaches. But he went out for the football team—and made it—only to turn in his helmet and pads after one day, prompting the student newspaper, the *Old Gold and Black,* to comment: "The gentleman states he is a poet by birth, a dreamer by nature, and a loafer by force of habit. He feared that the rough and tumble game and the violent contact with other members of his race would darken his bright, cheerful view of life. In this case, the poet claims that he would no longer be able to write, with beautiful simplicity, his touching verses on love, maidens and pastures green. Thus a good man was lost to the cause."[11]

Cash's intellectual emancipation began at Wake Forest. He excelled in C. Chilton Pearson's courses in American history and government and readily accepted an invitation from "Skinny" Pearson to join the exclusive Political Science Club, which discussed social issues, even the race question. Pearson was able to provoke thought in the wide-eyed youth. Though normally reserved, Cash chimed in with provocative rejoinders to Doc Pearson's contention that "the mind of Virginia" was more enlightened than the Tar Heel mind. From "Old Slick," the bald, soft-spoken, poetic professor of English, Benjamin Sledd, Cash gained renewed admiration for the classics of Western literature from Chaucer and Shakespeare to Hardy. Sledd, who judged Cash's work to merit several 85's and one 90, may have had a hand in introducing him to the writings of the Virginia fabulist James Branch Cabell and the seafaring Joseph Conrad, two vastly different writers who remained central to

10. Stallings is quoted in Sylvia Cheek, "Three Alumni Writers: Laurence Stallings," *Wake Forest Alumni Magazine,* 8, clipping in Morrison Papers; Edwin Holman to Joseph L. Morrison, September 20, 1965.

11. "Round About Town," *Old Gold and Black,* October 1, 1920.

Cash's intellectual and literary consciousness.[12] Cash's stories in the student literary magazine show the unmistakable influence of Conrad (and Edgar Allan Poe), and by the time Cash left school he was dreaming of writing a novel in the manner of Conrad. Cash read Theodore Dreiser and Fyodor Dostoyevski, gained a smattering of Karl Marx and Sigmund Freud, and became an unabashed disciple of H. L. Mencken, whose robust, iconoclastic style left a lasting impression on him. He had not been on campus long before he was having fun lobbing Menckenian barbs at the "skys," the Baptist preachers in the making, or expounding under a shady magnolia tree. "Wake Forest was a lush, green pasture for him because of the stimulating, liberal atmosphere—ready and waiting to be inhaled by the students," one of his classmates recalled. "And nobody gulped more abundantly than 'Sleepy' Cash."[13]

Sleepy learned a great deal at Wake Forest, probably more from his classes than he let on or his marks indicated. It was not so much what his teachers said as how they said it. They were rational, idealistic, moral. They were unpretentious embodiments of Ralph Waldo Emerson's American Scholar as "man thinking." They looked critically at things, but not with anger or denunciation. They embodied the Victorian notion that thinking was an ethical act. "If we turn out an occasional scholar, that will do no harm," said Old Slick, sounding the spirit of the school, "but the real business of this place is to turn out men. If we fail in that, an army of Doctors of Philosophy will not save us." One has the feeling that Skinny Pearson, Old Slick, and others had the wisdom to know that sometimes the best thing a good teacher can do for a bright, creative student is to get out of the way.[14]

At the center of Cash's world, and indeed of that of several generations of Wake Forest students, was the inspiring William Louis Poteat, a Wake Forest graduate, a gifted teacher of biology, and, after 1905, the college's tireless president. Dr. Billy was a native North Carolinian, a pious Baptist, a man of good cheer, a genuine leader, and an educator who happily reconciled Darwin and the Bible and had an open mind

12. Transcript of W. J. Cash, Wake Forest University, Winston-Salem, North Carolina.
13. Edwin Holman to Joseph L. Morrison, September 20, 1965, in Morrison Papers.
14. Gerald W. Johnson, "Old Slick," *Virginia Quarterly Review*, XXIV (1950), 206–207.

toward religion. As a tireless champion of social causes he combined
disparate elements of social conservatism and liberalism, supporting the
Anti-Saloon League and the Mental Hygiene Society, the latter an organization with a decidedly conservative Social Darwinist bent. He was
a founder of the Commission on Interracial Cooperation, a fact-finding
group of concerned editors and professors—Professor Pearson was a
member—that met for calm discussion and periodically issued calls for
humane treatment of blacks and an end to lynchings and racial violence.
Though Poteat was considered liberal at the time, today's judgment
would be that he was a paternalist who readily accepted segregation
and white supremacy but championed a benign application of white
rule. Thus, as at Wake Forest, the Poteats of the day warned against the
"extremists," the Coley Bleases on one hand and black leaders like
W. E. B. Du Bois on the other. The assumption that the race problem
was "out there" in the inflammable white masses and in black "trouble-
makers" was of a piece with their belief that improved schools and
public facilities such as parks and hospitals (mainly for whites) and
continued industrial growth guaranteed progress, however gradually
achieved.[15]

Poteat, a short, slightly portly man with a ready smile, courtly
nature, and customary red necktie, made an immediate impression
on every freshman who matriculated at Wake Forest, Cash included.
Dr. Billy was a wonderful model for Sleepy and other young men flee-
ing racist cultures and narrow religious households. Poteat's racial
stand, if paternalistic by today's standards, showed bravery and an attempt to break free from the racist past. His advocacy of Darwinism
reflected an engaging open-mindedness, and his piety combined with
his effervescent personality and charity toward his harshest enemies
made him an irresistible example of adulthood. Science opened his
mind to the reality of change; religion propelled him to work constantly for purposeful change. His well-known regard for religion and
old-fashioned values did not make him immune to criticism from
within the South, but southern traditions, intertwined with his personal piety, instilled in him a spirited love of his region. Intimates and

15. For a good portrayal of Poteat and reform see Suzanne Cameron Linder, *William Louis Poteat: Prophet of Progress* (Chapel Hill, 1966), 87–103. For a critical discussion of New South liberalism see Bruce Clayton, *The Savage Ideal: Intolerance and Intellectual Leadership in the South* (Baltimore, 1972).

admirers sensed immediately that Poteat respected the opinions of his neighbors even as he sought to change them. To a young man like Sleepy, who was in the process of throwing over his family's fundamentalism while quietly maintaining a lingering respect for disciplined religious feelings, Poteat was the very model of what a southerner should be. Dr. Billy was a reassuring figure for Sleepy Cash, who never felt close to his own taciturn, well-intentioned, but unprepossessing father.[16]

Poteat's influence on Cash was immediate, deep, and lasting. In the *Old Gold and Black*, which Cash edited in his senior year, he thwacked the fundamentalists who were denouncing Poteat for his stand on evolution. Cash vigorously lauded Poteat's work with the Commission on Interracial Cooperation and repeated the major points of New South liberalism. Poteat had a "true solution" to the race problem, said Cash. In the manner of his elders, Cash warned blacks not to listen to radicals like Du Bois, "whose policy is to wage bitter and aggressive war against the White race and their principles." (One wonders how many black readers editor Cash thought the student newspaper had at the all-white school.) Cash was so taken with Poteat's brand of paternalism that he repeated the familiar "we-know-the-Negro-best" litany—a self-congratulatory attitude he would outgrow and reject—and voiced the common liberal theme that Negroes would be given the vote "in time" when they were capable of using it intelligently. Meanwhile, blacks should remember that whites do not "intend for political equality to pave the way for social equality."[17]

In time, of course, Cash would reject this view categorically and denounce racism caustically both in his newspaper columns in the 1930s and on page after page of *The Mind of the South*. But however much he dismissed the creed of the New South liberal as shallow, class-bound, and blind to the inherent racism of the "better sort," the very class Poteat looked to for leadership, Cash never once publicly linked Poteat to that creed. To the end, Cash spoke approvingly of Poteat and

16. Linder, *Poteat*, 92, 100–101; Gerald W. Johnson, "Billy with the Red Necktie," reprinted in *South-Watching: Selected Essays by Gerald W. Johnson*, ed. with intro. by Fred Hobson (Chapel Hill, 1983), 191–99; Bruce Clayton, *W. J. Cash: A Life* (Baton Rouge, 1991), 27–28, 33–36.

17. [W. J. Cash], "Intolerance," *Old Gold and Black*, April 21, 1922; "The Negro Question," *ibid.*, February 3, 1922.

the Commission on Interracial Cooperation's work, particularly its efforts to stop lynchings. To Cash, Dr. Billy symbolized decency, liberality of spirit, and an open mind.

During the 1920s, as Cash fought off depression and worked in-
termittently as a journalist and would-be novelist, he watched Poteat
approvingly. Poteat's continued championing of free speech and battles
with antievolutionists who were seeking to throttle free inquiry in the
public schools elicited Cash's praise. He applauded as Poteat stood reso-
lutely but with customary good cheer against vicious critics in several
states and those in North Carolina, who in 1925 would enact legislation outlawing the teaching of evolution in the public schools. Thanks
in part to Poteat—one of those whom all "men of native good sense
and decency everywhere felt themselves bound to respect," said Cash in
The Mind of the South—North Carolina defeated the fundamentalists
and never went the way of Tennessee, home of the infamous "Monkey
Trial" in 1925. The trial of John T. Scopes, a high school biology
teacher, with William Jennings Bryan as chief witness for the prosecu-
tion, made the state the laughingstock of much of the civilized world
and deeply chagrined Cash (349).

Cash was pleased that Dr. Billy's retirement from Wake Forest in
1927 did not end his work for public enlightenment. During the heated
presidential election in 1928 that pitted Herbert Hoover, Republican,
Protestant, prohibitionist, and hero of the American heartland, against
Al Smith, Democrat, Catholic, wet, New Yorker, and son of an immi-
grant, Poteat remained a beacon of light in Cash's eyes by speaking out
against religious intolerance. That fall, Cash edited a short-lived country newspaper in his native Cleveland County and watched with horror
as his state relapsed into scurrilous nativism and anti-Catholic propaganda. His sharply worded editorials denounced those who interjected
religious bigotry into the campaign against Smith. Preachers and other
well-known clerics, led by Virginia's indefatigable Bishop James Cannon, were seeking to destroy the long-standing constitutional principle
of separation of church and state, Cash charged. But standing against
the political parsons, he noted admiringly, was Dr. Poteat. One of
Poteat's well-publicized speeches against mixing religion and politics
prompted Cash to quote him at length and to rhapsodize that "Dr.
Poteat has an almost uncanny way of being right. And I believe no man
in America better understands more clearly what Jesus, the most mis-

understood figure of all times, teaches."[18] (Interestingly, Cash passed over in silence Poteat's well-known work for Prohibition.)

In years to come, when Cash wrote for Mencken's *American Mercury* and later the Charlotte *News,* Poteat and a handful of people he called the "civilizing influence" were often in his thoughts. Writing for Mencken in 1929 in a prophetic and preliminary article he called "The Mind of the South," Cash assessed the region's intellectual successes and failures. He castigated screeds of New South liberalism such as Edwin Mims's ballyhooed book *The Advancing South* (1926), but he lauded James Branch Cabell, DuBose Heyward, and Julia Peterkin for trying to break free of the region's intense sentimentality. He praised the work of Howard W. Odum and the regionalists at the University of North Carolina. And, of course, Cash had high marks for "Poteat's teaching of evolution," which he had done, Cash said in his best Menckenian voice, "in face of the stake to young Baptists at Wake Forest College for the past thirty years." Even so, young Cash—twentynine in 1929—was far from sanguine and was in no danger of becoming, as he would one day describe Mims, one of the "professional glad boys." Cash concluded sadly and wearily that Poteat and the leading lights of the "civilizing influence" were "of that level of intelligence which is above and outside any group mind. They are isolated phenomena, thrown up, not because of conditions in the South, but in spite of them."[19]

Poteat and all that he and the civilizing influence represented remained fixed in Cash's thinking as he wrote the final sections of *The Mind of the South.* There, Cash once again lauded Poteat for fighting the fundamentalists and the Ku Klux Klan and their allies in the battle over the schools. Who, Cash asked rhetorically, courageously defended the civil liberties of the despised strikers during the anticommunist hysteria at the Gastonia textile strike of 1929? Poteat. Who, he went on, called for punishment of those who instigated violence against the maligned strikers? Poteat, said Cash, and only a handful of others. But to Cash, Poteat's greatness consisted of more than individual acts of courage. *The Mind of the South* practically credits Poteat's teaching of biol-

18. *Cleveland Press* (Shelby, N.C.), October 23, 1928. For a fuller discussion of Cash's brief editorial career and response to the election of 1928, see Clayton, *Cash,* 61–78.

19. Cash, "Mind of the South," 191–92.

ogy and his courageous stand against his critics with causing the spread
of evolution and modern science throughout the better schools of the
South (328–29, 349, 363).

To the still-awed Wake Forest graduate, Poteat's struggles and tri-
umphs represented far more than the victory of a theory, however well
grounded or controversial. To Cash, Poteat was a representative of the
"modern mind," by which Cash meant Darwinism and an intellectual
openness to Freud—who was indispensable for Cash's understanding
of the mind of the South—and a host of modernists from Marx and
Nietzsche to Oswald Spengler, John Dewey, Franz Boas, and Mencken.
To Cash, the modern mind was less a systematic philosophy than a
cosmopolitan perspective. It was critical of tradition, of dogma, of sentimentality, of prejudice, of the totems and taboos of the tribal mind.
The modern mind, said Cash in *The Mind of the South,* had found expression in the new history, in the new sociology as practiced by Odum
and his disciples, and in the new biology—Poteat's "biology without
equivocation." The modern mind exalted tolerance and "free inquiry."
In short, it was everything the "savage ideal," Cash's phrase for the
violent intolerance of the folk culture, was not (329, 330, 343, 350,
92–94, 137).[20]

Thanks in part to educators like Poteat, the modern mind was
within the gates, creeping stealthily into the southern mind. Young students were "returning home from school," said Cash, "to say that they
thought Mr. Darwin was right; echoing fearful ideas from that man
Freud, who sounded as though he were in the pay of the Kremlin;
quoting Henry Mencken and George Jean Nathan, and mocking the
ministers" (335). At one point in his great book, Cash was inclined to
believe that the modern mind, particularly that part Poteat symbolized
in his acceptance of Darwinism, had even penetrated the folk mind.
What he perceived (wrongly, probably) as the waning of fundamentalism and the mentality behind the Ku Klux Klan pointed in some small
way, he thought, to the "beginning of the subtle decay of the old rigid
standards and values, the ancient pattern" (350). None of this was theoretical to Cash. He was every inch a striving modern mind himself—as

---

20. For an analysis of Cash's modernism, see Bruce Clayton, "A Southern Modernist: The Mind of W. J. Cash," in *The South Is Another Land: Essays in the Twentieth-Century
South,* ed. Bruce Clayton and John A. Salmond (Westport, Conn., 1987), 171–86.

every page of his book makes clear. The modern mind was his mind, after all, the mind he had started to acquire at Wake Forest.

But, like Cash's life (and unlike Poteat's), the story does not have a happy ending. After musing on the possibility of the triumph of Poteat and his kind, second thoughts assailed Cash when he finished his book. The South had intellectual leadership "in its schoolmen, its literary men, its more enlightened editors." By 1940 the South had "the best intellectual leadership it had ever had." But that leadership "was almost wholly unarticulated with the body of the South." That the folk culture was affected by the new intellectual leadership "only remotely and sporadically" was, Cash lamented, "the final great tragedy of the South as it stood in 1940" (429).

Cash's famous, oft-quoted, penultimate paragraph reads: "Proud, brave, honorable by its lights, courteous, personally generous, loyal, swift to act, often too swift, but signally effective, sometimes terrible, in its actions—such was the South at its best. And such at its best it remains today, despite the great falling away in some of its virtues." But over and against those virtues stood the ancient enemies, still triumphant: "Violence, intolerance, aversion and suspicion toward new ideas, an incapacity for analysis, an inclination to act from feeling rather than from thought, an exaggerated individualism and a too narrow concept of social responsibility, attachment to fictions and false values, above all too great attachment to racial values and a tendency to justify cruelty and injustice in the name of those values, sentimentality and a lack of realism—these have been its characteristic vices in the past. And, despite changes for the better, they remain its characteristic vices today" (439–40).

Nothing had changed. Southerners, white and black, were still trapped in their history: that was the tragedy of the South. Cash was certainly not, as one distinguished historian said of him, someone who "betrays a want of feeling for the seriousness of human strivings, for the tragic theme in history." Just the opposite. To be trapped in history is to be imprisoned, unfree. But no southerner would ever admit that or even hint at it. The first and great commandment of the white South was to act as though everything was perfectly normal—and therefore right and good. Cash said none of this in happiness; his message was one of sorrow. His was no dispassionate, "objective" mind, eager to stand calmly outside the mind he felt obliged, even obsessed, to probe.

He could not coolly and with academic objectivity document how people's lives had been made wretched by race or class, perhaps snatched from them by the lyncher's rope or a diet of fatback. Neither his psyche, irrevocably shaped by both the folk culture and Wake Forest, nor his subject allowed such detachment. Nor, for all his admiration for Poteat, did his psyche and tragic vision allow him to look confidently to a happier tomorrow. In concluding that southern history was unbroken and dominated by a self-imposed savage ideal that was unyielding and stultifying, Cash was swimming in the very river of tragedy that flows quietly but relentlessly through the works of William Faulkner, Robert Penn Warren, even Thomas Wolfe. To know that southerners were enmeshed in history, the folk culture of his parents' world; to know that there was a liberating modern mind there for the taking; and to be obsessed with pointing out the gulf between the two—such was Cash's "burden of southern history." To bear such a burden took courage.[21]

Was there no hope for the future? Cash did not know. He doubted it. "But of the future," Cash writes in the last words of his great book, "I shall venture no definite prophecies. It would be a brave man who would venture them in any case. It would be a madman who would venture them in face of the forces sweeping over the world in the fateful year of 1940" (440).

21. C. Vann Woodward, "The Elusive Mind of the South," in Woodward, *American Counterpoint: Slavery and Racism in the North-South Dialogue* (New York, 1971), 280.

Behind a Veil: Black North Carolinians in the Age of Jim Crow

RAYMOND GAVINS

W. E. B. Du Bois, in *The Souls of Black Folk,* gives us the image of a veil, which characterizes the biracialism of W. J. Cash's world. Du Bois uses it as a metaphor for white-black segregation, for separate and unequal racial worlds, for a dialectic of domination and aspiration (*Mind,* 327).[1] It evokes the ever-present tension between the dominion of Jim Crow and the strivings of African-Americans. So absolute was the southern caste system before the 1950s that most whites could neither imagine nor discern the evolving black struggle for freedom. The modernist writer Cash was more discerning. If betraying a stereotype, he commented: "Behind that grinning face a veil was drawn which no white man might certainly know he had penetrated. What was back there, hidden? What whispering, stealthy, fateful thing might they be framing out there in the palpitant darkness?" (327). His subtle criticism of racism and his sense of blacks' growing protest in *The Mind of the South* are noteworthy for his time. My purpose in this essay is to describe the evolution of Jim Crow in Cash's adopted state and the black response, stressing politics, as a context for the comment quoted above.

Contradicting their reputation for liberalism and fairness in race relations, white North Carolinians strictly segregated blacks and periodically terrorized them. In 1943, when the former mayor of a Tar Heel town said, "Our attitude is that the white man is superior and the col-

---

1. See W. E. Burghardt Du Bois, *The Souls of Black Folk* (1903; rpr. New York, 1961), 16–17.

ored are looked on as servants," he described the ever-present oppression.[2] Social custom and the law were entwined and inseparable; the legacy of slavery influenced white attitudes and practices well into the twentieth century.

During slavery North Carolina had comparatively few laws mandating racial separation. Antebellum slave codes forbade intermarriage and common jails, and several acts passed between 1795 and 1839 reinforced these taboos. Since the inferior status of blacks was defined by involuntary servitude, most measures proscribing them related to labor and punishment. In towns such as Fayetteville and Wilmington, whose populations were over one-third black by 1860 and interracial contacts were extensive, town ordinances guarded less against commingling than the possibility of revolt. Even the battery of restrictions on free blacks, who lived mostly in rural districts, emphasized surveillance against insurrection. Authorities seemed to worry more about sedition than the physical proximity of blacks.[3]

Emancipation deprived slaveholders of human property and galvanized attempts to ensure their control. Former masters wanted to maintain power and privilege, segregate blacks, and exploit them as laborers. Coincidentally, former slaves viewed separatism as a tactical route to autonomy and independence. Despite the presence of northern missionaries, Republicans, and federal troops, the planter class soon reasserted its dominance. North Carolina's reputedly radical constitution of 1868 abolished slavery and legitimated black and mixed-race children born before its adoption. But it explicitly stated that "the children of the white race and the children of the colored race shall be taught in separate public schools." It also mandated a segregated militia.[4]

Continuing this trend, an act of 1874 decreed that a white child

2. Quoted in Charles S. Johnson, *Patterns of Negro Segregation* (New York, 1943), 195.

3. See James Howard Brewer, "Legislation Designed to Control Slavery in Wilmington and Fayetteville," *North Carolina Historical Review*, XXX (1953), 162–64; Ernest James Clark, Jr., "Aspects of the North Carolina Slave Code, 1715–1860," *ibid.*, XXXIX (1962), 148, 162–64; John Hope Franklin, *The Free Negro in North Carolina, 1790–1860* (1943; rpr. New York, 1971), 101–20; *The General Statutes of North Carolina of 1943* (4 vols.; Charlottesville, Va., 1943), II, 60; and Pauli Murray, ed., *States' Laws on Race and Color* (Cincinnati, 1951), 342–43.

4. *General Statutes of 1943*, II, 60; Murray, ed., *States' Laws*, 329, 343.

could not be apprenticed to a black person. Democrats mustered enough votes in 1875 to amend the state constitution, which reiterated school segregation and banned "all marriages between a white person and a Negro, or between a white person and a person of Negro descent to the third generation." Facilities for the mentally and physically handicapped were separated. Among the separatist bills the legislature enacted after Reconstruction was one to establish all-black agricultural, mechanical, and normal colleges. Other laws stipulated imprisonment for violators of the marital code and made Indians a third racial category.[5] Meanwhile, black and white steamboat and train passengers were separating without a statute.

Political conflict intensified the process of legalizing segregation. In 1892 Democrats proposed a law to segregate public transportation, but Populists and Republicans, hoping to woo black votes, blocked the measure. Bolstering the antisegregationists, President Joseph C. Price of Livingstone College led a delegation of black leaders before the legislature to deplore the proposal. "Jim Crow cars are products of those minds that fear the Negro's power to cope with his white brother," testified Professor John O. Crosby of Greensboro. "The heel of oppression lies heaviest upon the Negro that tries to be a man."[6]

Crosby's words were prophetic. Rampant oppression proved to be a major obstacle to black citizenship. For a while in the mid-1890s, by winning both legislative houses and the governorship, the Populist-Republican, or fusion, coalition contained the Democrats. But the tocsin of racism filled the air more than ever. "Before we allow the negroes to control this State as they do now," a Democratic congressman warned, "we will kill enough of them that there will not be enough left to bury them."[7]

It was just such an attack that led the Democrats to power and filled the statute books with Jim Crow. Backed by armed Ku Klux Klansmen and Red Shirts in 1898, the year of the bloody Wilmington riot,

---

5. *General Statutes of 1943,* I, 55, 67, III, 303, 305; Murray, ed., *States' Laws,* 329, 331–32, 338, 340, 342–43.

6. Quoted in Elwynn Webster Midgette, "Negro Baptists in North Carolina, 1865–1900" (M.A. thesis, North Carolina College, 1949), 89–90.

7. Quoted in Jeffrey J. Crow, "Maverick Republican in the Old North State: The Governorship of Daniel L. Russell, 1897–1901" (Ph.D. dissertation, Duke University, 1974), 201.

Democrats reclaimed control of the state. To keep future white chal-
lengers from exploiting the black vote, they devised a suffrage amendment with a literacy test that required the ability to read or understand
the state constitution, provided for a poll tax, and adopted a grandfather clause that protected illiterate white male voters whose ancestors
had voted prior to January, 1867.[8] After more than a generation of
voting, almost by a single blow in 1900 the black man had lost his
ballot.

Completing the process, legislators passed an omnibus segregation
package at the turn of the century. At least two acts outlawed racially
mixed fraternal orders and mental hospitals; five empowered the utili-
ties commission to "provide separate but equal accommodations for the
white and colored races at passenger stations or waiting-rooms, and
also on all trains and steamboats."[9] Clearly, custom had become law.

Statutory discrimination was the order of the day. When the voters
approved the suffrage restriction amendment, black communities began
to talk about leaving the state. Black educator Simon G. Atkins of
Winston-Salem thought it "unwise for the colored people to contemplate leaving the state in large numbers because of the result of the
(August) election . . . now is the time for the Negro to show his faith
in God and humanity." Atkins insisted that the "fear of mob violence
and uncontrolled outlawry" would pass. "I do not believe that the white
people of North Carolina have repudiated the spirit of Christ . . . I do
not believe that race hate can thrive in any considerable part of the
state's soil."[10]

Yet civic doors closed and prejudice against blacks spread across the
state. In 1910, for example, the county surveys of a white judge from
Pendleton disclosed flagrant injustices with no hint of regret. One registrar from a majority-black county wrote: "I will say that Negroes do
not serve on the jury in this county and have not since we, the white
people, got the government in our hands. When the Republican party

8. See Helen G. Edmonds, *The Negro and Fusion Politics in North Carolina,
1894–1901* (Chapel Hill, 1951), 179; and William Alexander Mabry, *The Negro in North
Carolina Politics Since Reconstruction* (Durham, 1940), 73–75.

9. *General Statutes of 1943*, II, 563, 634, 649, III, 351; Murray, ed., *States' Laws*,
339, 344–45.

10. S. G. Atkins, "The Situation in North Carolina," *Southern Workman*, XXX
(1901), 197, 199.

was in power Negroes were drawn." Another registrar asserted, "Negroes do not serve on juries in our County, nor are they allowed to vote or take part in county or municipal affairs."[11]

By 1910 the general assembly had drawn a color line across both the private and public domains. It authorized the state board of education to operate all-black school districts and the state librarian "to fit up and maintain a separate place for the use of the colored people who may come to the library." It incorporated a hospital to treat "persons of the colored race." It established benefits for "fire companies composed exclusively of colored men" and voided "contracts and agreements" of ten dollars or more with Indians. The assembly declared that "a person of negro descent to the third generation, inclusive," was to be considered black. Any officer who failed to confine black and white prisoners separately "shall be guilty of a misdemeanor," a prison statute declared. Other statutes similarly charged agents and conductors of streetcars and trains.[12]

Segregation had become what C. Vann Woodward terms the "invariable rule." Separate schools and a college were opened in 1911 "for the purpose of the education of the Cherokee Indians," extending tri-racial segregation. Yet Winston-Salem's 1912 residential segregation ordinance, a pacesetter in the urban South, demonstrated that the black-white or biracial structure was of greatest concern.[13] This was certainly true for Clarence Poe, editor of the Raleigh-based *Progressive Farmer,* who in 1913 warned that rural communities "are becoming blacker instead of whiter." He lobbied to segregate land in the country districts. A bill to that end was approved by a legislative committee and endorsed by the State Farmers' Union, but legislators eventually re-

11. Gilbert Thomas Stephenson, *Race Distinctions in American Law* (New York, 1910), 265–66.

12. *General Statutes of 1943,* II, 634, III, 305–20, 356; *Laws and Resolutions of the State of North Carolina . . . Adjourned Session of 1900* (Raleigh, 1900), 58–60; Murray, ed., *States' Laws,* 331, 339, 341–44, 347–48; *Private Laws of the State of North Carolina . . . Session of 1901* (Raleigh, 1901), 368–69, 565; *Public Laws and Resolutions of the State of North Carolina . . . Session of 1901* (Raleigh, 1901), 804; Stephenson, *Race Distinctions,* 147; Archer Rudder Turner, "The Development of Statutory Racial Segregation in North Carolina Since 1890" (B.D. thesis, Duke University Divinity School, 1945), 45, 60.

13. Johnson, *Patterns of Negro Segregation,* 174; Murray, ed., *States' Laws,* 341; C. Vann Woodward, *American Counterpoint: Slavery and Racism in the North-South Dialogue* (Boston, 1971), 237.

jected it. Perhaps they accepted the argument that "the segregation of the races in the country would . . . cause still more of the negroes . . . to move to the city."[14]

Though it discarded Poe's proposal, the assembly added a host of other restrictions. Accommodations for Indians only were allotted in jails, homes for the aged, and "Hospitals for the Insane." Black normal schools were permitted to provide the minimum feasible "academical and classical instruction." Toilets had to be "lettered and marked in a distinct manner, so as to furnish separate facilities for white males, white females, colored males and colored females." Benevolent societies must retain exclusive memberships, and black-Indian or white-Indian marriages would be "declared void." Indeed, by the eve of World War I, little remained for the legislators to address except reenactments on the militia and prisons. The state denied the "organization of colored troops . . . where white troops are available, and while permitted to be organized, colored troops shall be under the command of white officers." A breach of the code on convicts meant a fine or jail sentence.[15]

Discriminatory laws continued to pile up, supporting Woodward's view that "they were constantly pushing the Negro further down."[16] Black migration to cities, job competition between the races, and unequal public services tended to elaborate and extend segregation. One-party rule justified Jim Crow politics, and vice versa, as the most successful candidates preached white supremacy.

A random sample of statutes passed in North Carolina from 1917 to 1945 reveals the kaleidoscopic nature of Jim Crow. Of sixty-one laws, three concern black aliens, such as a 1940 measure denying "persons of African nativity or descent" the right to become naturalized citizens. Education is the subject of nineteen, including a 1935 stipulation that "books shall not be interchangeable between the white and colored schools, but shall . . . be used by the race first using them."

14. See Raleigh *Progressive Farmer*, March 15, June 7, 14, 1913; Gilbert T. Stephenson, "The Segregation of the White and Negro Races in Rural Communities of North Carolina," *South Atlantic Quarterly*, XIII (1914), 114; and Clarence Poe, "Rural Land Segregation Between Whites and Negroes: A Reply to Mr. Stephenson," *ibid.*, 207, 208, 210.

15. *General Statutes of 1943*, II, 339, 882, III, 303–305; Murray, ed., *States' Laws*, 332, 339, 340–44; Turner, "Statutory Racial Segregation," 45, 63.

16. C. Vann Woodward, *The Strange Career of Jim Crow* (3rd rev. ed.; New York, 1974), 108.

Three regulations expand separate schooling for Indians; an equal number segregate companies "doing the business of insurance." A single act prescribing punishment for violating the provision of separate toilets applies to all categories of labor. Seventeen codes cover special institutions, including the segregation of "deaf-mutes and blind children," and fifteen reinforce segregated transportation. Not until 1947 did the legislature pass a Jim Crow cemetery law.[17]

The permission to segregate granted by the state produced a wide range of local variants. Some cities copied Winston-Salem's housing plan, which prohibited persons of one race from living where most of the residences were occupied by the opposite race. Over time concentrations of blacks—across a railroad track or similar fixed barrier—marked the urban landscape. Black ghettos took shape, with their by-products of crime, disease, joblessness, and poverty. Cash's biographer Bruce Clayton writes of his investigations and exposure of such conditions in the late 1930s as a muckraking journalist for the Charlotte *News*.[18]

City councils and county commissions multiplied the number of Jim Crow ordinances relating to public accommodations and places of assembly. Lest there be trespassing, "White Only" and "Colored" signs guarded entrances and exits. Banks and railroad, textile, tobacco, and utility companies not only segregated the workplace but confined blacks to labor-intensive and low-wage jobs.[19]

According to a survey of the South, tobacco plants in Durham, Reidsville, and Winston-Salem assigned "Negro and white workers to separate parts of buildings, or to different workrooms even when performing the same tasks, or to separate sides of the same room, or even to separate rows in the same room." Drugstores in rural Johnston

17. *General Statutes of 1943*, II, 634, 649, 662; 1949 Cum. Supp. to II, 230; III, 223, 227, 238, 303–305, 311; 1949 Cum. Supp. to III, 167; IV, 34; Murray, ed., *States' Laws*, 329–33, 338–48.

18. See Johnson, *Patterns of Negro Segregation*, 9–10; Richard Kluger, *Simple Justice* (New York, 1977), 88; Thomas Jackson Woofter, Jr., *Negro Problems in the Cities* (Garden City, N.Y., 1928), 67, 79; Donald W. Wyatt, "Negro Youth in Greensboro, North Carolina," in *Thus Be Their Destiny*, ed. J. Howell Atwood, Donald W. Wyatt; Vincent J. Davis, and Ira D. Walker (Washington, D.C., 1941), 8, 11; Bruce Clayton, *W. J. Cash: A Life* (Baton Rouge, 1991), 140–42.

19. See Kluger, *Simple Justice*, 88; and Woodward, *Strange Career of Jim Crow*, 97–102.

County doubled as bus stations. Blacks bought tickets and waited out-side, usually standing, though benches for passengers were unlabeled.[20] Such informal practices widened the racial gulf in every community.

Through the period, moreover, many blacks died in periodic out-breaks of lynching, Klan night riding, and rioting, all expressions of what Cash would call the "savage ideal." North Carolina joined the reign of terror. Between 1900 and 1931, when 566 lynchings, of which 97 percent of the victims were black, were reported throughout the South, mobs in North Carolina lynched 36 persons, all but 3 of them black. The state's worst riots, two in 1918 and four in 1943, claimed over two dozen black and white lives. Scores of blacks and sympathetic whites were intimidated, jailed, maimed, whipped, or otherwise perse-cuted for dissent (93–94).[21]

Race prejudice, which united all classes of whites and shaped Cash's concept of the "Proto-Dorian Convention," permeated popular litera-ture. A 1936 novel on the Wilmington riot gave as the reason for the unfortunate conflict that "Wilmington was really becoming a Mecca for Negroes and a City of Lost Opportunities for the working class whites." This fictional work echoed the reigning political orthodoxy: "The North Carolina Clause is in effect a 'toll bridge' over which igno-rant Negroes cannot cross to the polls, but intelligent Negroes can cross this 'bridge' and cast their votes, if they have the temerity to do it."[22]

A beleaguered remnant of black Carolinians tried to cross that bridge in the age of Jim Crow. Their actions attest to a black mind, to another world. To what extent did blacks undermine disfranchisement? How were they able to forge a politics of shared risk and uplift? What contribution did they make to the emerging civil rights movement?

In politics black North Carolinians fought as best they could. Only 12 were registered in heavily black Warren County in 1902, a year when fewer than 5,000 of them voted statewide. At 624,480, blacks made up nearly a third of the state's population, and 120,000 of them

20. Johnson, *Patterns of Negro Segregation,* 48, 100.

21. Raymond Gavins, "North Carolina Black Folklore and Song in the Age of Seg-regation," *North Carolina Historical Review,* LXVI (1989), 414–15, and n. 8.

22. Bruce Clayton, "The Proto-Dorian Convention: W. J. Cash and the Race Ques-tion," in *Race, Class, and Politics in Southern History: Essays in Honor of Robert F. Durden,* ed. Jeffrey J. Crow, Paul D. Escott, and Charles L. Flynn, Jr. (Baton Rouge, 1989), 275–76; Harry Hayden, *The Story of the Wilmington Rebellion* (Wilmington, N.C., 1936), 2, 26, 30.

were males of voting age. Most were uneducated and would never become voters. It is instructive that one school principal published a handbook that helped them "learn step by step to spell, and to read and write any section of the State Constitution." He also encouraged them to "be thrifty, every one of you, accumulate property, build homes, educate yourselves and children, rear religious families, and then let's go to the ballot box."[23]

Urban blacks were active in politics in greater numbers than their rural brothers and sisters, who were more vulnerable to violence and extralegal oppression. Gradually, a cadre of black voters emerged in piedmont cities. Buck Waller started out as a ward heeler in Durham around 1911. "Only a few Negroes were voting, but they were not interested in the other fellow voting. I was, so I began working to build up a bloc of voters to give [to] the best candidate," he recalled, estimating his following at "300 to 400 people." Assisted by "some ten or eleven youngsters I'm trying to get interested in politics," Waller would "deliver the vote" on election day for cash. "I love money, but don't bow to it," he insisted. Unlike the "big niggers, I still am recognized 'downtown' as the power and the real father of Negro voting in Durham." One of the pioneer black voters in Winston-Salem was a journalist, who stated: "When I came back to Winston in 1917, the registrar refused to register me, and so I made a speech: 'I have just returned from the war, fighting for democracy and now I come here, and democracy in its elemental form—the vote—is denied. Oh, no! I wasn't scared over there and now I'm not scared, and I'm here to stay until you register me.'"[24]

World War I accelerated aspirations for the ballot across the state, particularly among women. Blacks in Raleigh, Durham, Greensboro, and Winston-Salem organized chapters of the National Association for the Advancement of Colored People (NAACP). By 1919, such organizing in Fayetteville and Winston-Salem had led to race riots. Both the Democratic party and the Invisible Empire resisted the black demand for civil rights.

---

23. North Carolina Civil Rights Advisory Committee, *Restrictions on Negro Voting in North Carolina History* (N.p., 1962), 7; *Fourteenth Census, 1920: State Compendium, North Carolina,* 7; Mabry, *Negro in North Carolina Politics,* 73, 75–77; G. Ellis Harris, *North Carolina Constitutional Reader* (Raleigh, 1903), 3, 9.

24. Quoted in Ralph J. Bunche, *The Political Status of the Negro in the Age of FDR,* ed. Dewey W. Grantham (Chicago, 1973), 317, 447.

In Raleigh, a storm center of debate over woman suffrage, segregated black clubwomen demanded equal enfranchisement of their gender and race. Opponents of woman suffrage in the 1920 legislature blocked white women and their would-be black sisters. One editor, fearing the Nineteenth Amendment would be inevitable, promised that whites would handle "negro women in some such manner as they have . . . so large a proportion of the negro men who got their right to vote through a similar constitutional amendment." A suffragist broadside, however, erased any doubt about white women's racial allegiance or about interracial female bonding. "If white domination is threatened in the South, it is, therefore, doubly expedient to enfranchise the women quickly in order that it be preserved," it stated.[25]

Despite these obstacles, the intercity Colored Women's Rights Association continued to crusade. From its Raleigh headquarters in 1920 came a pro-Republican letter asserting that "when we get thousands of voters on the registration books, the white Republicans of North Carolina and the South will be glad to recognize us as their political equals." Democrats scurried. Fearing that they might retaliate by cutting appropriations for black educational institutions, James B. Dudley, president of the Agricultural and Technical College in Greensboro, was much alarmed. "It is unnecessary" to organize politically, he told black women. "The latent power that you now possess and can develop away from the polls, is far greater than any power you can secure at the ballot box." Black newspapers reacted by calling Dudley a male chauvinist and an "Uncle Tom."[26]

Blacks persevered in their quest for enfranchisement and equal protection under the law. As lily-whitism was pushing them from the Republican fold, they sometimes joined segregated Democratic auxiliaries. Raleigh had a strong one, "but in Winston-Salem . . . a Negro Democratic club organized by a local restaurant keeper . . . in 1928 was frowned out of existence." Regular black Democrats were a token lot.

25. Marjorie Julian Spruill, "White Supremacy and the Southern Ideal of Woman: A Study of the Woman Suffrage Movement in North Carolina" (Honors thesis, University of North Carolina at Chapel Hill, 1973), 16, 17, 37, and appendix.

26. North Carolina Civil Rights Advisory Committee, *Restrictions on Negro Voting,* 8; Winston-Salem *Union Republican,* January 24, 1918; Ewa U. Eko, "Black Women in Politics, 1912–38: Perspectives from the Collections of Monroe Nathan Work" (Paper presented at the Association for the Study of Afro-American Life and History, New York City, October 20, 1973), 6–10.

Though statewide black registration in the 1920s ranged from 12,000 to 20,000, most blacks were registered Republicans, and they usually had trouble voting. Of Asheville's 3,360 eligible blacks, 100 to 200 were voters. Durham, where 3,105 blacks were eligible, and Greensboro, counting 2,678, led the state with 500 to 700 black voters, respectively. Raleigh, reporting 3,897 eligible, had 582 actual voters. Winston-Salem, with 9,452 eligible, reported 326.[27]

During the 1930s these urban communities became focal points of black political action. Social service needs, intensifying with each wave of poor migrants from rural areas, sharpened the deprivation and neglect that the Charlotte *News* and Cash condemned. Blacks lined up behind President Franklin D. Roosevelt and the New Deal, but they found Tar Heel Democrats to be most difficult. Voter registration drives by NAACP chapters and civic organizations encountered many obstacles, including legislation such as a 1935 law eliminating "haulers and markers" from primaries. Registrars refused potential black registrants, and white vote-buying from ward heelers undermined attempts at bloc voting. A nearly discouraged captain of a Raleigh black precinct sighed, "For a drink, a free shindig at a piccolo center, and a barbecue, they'll vote." Lest they lose out to the vote-buyers and white supremacists, black leaders took steps to unify their constituencies.[28]

They organized. In 1933, when the NAACP was suing the University of North Carolina at Chapel Hill to admit a black student and staging a mass antilynching rally in Raleigh, blacks from across the state met in Durham and formed the Independent Voters League, "the first organization of its kind in the South." Two years later, a handful of middle-class black professionals caucused at North Carolina Mutual Life Insurance Company and named themselves the Durham Committee on Negro Affairs. In 1936 the committee hosted a conference "to centralize all civic organizations throughout the state by encouraging affiliation with the North Carolina Committee on Negro Affairs."[29]

27. Paul Lewinson, *Race, Class, and Party* (New York, 1932), 185, 141–43, 153, 158, 219, 269; Mabry, *Negro in North Carolina Politics*, 78–79.

28. Bunche, *Political Status of the Negro*, 249, 318, 446, 482–84; Rayford W. Logan, ed., *The Attitude of the Southern White Press Toward Negro Suffrage, 1932–1940* (Washington, D.C., 1940), 49–52.

29. Bunche, *Political Status of the Negro*, 315–16; Robert Cannon, "The Organization and Growth of Black Political Participation in Durham, North Carolina, 1933–1958" (Ph.D. dissertation, University of North Carolina at Chapel Hill, 1975), 9–12; Mabry, *Negro in North Carolina Politics*, 78.

Five cities had branches of the committee. Charlotte's, run by a few educators and a minister, railed against the "votin' don't git you no-where" attitude and worked for clinics, libraries, paved streets, playgrounds, and better schools. A black man ran for city council and a black woman for the board of education in a 1937 Democratic primary, but both lost. Durham's committee enhanced its reputation through campaigns to end police brutality, hire black clerks, and stop the old ward heelers. It controlled approximately three thousand votes. In elections it regularly turned out up to 16 percent of the city's total vote. Accordingly, the committee defeated a 1938 bond issue for an airport "that Negroes would not be permitted to use."[30] Democratic registrars suddenly became cooperative and party candidates courted the committee's endorsement.

Activist ministers led the Greensboro branch, although they had trouble unifying the flock. The bosses at Cone Mills, who wielded considerable control over their black employees, posed a serious problem. One black worker revealed: "At voting time, party come out here and git us. . . . You understand, one who you works for wants you to vote like they want." Despite its constituency of 4,550, the Raleigh committee dissipated itself fighting "the Negro undertaker or doctor whose boss is the white politician with the money bag" and warding off a hostile white press. No blacks held public office in Winston-Salem, where the powerful hosiery and tobacco companies were determined to maintain the status quo.[31]

That slow breakthroughs did occur in these communities indicates the valuable role of black politics under Jim Crow. Durham and Raleigh reported that each had a black justice of the peace. Each man craftily waited until the last minute to file his candidacy and ran unopposed. Otherwise, whites held every important elective office. Municipal employment also followed the color line. Charlotte, whose Good Samaritan Hospital "was the first . . . in the United States built and operated exclusively for blacks," hired black people mostly to carry messages and sweep floors. Charlotte, Greensboro, and Raleigh each employed a black truant officer. Durham had two black postal workers. Greens-

<hr>

30. Bunche, *Political Status of the Negro,* 447.

31. *Ibid.,* 202, 316, 482–84, 550–51, 567; Cannon, "Black Political Participation in Durham," 49, 51, 58; William R. Keech, *The Impact of Negro Voting* (Chicago, 1968), 26, 28, 30; Logan, ed., *Attitude of the Southern White Press,* 47–48; Winston-Salem *Journal-Sentinel,* June 30, 1957.

boro had a few blacks in its Unemployment Compensation Commission office. Raleigh hired two black caseworkers and a handful of clerks. Most blacks in the capital city and elsewhere were elevator operators, garbagemen, maids, messengers, scrubwomen, and watchmen. One could find black principals and teachers, but no firemen or policemen. Nor were facilities and services improving fast enough. After visiting them, political scientist Ralph J. Bunche described black neighborhoods in Charlotte, Greensboro, and Winston-Salem as "woefully inadequate . . . typical squalor." Still, blacks' guiding assumption was that political participation would enable them to end such discrimination and neglect.[32]

Considering the odds, quitting would have been tempting. By 1940 about 35,000 black voters were registered in the state, or 10 percent of voting-age blacks, most of them city dwellers. The vast majority of blacks in the country districts were still essentially disfranchised. In 1940, when Richmond County submitted its roster of 8,746 voters, only 68 of them were black. At the time, a white newspaper reported: "This year, for the first time since 1900, with just an occasional exception, Negroes will vote. Not a Negro has voted in the county in the past dozen years."[33]

The fight for democracy at home escalated during World War II. North Carolina did not have a white primary when the Supreme Court invalidated this practice in *Smith* v. *Allwright* (1944). But the landmark decision inspired black Carolinians' hope for the "new charter" on race relations that their leaders had demanded in the "Durham manifesto" of 1942. Rejecting the cant that "a black skin was prima facie evidence of inability to read in some of the eastern counties," the infant North Carolina State Conference of NAACP Branches launched an aggressive campaign to educate and register black voters. It sponsored voting rights suits, which resulted in fines against local registrars in 1945–1946 and framed a statewide civil rights agenda.[34]

32. Bunche, *Political Status of the Negro,* 550–52, 558–59, 567, 570; Thornton W. Mitchell, *Preliminary Guide to Records Relating to Blacks in the North Carolina State Archives,* Archives Information Circular No. 17 (Raleigh, 1980), 18.

33. Raleigh *News and Observer,* May 16, 1940.

34. North Carolina Civil Rights Advisory Committee, *Restrictions on Negro Voting,* 9; Committee of Editors and Writers of the South, *Voting Restrictions in the 13 Southern States* (Atlanta, 1945); Luther P. Jackson, "Race and Suffrage in the South Since 1940," *New South,* III (1948), 10; Raleigh *News and Observer,* May 16, 1940, April 5, May 9,

Black political consciousness had been raised, forming the base for North Carolina's postwar freedom struggle. Black communities organized scores of NAACP branches and chartered labor union locals, and a black man was elected to the Fayetteville city council. Congress of Industrial Organizations (CIO) Local 22—Food, Tobacco, and Agricultural Workers—became "the number-one political power" among Winston-Salem blacks, whose local organizations preached ballots over bullets. They elected a black councilman in 1947. Some seventy-five thousand black Carolinians (15 percent of the black voting-age population) were qualified voters. Although still minuscule, the black electorate had doubled since 1940, ranking third after Texas and Tennessee in the South.[35] Imperceptibly, black struggles behind the veil were undermining Jim Crow in the Old North State.

Segregation, an inviolable institution during Cash's career in the Carolina piedmont, fixed a boundary between black and white. These separate worlds coexisted in an ambience of fear, hate, and tension that neither race could escape. As they survived and resisted, blacks essentially lived Du Bois' definition of a "double-consciousness, this sense of always looking at one's self through the eyes of others, of measuring one's soul by the tape of a world that looks on in amused contempt and pity."[36]

Blacks constantly felt the strain of the twoness. "We were bottled up and labeled and set aside—sent to the Jim Crow car, the back of the bus, the side door of the theater, the side window of a restaurant. We came to know that whatever we had was always inferior," protested former Durhamite Pauli Murray. "We came to understand that no matter how neat and clean, how law abiding, submissive and polite, how studious in school, how churchgoing and moral, how scrupulous in paying our bills and taxes we were, it made no essential difference in our place."[37]

As his lines on the grinning but veiled black face imply, Cash did

1944; Raymond Gavins, *The Perils and Prospects of Southern Black Leadership: Gordon Blaine Hancock, 1884–1970* (Durham, 1977), 122–27; William H. Towe, *Barriers to Black Political Participation in North Carolina* (Atlanta, 1972), 10.

35. Jackson, "Race and Suffrage," 3–4; Towe, *Barriers to Black Political Participation,* 13; Winston-Salem *Sentinel-Journal,* June 30, 1957.

36. Du Bois, *Souls of Black Folk,* 16–17.

37. Pauli Murray, *Proud Shoes: The Story of an American Family* (New ed.; New York, 1978), 270.

discern a complexity in black response. He speaks as an outsider and, from a humanistic perspective, as a victim. For he could not and did not engage or exchange with enriching minds such as Pauli Murray's. The contrast is telling: he attended Wake Forest College while she went to a "seedy run-down school" in Durham. When he was writing *The Mind of the South,* she was being denied admission to the University of North Carolina at Chapel Hill because of her race.[38]

Cash's perceptions in the book are ambivalent. He gratuitously describes post–World War I southern blacks, whose strivings I have discussed, as "a simple and wistful people greatly susceptible to and enamoured of the outward appearance of things." Paradoxically, he perceives that their progress in education and in farm and home ownership had instilled "a pride which was at bottom quite incompatible with the established Southern view." They were also protesting. "Throughout Dixie, in short," Cash writes of the 1930s, "the Negro was slowly lifting his head and beginning to grow perceptibly more assertive. And everywhere there was in evidence a subtle but quite real change in attitude—a rising sullenness before brutality and indignity, a growing tendency to fierce outburst when pressed too hard, a mounting reluctance . . . toward acting out the role of Jim Crow or Uncle Tom." He concludes: "So far did the new assertiveness go that in some places—as Richmond, Charlotte, Raleigh, Greensboro, Atlanta, and Memphis—the Negroes would be reaching out cautiously to claim the ballot" (320, 323–324). Beyond contemplating and intuiting the forms and shadows of such protests, however, Cash could not penetrate the veil. He did not foresee that black Carolinians and southerners were creating a mass social movement that would rend the veil of segregation and ultimately force the South to become a racially integrated society.

38. Clayton, "Proto-Dorian Convention," 268–70; Murray, *Proud Shoes,* 270; Pauli Murray, *The Autobiography* (Knoxville, 1989), 114–29.

W. J. Cash: Creativity and Suffering in a Southern Writer

BERTRAM WYATT-BROWN

V. O. Key noted in his famous 1947 study, *Southern Politics in State and Nation,* that "a depressingly high rate of self-destruction prevails among those who ponder about the South and put down their reflections in books. A fatal frustration seems to come from the struggle to find a way through the unfathomable maze formed by tradition, caste, race, poverty." The statement is arresting in its allusions to enigma, despair, and predetermination. Almost twenty years later, Joseph L. Morrison, Cash's first biographer, was unimpressed with Key's argument. He discovered that the political scientist had in mind three suicidal authors: Cash; Clarence Cason, who in 1935 published *90° in the Shade;* and an unnamed third. Morrison argued that before his self-inflicted death, Cash had by no means feared the weight of southern conformity or tradition. Nor was he worried over the South's future. With a journalist's customary glibness, the biographer dismissed Key's proposition out of hand on statistical grounds. "Since the incidence of three suicides," Morrison wrote, "cannot rightly be construed as 'a depressingly high rate of self-destruction,' Key's engagingly written generalization must be set down to artistic license, no more." [1]

I wish to thank the Earhart Foundation, the National Endowment for the Humanities, and the National Humanities Center, Research Triangle Park, North Carolina, for making the research for this essay possible. I also thank Anne Wyatt-Brown for contributing many of the insights herein and David H. Fischer for a variety of helpful suggestions.

1. V. O. Key, Jr., *Southern Politics in State and Nation* (New York, 1947), 664; Joseph L. Morrison, *W. J. Cash, Southern Prophet: A Biography and Reader* (New York, 1967), 140. Alexander Heard, Key's research associate and source for Morrison's information, could not remember the third suicide Key alluded to.

Both writers present plausible but imperfect answers. Yet V. O. Key's notion cannot be casually dismissed. Particularity, not statistics, informs the proposition. From the Civil War to our own day, the South's rate of suicide has been much lower than the national average and the incidence of homicide much higher.[2] At a time when the region was still mired in those conditions that Key named, intellectuals were isolates. They belonged to a special breed—a very rare one in the agrarian South. By no means was the intellectual a "man at the center," as Cash designated the ordinary southerner. In fact, he wrote bitterly in an essay published in 1929, "a thinker in the South is regarded quite logically as an enemy of the people," whom the people ought to sup-press. The very act of thinking, said Cash, made it "necessary to repu-diate the whole Southern scheme of things, to go outside God's ordered drama and contrive with Satan for the overthrow of Heaven."[3] Such an alienated individual as Cash described could well have reached some gloomy conclusions regarding both self and society, with sometimes fatal consequences.

Thus Key, it might seem, was offering an arresting point. Yet, like Morrison's, it is not wholly convincing. A brief review of Cash's illness and death reveals its weakness. During the summer of his Guggenheim year in Mexico City, 1941, the recently published author of *The Mind of the South* showed alarming signs of hallucination and mental collapse. Long exercised by the rise of Hitler, the Charlotte *News* editorialist believed that Nazi agents were whispering among themselves nearby to prepare his assassination.[4] Frightened by his fantasies, he bolted out of the hotel room shortly after his wife, Mary, greatly alarmed, had left to look for help. In his own way, Cash was also looking for help—for a permanent escape from the voices and the madness they represented. Like Virginia Woolf, the great English novelist with similar mental ail-ments, Cash feared Nazi victory and the end of civilization. Earlier that same year, Woolf, before drowning herself, wrote her sister and hus-band in joyless words that perhaps reflected the desperation Cash also

2. See Sheldon Hackney, "Southern Violence," *American Historical Review,* LXXIV (February, 1969), 906–25. Also see Louis L. Dublin, *Suicide: A Sociological and Statistical Study* (New York, 1963), 33–35, 218–19.

3. W. J. Cash, "The Mind of the South," *American Mercury,* XVII (October, 1929), reprinted in Morrison, *Cash,* 193.

4. Mary Cash Maury to Joseph Morrison, August 20, 1964, in Joseph L. Morrison Papers, Southern Historical Collection, University of North Carolina, Chapel Hill.

experienced under similar circumstances. "I am always hearing voices," Virginia Woolf told them in late March, 1941, "and I know I shant get over it now. . . . It is this madness."[5] For both Woolf and Cash death was preferable to enslavement under minds out of control. On July 1, 1941, in a dingy hotel room across town, the police found him dead. He had hanged himself with his necktie on the back of a bathroom door.[6] Contrary to Key's view, these factors suggest physiological, not cultural factors alone, in Cash's suicide.

Morrison's contrary argument also has flaws. Cash's erratic behavior and hallucinations might suggest a severe alcoholic reaction, particularly since depression and alcoholism have been shown to be closely connected in many cases of suicide. Mary Cash Maury claimed that Cash had few if any difficulties with addiction, particularly in Mexico City. But she did recall that shortly after their marriage and the completion of the book, he began to drink very heavily, even though he had almost no tolerance for liquor. Moreover, Cash had apparently missed many a Monday workday at the Charlotte *News* because of hangovers from solitary weekend boozing. Despite these clear indications of a chronic rather than unpredictable illness, Morrison claims that Cash's physician denied that his patient was a genuine alcoholic. Further, he argues that a cold-turkey withdrawal would have produced uncomfortable symptoms for only a few days afterward.[7] Mary Cash may have had her own reasons for dismissing the stigma of alcoholism; Morrison sought to defend his subject's virtue, as if overdrinking were not a disease but a moral stain.

One suspects that Cash's psychotic state may have resulted from either overindulgence or teetotal reaction, either one of which would have had very severe effects on his body and its chemistry. Newly mar-

5. Virginia Woolf to Vanessa Bell, March 23[?], 1941, and to Leonard Woolf, March 28, 1941, in Nigel Nicholson and Joanne Trautmann, eds., *The Letters of Virginia Woolf, 1936–1941* (6 vols.; New York, 1975–80), VI, 485, 487. See also Thomas C. Caramagno, "Manic-Depressive Psychosis and Critical Approaches to Virginia Woolf's Life and Work," *PMLA*, CIII (January, 1988), 10–23.

6. Ben F. Meyer to Morrison, August 11, 1964, in Morrison Papers; see also Maury's lengthy account, "Suicide," *ibid.*

7. Ronald Maris, *The Biology of Suicide* (New York, 1986), 173–74; Susan J. Blumenthal and David J. Kupfer, eds., *Suicide over the Life Cycle: Risk Factors, Assessment, and Treatment of Suicidal Patients* (Washington, D.C., 1990), 7–8, 26–29; Maury, "Suicide," in Morrison Papers; Morrison, *Cash*, 145–46.

ried, with his book completed and fresh plans to fulfill, he might have sworn to cut back on his consumption, unaware of the effect that might have. His wife, however, left unrecorded many events in the three weeks before his last nervous seizure and death. Thus we do not know whether the pair gave up or overdid their drinking. After forty years on bourbon and gin, William Styron discovered that he could no longer take a drop of hard liquor. Yet, the novelist says, almost at once he plunged into a caldron of physical and mental woes that continued for months thereafter. Misery almost drove the author of *Sophie's Choice* to suicide.[8] Like Styron, Cash experienced the insomnia, loss of vocal control, and deterioration of hand-eye coordination that mark the severely depressed—and perhaps the alcoholic as well.

Morrison argued that Cash suffered from neither intoxication nor depression but rather from a sudden, highly "acute brain syndrome—almost certainly toxic in origin." He treats the condition as if Cash had contracted viral pneumonia. We now know much more about the biochemistry of depression than we did thirty years ago when Morrison wrote. It does seem likely that physiological changes in the brain triggered Cash's mental disorder—low levels of what is called 5-HIAA, a metabolite of serotonin and high levels of various urinary compounds that have been found in the brain fluids of most suicides.[9] Nonetheless, the biographer ignores Cash's long history of depression, stretching back to childhood, that preceded the final episode. No doubt if lithium or Prozac had been available to counteract the chemical imbalances, the writer might have overcome the suicidal impulse.

Morrison did recognize that medical not just social or literary issues were involved, but he failed to see how chronic depression might be linked to Cash's death and also to the character of the book he wrote. Key discerned some connection between the suicide and Cash's critical imagination, but he thought his death a consequence of reactions to externalities, not of problems within. W. J. Cash was not terrorized by the thought of critical rejection per se, nor, as later explained, by justifiable fears of ostracism and rejection, but rather by a psychotic episode that had its origins in a long-standing inclination to melancholia. Key would

8. William Styron, *Darkness Visible: A Memoir of Madness* (New York, 1990), 43–50.

9. Morrison, *Cash,* 147; Maris, *Biology of Suicide;* Blumenthal and Kupfer, eds., *Suicide over the Life Cycle,* 128–29.

have been on firmer ground, however, if he had seen the alienation of the southern intellectual as a product rather than a cause of chronic depression and suicidal impulse. Such a mental state could find release in literary expression, particularly when the alienated thinker found the means to challenge imprisoning social conventions and mores. In other words, Cash killed himself for reasons deeply rooted in his own psychological makeup, but his writing served as a form of momentary therapy that eased some of the agony that melancholia entailed.

Three issues thus become significant, particularly as they relate to Key's speculations about the enigma of southern society: the relation of depression and suicidal inclination to creativity; the problem of cultural, regional sources for both depression and creativity; and the character of Cash's *Mind of the South* when considered in light of its author's own state of mind. All three categories lend themselves more to conjecture than to hard evidence. Much has yet to be learned about depression in both its cultural and personal manifestations. The relationship between the operation of the brain—the neurophysiological functions—and the mind, that is, consciousness, is as mysterious as ever. Yet we do not know that the Cartesian division between mind and body is a purely convenient but false distinction. Likewise, "about creativity almost everything has been said and almost nothing is known," as Daniel Dervin has declared. Despite these pitfalls, approaching the issue of depression and original expression may help to illuminate the understanding, and medical investigation provides much testimony. John Dryden expressed a Senecan maxim in verse: "Great wits are sure to madness near allied, / and thin partitions do their bounds divide." In the mid-nineteenth century, Cesare Lombroso and Francis Galton introduced the notion that genius arises in part from early and severe emotional adversities. Then in 1921, Sigmund Freud pioneered the idea that repressed anger in a distorted mourning process, usually over a lost father, induces the victim to write, paint, experiment, or compose as a pathological means of compensation and release from the sense of despair and degraded self-esteem that the illness involves. As a self-consciously literary writer and connoisseur of art himself, Freud admitted, "Before the problem of the creative artist, psychoanalysis must, alas, lay down its arms." Nevertheless, his own analyses of artists and writers stressed the deviant, not the creative, aspects of his subjects' lives. Presumably, if Leonardo da Vinci and Fyodor Dostoyevski could have consulted analysts and rejected the childish toys of fantasy, they would have lived normally—without, one might guess, leaving behind a trace of artistry, discovery, or invention.[10]

Taking a more benevolent view, Anthony Storr, George H. Pollock, George Pickering, Felix Brown, and others, largely of the Jungian school, have celebrated the apparent linkage between the urge for self-expression and the Freudian propositions: death or desertion of parents early in an author's life, irremediably unhappy childhoods, and hidden fears of and rages against these and other forms of early mistreatment. The examples are extraordinary. They range from Isaac Newton and Robert Schumann to Sylvia Plath and Anne Sexton. George Pollock, a Chicago analyst, claims that he has tabulated more than two thousand major literary figures who suffered from chronic depression.[11]

The difficulty is that the more we learn about depression and the

10. Cash was scarcely alone in suffering from an ailment all too prevalent in the United States. Estimates in 1974–75 concluded that 18.5 million people, or 17.3 percent of the population between ages twenty-five and seventy-four, were chronically affected. See Rona Beth Sayetta and David P. Johnson, "Basic Data on Depressive Symptomology," in *DHEW Publication No. (PHS) 80-1666* (Washington, D.C., 1980), 1; Daniel Dervin, *Creativity and Culture: A Psychoanalytic Study of the Creative Process in the Arts, Sciences, and Culture* (Rutherford, N.J., 1990), 9; John Dryden, *Absalom and Achitophel,* verses 163–64, quoted in Anthony Storr, "Genius and Psychoanalysis: Freud, Jung, and the Concept of Personality," in *Genius: The History of an Idea,* ed. Penelope Murray (London, 1989), 224. George Sand, Napoleon's romantic contemporary, echoed Dryden (who in turn had borrowed from Seneca): "Between genius and madness there is often not the thickness of a hair" (quoted in D. Jablow Hershman and Julian Lieb, *The Key to Genius* [Buffalo, N.Y., 1988], 8). See also Cesare Lombroso, *The Man of Genius* (London, 1891); Sir Francis Galton, *Hereditary Genius: An Inquiry into Its Laws and Consequences* (1892; rpr. New York, 1978); and Sigmund Freud, "Dostoyevsky and Parricide," in James Strachey, trans. and ed., *The Standard Edition of the Complete Psychological Works of Sigmund Freud* (24 vols.; London, 1953–74), XXI, 175–98, and "Leonardo Da Vinci and a Memory of His Childhood," *ibid.,* XI, 63–137. Storr criticizes the Freudian mistrust of fantasy in "Genius and Psychoanalysis," 214–15.

11. George H. Pollock, "The Mourning Liberation Process in the Older Patient" (Paper presented at the Psychotherapy and the Older Patient Conference, Bruce Draper Memorial Symposium, February 17, 1989, University of South Florida and the Psychoanalytic Group of Tampa, Tampa, Florida); Pollock, "The Mourning Process," *Chicago Theological Seminary Register,* LVII (December, 1966), 15–23; Pollock, "Mourning and Adaptation," *International Journal of Psycho-Analysis,* XLIII (July–October, 1962), 341–61; Anthony Storr, *Solitude: The Return to the Self* (New York, 1988); Storr, *Churchill's Black Dog, Kafka's Mice, and Other Phenomena of the Human Mind* (New York, 1988); Sir George White Pickering, *Creative Malady* (New York, 1974); Felix Brown, "Bereavement and Lack of a Parent in Childhood," in *Foundations of Child Psychiatry,* ed. Emanuel Miller (London, 1968), 435–55, an excellent review that suggests a connection between creativity and loss of a parent.

role of creativity the less likely, it seems, that the connection has purely emotional roots. Perhaps Ernst Kretschmer in 1931 carried matters a little far when he asserted, "The spirit of genius . . . is no free-floating absolute power, but is strictly bound to the laws of blood chemistry and the endocrine glands."[12] Nonetheless, recent neurological findings suggest that certain genetically controlled chemical compounds may induce the malfunctioning of the neurotransmitter, neuroendocrine, and automatic nervous systems in the brain.[13] The emotional repercussions vary in severity from serious swings of mood to delusional psychosis. If genetics, not environment, predominate in creating the depressive personality, it might appear that the connection between the malady and creativity is simply coincidental. But instead, an interaction develops between the biological and psychological factors: the depressive may suffer episodic bouts, but in the more normal intervals, a sense of emotional well-being has been permanently damaged. As the English analyst Donald W. Winnicott points out, for healthy individuals, "*Depression has within itself the germ of recovery*." Loss and response to loss imply that something—love—was there to begin with. Its absence triggers regret, guilt, and other feelings connected with our emotional maturing. To be sure, those who despair as severely as Cash did should seek treatment. Yet even they have periodic respites from the full weight of the mental yoke.[14] For reasons by no means fully understood, Winnicott's observation seems to hold true: the mind's agony apparently stimulates the imaginative process. According to one study, poets are the most vulnerable to the problem. Biographers, it seems, are the least susceptible.[15]

12. Ernst Kretschmer, *The Psychology of Men of Genius,* trans. Raymond B. Cattell (College Park, Md., 1970), 128.

13. Arnold J. Mandell, "Toward a Psychobiology of Transcendence: God in the Brain," in *The Psychobiology of Consciousness,* ed. Julian M. Davidson and Richard J. Davidson (New York, 1980), 410–12.

14. Donald W. Winnicott, *Home Is Where We Start From: Essays by a Psychoanalyst,* ed. Claire Winnicott, Ray Shepherd, and Madeleine Davis (New York, 1986), 72. See also Randy S. Milden, "Affective Disorders and Narcissistic Vulnerability," *American Journal of Psychoanalysis,* XLIV (Winter, 1984), 345–53.

15. See Kay Redfield Jamison, "Mood Disorders and Patterns of Creativity in British Writers and Artists," *Psychiatry,* LII (May, 1989), 125–34; John E. Drevdahl and Raymond B. Cattell, "Personality and Creativity in Artists and Writers," *Journal of Clinical Psychology,* XIV (April, 1958), 107–11; T. F. McNeil, "Prebirth and Postbirth Influence on the Relationship of Creativity and Mental Illness," *Journal of Personality,* XXXIX (September, 1971), 391–407.

Affective disorder, as manic-depression is now called, tends to run genetically in families.[16] Studies of separated twins and foster children, conducted by Danish researchers, demonstrate the point. According to the latest work (1988), Nordic mental care specialists have found that schizophrenia and depression are much more frequent illnesses in the relatives of artists, writers, scientists, and mathematicians than they are in the general populace. Kay Redfield Jamison, the leading statistical expert on the topic, found that of forty-seven notable British writers, 38 percent had sought psychiatric help for depression. A third of the forty-seven suffered from intense swings of mood. Most believed that their disorder, when under control, enabled them to write.[17]

Granted that a close correlation exists, the question remains, Is manic-depression a *necessary* component of great achievement? Prominent writers themselves, an often reticent breed, offer little enlighten-

16. There are two major forms of chronic depression: unipolar and bipolar. The former involves downswings of great severity in which the afflicted feel totally lost, lethargic, and disengaged from normal personal feelings and relationships. The latter is also cyclical, but the upswings induce a sense of false omnipotence, hyperactivity, and volatile storms of temper and glee before a plunge into inanition and hopelessness. See *Diagnostic and Statistical Manual of Mental Disorders (DSM-III-R)* (Washington, D.C., 1987), 901–10.

17. L. J. Eaves, H. J. Eysenck, and N. G. Martin, *Genes, Culture, and Personality: An Empirical Approach* (London, 1989), 299–314. This study, based on data for twins, shows that genetic factors are consistently significant but that social attitudes, derived from both family environment and genetic predispositions, also play a role in the development of personality traits, including chronic forms of depression. See also Seymour S. Kety, "Observations on Genetic and Environmental Influences in the Etiology of Mental Disorder from Studies on Adoptees and Their Relatives," in *Genetics of Neurological and Psychiatric Disorders*, ed. Seymour S. Kety *et al.* (New York, 1983), 105–14; Eugene S. Paykel, "Life Events and Early Environment," in *Handbook of Affective Disorders*, ed. Kety *et al.* (New York, 1982), 147–61; Ruth Richards *et al.*, "Creativity in Manic-Depressives, Cyclothymes, Their Normal Relatives, and Control Subjects," *Journal of Abnormal Psychology*, XCVII (August, 1988), 281–88; A. Bartelsen, "A Danish Twin Study of Manic-Depressive Disorders," in *Origin, Prevention, and Treatment of Affective Disorders*, ed. M. Schou and E. Stromgen (Orlando, Fla., 1979), 439–76; Leonard L. Heston, "Psychiatric Disorders in Foster Home Reared Children of Schizophrenic Mothers," *British Journal of Psychiatry*, CXII (August, 1966), 819–25. For examples of professional West European artists and affective disorder, see N. C. Andreasen and Arthur Canter, "The Creative Writer: Psychiatric Symptoms and Family History," *Comprehensive Psychiatry*, XV (March–April, 1974), 123–31; N. C. Andreasen, "Creativity and Psychiatric Illness," *Psychiatric Annals*, VIII (March, 1978), 113–19; and Kay Redfield Jamison, "Mood Disorders and Patterns of Creativity in British Writers and Artists," *Psychiatry*, LII (May, 1989), 125–34. See also Frederick K. Goodwin and Kay Redfield Jamison, *Manic-Depressive Illness* (New York, 1990).

ment. Styron, for instance, has eloquently recounted his own case history, but, still gripped in the vise of what he calls a "darkness visible," he stresses only the torment, not the creative process. Others—Charlotte Brontë, Friedrich Nietzsche, Gustav Mahler, Virginia Woolf, and Thomas Mann, for instance—testified that pains of mind, body, or both stimulated creative reactions and even inspired and informed their work. They did not elaborate much, however, on how the mechanism worked.[18]

One can only offer suggestions. Probably the most significant factor is the depressive's need for perfection, a constant worrying of the subject at hand until the thinker meets a self-imposed criterion beyond the ordinary. Dread of being rejected and diminished self-regard are complements to the depressive's drive. The remedy, it would seem, is to aim higher and farther than others. Analyst Albert Rothenberg recognizes this factor even as he observes that creative people, whether artistic, philosophical, or scientific, are only somewhat above average in intelligence yet equipped with some innate faculty that must be practiced and painstakingly developed. According to his researches with Nobel laureates and Pulitzer Prize–winning poets and novelists, these talented few do not conform to a single personality type. Some are extroverts, but all are meticulous, perfectionistic, and extraordinarily motivated toward doing something new and dramatic. Even he admits, however, that "there is a thin *but definite* borderline between the most advanced and healthy type of thinking—creative thinking—and the most impoverished and pathological types of thinking—psychotic processes." A shifting back and forth takes place, but the creative individual can conceive multiple opposites or antitheses simultaneously, "a leap that transcends ordinary logic." He identifies the mechanism as the "janusian process," after the Roman god Janus. He means a marked facility for looking backward and forward at the same time that makes possible an original perspective by exploiting the tension between apparently antithetical or opposite elements. "The janusian process," says Rothenberg, "serves to bring together specific interrelated elements out of the relatively diffused substratum of experience and knowledge."[19]

18. Styron, *Darkness Visible;* Philip Sandblom, *Creativity and Disease: How Illness Affects Literature, Art, and Music* (Philadelphia, 1982), 15–24.

19. Albert Rothenberg, *Creativity and Madness: New Findings and Old Stereotypes* (Baltimore, 1990), 12, 15, 33. See also Rothenberg, *The Creative Process of Psychotherapy* (New York, 1988), 3–16.

In light of this process of connecting disparate elements, one might see as a central theme in Cash's work a union of opposites. First there is the basic antinomy that linked the South as primitive in conduct yet refined and religious. Still more dichotomous is the notion of a southern individualism, which Cash celebrates, while he recognizes timid subservience to community conventions and values. Southerners, he realized, insisted on their sense of independence even as they prided themselves on their loyalty to kin and neighbors. Other observers of the South had come to similar conclusions, but Cash extended these tropes, as it were, so that the insights were seen as central and pervasive over the course of time and extended into various areas of cultural life.

Cash came to these conclusions not when he was paralyzed or distracted by despair but when he was released from its toils. The impulse to create, as Rothenberg demonstrates, can arise only when the ravages of hopelessness and inanition have abated. During the period after depression and, in some cases, before the onset of an opposite and distracted manic state, Cash and other gifted thinkers could find a greater than customary access to metaphor and simile, a vision of interconnected ideas, and a heightened eloquence. According to Anthony Storr, these capacities emerge because the depressive requires an enhancement of self-confidence that reputation alone can supply. But because the dejected writer tends to be overly dependent on others and yet resentful of the weakness within, such a figure finds critical acclaim a temporary respite at best. Although the creation arises from insights well within the spectrum of rationality, the form of the literary outpouring may itself be so aggressively different from orthodox standards that its anticipated appearance before the public can frighten the perpetrator. The author dreads the disapproval of those upon whom he or she relies and worries that society at large will mock or ignore the accomplishment. Writer's block ensues.[20]

So it was with W. J. Cash. Composing *The Mind of the South* was a veritable agony of fleeting inspirations, furious destruction of drafts and footnotes, and renewed beginnings. As a result, starting in 1929, Cash took over a decade to complete the work. The problem of depression that so hobbled his progress stretched back to his earliest days when he needed and yet chafed under the rule of his "Hell-fearing fundamentalist" parents. After his years at Wake Forest, explains Bruce

20. Anthony Storr, *The Dynamics of Creation* (New York, 1972), 79–80.

Clayton in his recent biography, Cash entered the shadows. "The stray bits and pieces of evidence . . . suggest that he suffered through aimless years, characterized by nervousness and depression and stalled attempts to write something important. His stern self-consciousness of his limitations" bedeviled him. Hating himself, he later converted that anger into the prose of *The Mind of the South*. All he found, says Clayton, was "recurring melancholia." A year's teaching at Georgetown College in Kentucky proved disastrous to his pride. He fell for Peggy Ann, a freshman, but on their sole attempt at lovemaking, he did not perform successfully.[21]

The experience would have been humiliating for any rather chaste young man. For someone who grew up in the honor-conscious South it was particularly shameful. Clayton recounts that the incident "haunted him for years." Dissatisfied with himself, he could not settle into any regular writing, teaching, or journalistic job for very long. Briefly he taught school in Hendersonville, North Carolina. In 1927 he apparently came close to a nervous collapse. A tour of Europe helped his recovery, but it was scarcely complete. In 1936, he wrote Alfred Knopf, "Five years ago I was a complete neurasthenic, but I have since largely cured myself." That evaluation was unhappily inaccurate; he had not healed himself. As late as 1940, he again reported to his publisher-friend, "I am a confirmed neurasthenic, habitually expecting the worst."[22]

Like his contemporaries the English novelist Barbara Pym and the Mississippi poet William Alexander Percy, Cash had spent several of his postcollegiate years living under his parents' roof. The return to the family nest scarcely signified a growing independence. Even after leaving home, he found parental substitutes in the new surroundings, among them women whom he designated to take his mother's place. Katherine Grantham Rogers, a reporter at the Charlotte *News,* where Cash was temporarily employed in 1928, was an early friend to whom he sometimes turned for nurture. Cash once told her the story of his

21. Sigmund Freud, "Mourning and Melancholia," in Ernest Jones, ed., *Collected Papers of Sigmund Freud,* trans. Joan Riviere (5 vols.; London, 1948), IV, 152–70; Maury to "Miss Milam," May 6, 1957, copy in Morrison Papers; Bruce Clayton, *W. J. Cash: A Life* (Baton Rouge, 1991), 41.

22. Clayton, *Cash,* 46; Katherine Grantham Rogers to Morrison, September 30, 1964, in Morrison Papers; Cash to Knopf, quoted in Joseph L. Morrison, "The Obsessive 'Mind' of W. J. Cash," *Studies in Journalism and Communications,* IV (May, 1965), 8.

affair with Peggy Ann, ending the confession by bursting into tears. Knowing that he would later be ashamed of his indiscretion and try to avoid her, she confronted him at once with blunt truths. "You come out here acting the crucified Christ and treating me as an all-understanding Madonna. Well, you ain't and I ain't. You're awash in self-pity." Basically, she went on, "you are subconsciously just another sentimental Victorian male, strictly dividing females into just two classes—the all-good and all-bad." Simply "chalk up your 'first failure' with your lovely lady to the taboo that your subconsciously-held code imposed."[23] Cash did not last long at the *News;* after three or four weeks on the job, he returned to Boiling Springs to live with his parents.

The very difficulties he underwent in composing *The Mind of the South* no doubt contributed to the extraordinary depth of his insights, but those problems were indeed substantial. A hyperthyroid condition, panicked moments of hypochondria with such emotionally related signs as vertigo, impaired vision, slight muscular convulsions, and bronchial attacks became genuine impediments.[24] But these manifestations were not the heart of the trouble. Despite all the financial advances and reassurances of the Knopfs, for over a decade he could not bring himself to complete the work.

Mary Cash Maury, Cash's widow, recalled his procrastination: "There was some ill health, some frustrating blank-minded periods when he could accomplish nothing at all." His resulting "anger and despair," she said, "pyramided his failures." At times, she continued, Cash thought he had written "an utterly loathsome textbook fit to be read only by learned sticklers for minutiae." In his gloomier moments, his most notable phrases, like the "Proto-Dorian Convention," struck him as inappropriate because he wished above all to be "read by the people it actively concerned." Clearly, he grew ever more obsessional "as the book inched to a close." It made him feel helpless when fellow Americans dismissed his almost southern revivalist prophecies of the Nazi threat. His widow remembered that he "would stand by the radio savagely biting his hands until he left the house to walk the streets all

23. Rogers to Morrison, October 2, 1964, in Morrison Papers.
24. Silvano Arieti and Jules Bemporad, *Severe and Mild Depression: The Psychotherapeutic Approach* (New York, 1978), 167–68; James P. Sayers, "Depression May Reduce Activity of Natural Killer Cells," *Research Resources Reporter,* XIII (November, 1989), 1–4.

night." Morrison claimed that his preoccupation with Hitler's rise caused the journalist to put aside the text of *The Mind of the South*.[25] Not so. Obsession with Nazi encroachments was part of the problem—a projection of his own feelings of violence that had to be exorcised or transferred in such a manner. Of course, Cash had legitimate reasons for concern about European politics and war but not at the expense of his own stability.

Then, at last, the work was completed in a brief, miraculous burst of tranquil, almost effortless composition. No doubt Mary Ross Northrop, whom Cash was shortly to marry, provided him with encouragement and love that freed him from old terrors and indecisions. Writing, however, was not an activity that gave him complete self-confidence. As Albert Rothenberg argues, "A work of art may reduce anxiety to some extent for both creator and recipient, but it also stimulates the anxieties of both to a degree." Even though creation can serve as a means to cope with unmanageable feelings, it is "not a form of therapy." No sooner was the work completed than doubts set in. "Weren't they, if any of 'them' ever bothered to read it, likely to think him filled with hatred of his own land?" his wife recalled. "Wouldn't they damn him from the pulpits, at the meetings of Rotary, the D.A.R., the U.D.C.?" Like Virginia Woolf, another suicide in those fateful years of Hitler's military domination, Cash fretted that critics far less gifted than he would ridicule or, still worse, neglect his work.[26]

So long were the delays in completing *The Mind of the South* that, for him, they constituted normal dysfunction, as it were. He was used to his illnesses, excused them, pampered them. At one point, bronchitis was the alibi. "I am thoroughly depressed about the delay," he wrote his publisher in the summer of 1939. "But the matter has been out of my control." Not coincidentally, Mary was away on vacation during this long bout of procrastination and respiratory ailment.[27]

By contrast, under the influence of hypomania, a mild and productive state of mind, writing seemed exceptional and wholly out of his control. Unfortunately, hypomania, in which the underlying depression

25. Maury to "Miss Milam," May 6, 1957, Maury to Morrison, May 31, 1965, Maury to Morrison, n.d., pp. 6, 7, and Everette A. Houser, Jr., to Morrison, September 11, 1964, in Morrison Papers; Morrison, *Cash*, 80, 94–98.

26. Rothenberg, *Creativity and Madness*, 47; Maury to "Miss Milam," May 6, 1957, Maury to Morrison, n.d., p. 11, in Morrison Papers.

27. Cash quoted in Clayton, *Cash*, 153; see also 153–54.

is often denied, served Cash only as a temporary respite, a common phenomenon among afflicted artists. When the act of writing was completed, depression inevitably returned, for him as for others of similar disposition. According to analyst Marion Milner, Winnicott has argued that "the actual work of art, the finished creation, never heals an underlying lack of sense of self."[28] Cash doubtless experienced that mood of inner emptiness and loss before his act of fatal madness.

Completing the text, in other words, did not merely produce postpartum blues that writers often experience when letting go their literary "baby." Rather, it prompted grave misgivings of future capacity. During his Guggenheim year, 1941, he planned to write in Mexico City a novel about a three-generation southern dynasty, based in part on his own family.[29] According to Mary Cash, his marriage was successful, contributing much to his newfound sexual confidence. Nonetheless, Mary, who had helped him so much with the completion of *The Mind of the South* during their courtship, could do little for him at this juncture. The more he stared at the blank page the greater became his panic and fear of lost self-mastery. Delving into material that would confront his kinfolks and parents was bound to make matters worse.

The second category, the relation of depression to regional culture, is perhaps still more problematic and complex than the link between imaginative toil and melancholia. First, affective disorder is hardly peculiar to any specific place or time. The disease has appeared in nearly all cultures, though the reactions to it and the explanations of its nature vary widely. Insofar as the Anglo-American experience is concerned, Howard I. Kushner has recently agreed that all three aspects of depression must be seen as interrelated—the genetic, the psychological, and the cultural—the last ingredient being the contribution of Emile Durkheim's study *Suicide*.[30]

Indeed, the latter aspect helps to substantiate Key's observation, at

28. See Winnicott, *Home Is Where We Start From,* 78; quotation in Marion Milner, *The Suppressed Madness of Sane Men: Forty-Four Years of Exploring Psychoanalysis* (London, 1987), 283.

29. See Rogers to Morrison, September 30, 1964, in Morrison Papers.

30. See Arthur Kleinman and Byron Good, eds., *Culture and Depression: Studies in the Anthropology and Cross-Cultural Psychiatry of Affect and Disorder* (Berkeley, 1985), esp. 1–41; Howard I. Kushner, *Self-Destruction in the Promised Land: A Psychocultural Biology of American Suicide* (New Brunswick, N.J., 1989).

least in part. The particularities of southern life that the political scientist offered, most especially the subordination of individualism to a "hell-of-a-fellow" conformity, as Cash put it, and the traditions of honor and the fear of shame played a role. As Drew Faust so acutely observed in *The Sacred Circle,* the antebellum southern thinker had a special burden because solitude and the life of the mind aroused deep public suspicion. Such preferences were considered antisocial, subversive, and effeminate.[31] Of course, in many societies intellectuals have always faced prejudice. Nonetheless, in the American setting, where individual freedom has been exalted, the southern ideologue, whether on left or right, has encountered the contradictory force of community mistrust. He or she has had to face whispers of being either a dangerous incendiary or, still more demeaning, a harmless eccentric. The intellectual, stigmatized in this way, might well turn morbid.[32] Equally significant is the role of fatalism in southern culture and its connection to a gloomy, personal state of mind. Throughout southern history, but most especially in the aftermath of Civil War and emancipation, white southerners, having lost so much, had little reason to expect to experience the progress that northern society celebrated. Despite the rhetoric of New South boosters, in the early twentieth century the region still had not reached the level of prosperity that the rest of the nation then enjoyed. Cash argued that the South was too primitive, too "uncomplex, unvaried, and unchanging." As a result, its people let matters take their course, without intervention, but most of all, without thought. Such a society did not bend every purpose toward harnessing the future but willingly let God direct and fate determine. A Calvinistic religiosity, Cash thought, underscored the old predisposition. To explain the white southerner's antipathy to unions and strikes in the 1920s, Cash wrote that many times he had personally heard in North Carolina "the conviction that God had called one man to be rich and master, another to be poor and servant, and that men did well to accept what had been given them, instead of trusting to their own strength and stirring up strife" (*Mind,* 359). He deemed the prospect for change and advance anything but hopeful.

Other intellectuals who shared Cash's temperament as well as his

31. Drew Gilpin Faust, *The Sacred Circle: The Dilemma of the Intellectual in the Old South* (Baltimore, 1977).

32. Bertram Wyatt-Brown, *Southern Honor: Ethics and Behavior in the Old South* (New York, 1982), 98–99.

troubled parental relationships also shared his tragic vision of a doomed South. Some, as V. O. Key suggested, committed suicide, although he had only three in mind. The unnamed third was most likely Hinton Helper, North Carolina author of *The Impending Crisis,* an antislavery pamphlet directed at the poor whites of the South. The hard-hitting tract assisted the plunge toward secession and war. Helper thought southern progress was impossible until blacks, slave or free, were forcibly removed. Like many other literary suicides, Helper was fatherless from an early age. His manic episodes, marked by a hysterical racism, grew ever more virulent in the postwar years. He killed himself in 1909.[33]

Clarence Cason, the liberal-minded Alabama journalist, like Cash, dreaded an explosion of criticism in light of his opposition to racist demagoguery. More deeply personal factors prompted him to shoot himself shortly before *90° in the Shade* arrived at the bookstalls. Yet, as in Cash's case, Cason's anxieties were greatly exaggerated.[34] But the list goes on. Motherless at age five, fatherless at sixteen, Edmund Ruffin, who belonged to a much earlier generation, at once springs to mind. A depressive all his life, the Virginia secessionist had discovered in 1840 the self-slaughtered body of his former guardian, Thomas Cocke. It shocked but also intrigued him. The irascible fire-eater quarreled with his homeland, damning for decades its complacency in the face of abolitionist danger, then cursing Yankee conquerors as he put a gun muzzle in his mouth in 1865.[35]

The other writers who published their reflections on southern life in the year *The Mind of the South* was published were also melancholy souls, though neither took his own life, except indirectly. In 1941 James Agee and Walker Evans published *Let Us Now Praise Famous Men,* a

---

33. James De Roulhac Hamilton, "Hinton Rowan Helper," *Dictionary of American Biography,* IV, 517–18; Hugh C. Bailey, *Hinton Rowan Helper: Abolitionist-Racist* (University, Ala., 1965).

34. See Wayne Flynt, Introduction to Clarence Cason, *90° in the Shade* (University, Ala., 1989), v–x, and Flynt, *Ban, Burn, and Ignore: Writing and Publishing Books in the South* (University, Ala., 1989); "C. E. Cason Ends Life," New York *Times,* May 9, 1935, p. 12; John Chamberlain, book review, *ibid.,* May 30, 1936; C. McD. Puckette, "The South's Special Character," *New York Times Book Review,* May 19, 1935, p. 2.

35. See Edmund Ruffin, "Statement of the Closing Scenes of the Life of Thomas Cocke," Appendix 2, in David F. Allmendinger, Jr., ed., *Incidents of My Life: Edmund Ruffin's Autobiographical Essays* (Charlottesville, 1990), 179–88; Allmendinger, *Ruffin: Family and Reform in the Old South* (New York, 1990), esp. 87–88, 175.

classic probing of the southern soul in prose and photographs. Like
Ruffin, James Agee lost his father. The calamity scarred him for life.
Once he nearly killed himself in a car crash that was a conscious repli-
cation of his father's own accidental death. He saw that his abuse of
alcohol and excesses both sexual and otherwise were self-destructive.
Yet he could find no equilibrium. In May, 1955, he died of heart
trouble, hastened by his depression-induced alcoholism.[36]

Like Cash, Will Percy, the third in this triumvirate and author of
Lanterns on the Levee, held a book contract with Alfred and Blanche
Knopf in New York. According to Percy's friend David Cohn, the me-
morialist for a long-departed southern ethic "was one of those who
have been 'half in love with easeful Death, call'd him soft names in many
a musèd rhyme.'" Will Percy died at only fifty-seven from a series of
strokes, an illness that, in his case, cannot be wholly separated from
psychological factors. His father, Senator LeRoy Percy, had himself
given up on life, following the suicides of both his brother and his
brother's son and the death of his wife.[37]

All three writers—Cash, Agee, and Percy—could not deal openly
and evenhandedly with conflicts regarding themselves and their relationship to their fathers. They loved their fathers yet hated themselves,
believing that they could not achieve much in life that was worth-
while.[38] John William Cash, working at the store of his father-in-law in
Boiling Springs, North Carolina, and LeRoy Percy both questioned
their sons' manhood. As very conventional southern males, they worried that the minds their offspring possessed would deny them entry
into the community of other men. Both fathers feared the disgrace that
their sons might bring down on their heads. In fact, to his own death,
John Cash insisted that Nazi agents really did kill his son. Suicide for

36. See Laurence Bergreen, *James Agee: A Life* (New York, 1984), esp. 168–69,
380–82, 390–91, 405–407.
37. David L. Cohn, "Eighteenth-Century Chevalier," *Virginia Quarterly Review,*
XXXI (Autumn, 1955), 562–63. See also Bertram Wyatt-Brown, "Walker, Will, and
Honor Dying: The Percys and Literary Creativity," in *Looking South: Chapters in the Story
of an American Region,* ed. Winfred B. Moore, Jr., and Joseph F. Tripp (Westport, Conn.,
1989), 228–58; Lewis Baker, *The Percys of Mississippi: Politics and Literature in the New
South* (Baton Rouge, 1983), 149.
38. See Wilbur J. Cash to John Cash, May 1, 1941, in Morrison, *Cash,* 286–89.
Like Will Percy in regard to LeRoy Percy, W. J. Cash readily expressed affection for his
father, but underneath was an attitude he refused to recognize.

the elder Cashes was the great "Unpardonable Sin so Wilbur could not have killed himself."[39]

Reflecting southern attitudes about self-dissolution, parental denials and repressions had similar but opposite effects upon the authors' understanding of themselves as they translated those selves into projections of southern culture. Percy denied the negative aspects of regional life and extolled those virtues of honor, glory, and stoic fortitude that, as Will imagined, his father represented. Conventional in more ways than he knew, W. J. Cash himself had no greater understanding of suicide than did his father. In July, 1940, he boasted in the Charlotte *News* that South Carolinians had the lowest suicide rate in the country. Making reference to that fact and the current menace of Hitler, he declared, "They never were a people to scare easily."[40] Like most other southerners, he accepted the sadly common but simple-minded notion that suicides were cowards. Nevertheless, in the tone and generalizations of *The Mind of the South,* Cash demonstrated an inner despair. He pushed aside the positive features of the region and dwelt upon the sins of the fathers.

Depression, however, was scarcely the sole source of inspiration for that point of view. The apocalyptic rhetoric of the preachers he had heard as well as his own reading of the Old Testament prophets in the monumental prose of the King James Version also influenced his style and content. Having rejected the faith of his parents, the author, a stern moralist for himself and his region, no doubt found it hard to proceed in the vein of the biblical jeremiad. Perhaps it even further inhibited his progress in writing—his awareness of how disapproving the old man would be of his apparent perversity, by southern standards. For Cash was ridiculing "sin" in the manner of the old prophetic tradition upon which he was raised. The transgressions to which Cash referred were not the ones his father and other white men of the South would recognize. Rather, in Cash's anti-Baptist theology, they were racial bias, blind materialism, violence, and paganlike conventions—all offenses of a Bible-thumping culture, Christian only in the narrowest sense. *The Mind of the South* was a bold, even perilous enterprise, but behind it lay matters of a subtler nature.

39. Maury to Morrison, August 20, 1964, in Morrison Papers.
40. See Charlotte *News,* July 24, 1940, quoted in Morrison, *Cash,* 269.

To assail the region as a whole was perhaps a way of deflecting feelings that could otherwise explode closer to home. Cash's inner rage against the family, whose members he both loved and feared, stimulated an embittered wit and sense of indignation against other, more public and therefore less internally threatening targets. How impossible it was for Cash ever to confront his dismissive father. He never even tried. His resentments found other outlets. Cash, reminisced Edwin Holman, a college chum, "did a pretty good job of hating in several categories." Among his favorites were revivalist "false-fronters," demagogues, big-mule industrialists, and Adolf Hitler.[41]

With regard to the latter, Cash's belligerence, as if he were at war, was quite in keeping with a depressive state of mind. The perils of combat yield up opportunities for death or glory or both. Some depressives, like World War I hero William Alexander Percy, also welcomed the drama, the crises of battle. Having taken extraordinary risks, Percy was honored by the French with the Croix de Guerre. "Heroism," declares Howard I. Kushner, "shares with suicide a fantasy of remembrance. In both we uncover a wish to transcend death."[42] In the very risks of blood and death that war engenders, the depressive may find outside himself reasons for existence that elude him in the "everydayness" of an apparently unchallenging state of peace. In wartime the mind is not permitted the luxury of introspection. Yet the hatred and desire for apocalyptic events that Cash invested in his anti-Hitler passions did not make his task of writing an easy process.

By no means was Cash unusual among southern thinkers in apprehending how central manliness and martial valor were to the southern male experience. Nor did he entirely disapprove. Cash could write, "Proud, brave, honorable by its lights . . . swift to act, often too swift, but signally effective, sometimes terrible, in its action—such was the South at its best" (439). But virility had its darker, menacing side. Cash assailed the "savage ideal" as if his life depended upon its defeat—his campaign to overthrow the fathers.

Certainly a surprising number of white southern writers, apart from Cash himself, bore similar relationships to their fathers and the social bond of honor—often with depressive results. Among those with some form or another of affective disorder in the twentieth century are

41. Edwin Holman to Morrison, October 1, 1964, in Morrison Papers.
42. Kushner, *Self-Destruction in the Promised Land,* 143.

Walker Percy, Conrad Aiken, William Faulkner, William Styron, Carson McCullers, Ellen Glasgow, John Peale Bishop, John Gould Fletcher, Randall Jarrell, John Kennedy Toole (the last three suicides), Evelyn Scott, Caroline Gordon, Truman Capote, and Tennessee Williams. Yet, apart from the patriarchal aspects of southern life, in the upper ranks of post–Civil War southern society, from which so many literary figures emerged, suicide may well have arisen from other sources. One of them was the late nineteenth-century transition from a primitive planter culture to a more modern and secular style. Long ago, Emile Durkheim found a connection between rapid social change in modern, commercializing Protestant societies and an increase in suicide. In the post–Civil War South, the code of gentlemanly honor fell into disfavor. Men no longer exchanged fire in the semisuicidal ritual of the duel. Instead, the self-aggrieved took a different, a Durkheimian course, as it were: the self-aimed shot to the head. Perhaps Walker Percy spoke more generally than one might guess in *The Last Gentleman*. The novelist explains that, after a succession of grandsires who knew their aims and acted accordingly, Will Barrett's father, a modern southerner, had turned inward and "was killed by his own irony and sadness and by the strain of living out an ordinary day in a perfect dance of honor."[43]

As criminologists know, suicide and homicide are more closely linked than laymen might suspect. Colonel Ellerbe Boggan Cash, one of Jack Cash's forebears, fought and won one of the last duels in South Carolina in 1881. Colonel Cash, an old-fashioned squire, was much more mentally disturbed than the future writer. Earlier Cashes also had reputations for extreme violence and compulsive behavior. Before the Civil War, a Bogan Cash of Cheraw, South Carolina, was wanted in several counties for highway robbery—or so a family story had it.[44]

*   *   *

43. Walker Percy, *The Last Gentleman* (New York, 1968), 16; on the psychology of duels, see Wyatt-Brown, *Southern Honor*, 349–61.

44. Hackney, "Southern Violence," 907; see also Austin L. Porterfield, "Indices of Suicide and Homicide by States and Cities: Some Southern–Non-Southern Contrasts with Implications for Research," *American Sociological Review*, XIV (August, 1949), 481–90; E. B. C. Cash, *The Cash-Shannon Duel* (Greenville, S.C., 1881); S. W. Henley, *The Cash Family of South Carolina: A Truthful Account of the Many Crimes Committed by the Carolina Cavalier Outlaws* (Wadesboro, S.C., 1884); Lewis Shore Brumfield of Yadkinville, North Carolina, "Thomas Lanier Clingman and the Shallow Ford Families" (Unpublished genealogical study in the possession of the author), 75–76. Mr. Brumfield has supplied me with a two-page account of the relationship of W. J. Cash to these Cashes. Circumstantial evidence, he concludes, strongly suggests a linkage.

The final issue concerns the relation of depression to Cash's achievement. The outstanding characteristic of the book is its intensely personal tone, particularly for a work that seeks to define in ostensibly
value-free fashion the lineaments of a regional culture. Interestingly,
writer David Cohn, Will Percy's friend, detected this feature when the
book first appeared. He declared that *The Mind of the South*, "for all the
author's heroic attempts at objectivity, is often a strangely embittered
book. It is obvious that he is, in the Nietzschean phrase, a great despiser
because he is a great adorer. And being such, he lashes out in language
which reveals not only his admiration of the South but his own essential
Southernness; he is no stranger to that Southern violence which he
deplores."[45] As Cohn implies, dependency and unexamined admiration
were one side of Cash's personality and violence and rage another—
poles of feeling that the depressive experiences. Such an inner conflict,
however, made for memorable prose.[46] Nor did the source of his imaginative impulses interfere with his understanding of the South's history.
He worked assiduously with statistical reports, old files of newspapers,
and other materials to produce his great work. Attracted to fiction from
an early age, he treated such literary sources as Joseph Glover Baldwin's
Flush Times as if it were as trustworthy as a courtroom document
(12–13). Nonetheless, the chief foundation of the book lay not in his
reading but rather his own experience and that of others who told him
stories about the past or gossip about local events. He used to slump in
his chair, "balding head propped against a wall," eyes shut. "This was
the posture he managed to get into," Katherine Rogers recalled, "during every conversation I ever had with him."[47]

These sources, heightened by his romantic tendencies, suggest an
imaginative, sometimes almost gothic approach that was in keeping
with his "neurasthenia," as he liked to call it. Yet by no means do they
invalidate his work. Far from it. In handling the "savage ideal" or the
"Proto-Dorian Convention" as well as other themes, Cash might seem
to exaggerate, to adopt the role of the clownish tall-tale teller. Some
critics have accused him of intellectual sloppiness as a result. But Cash
knew exactly what he wished to say and how to say it. Like so many

45. Cohn quoted in Clayton, *Cash,* 168; see Cohn in *Saturday Review of Literature,*
XXIII (February 23, 1941), 7, 16–17.

46. See Bertram Wyatt-Brown, "Introduction: The Mind of W. J. Cash," in W. J.
Cash, *The Mind of the South* (1941; rpr. New York, 1991), vii–xli.

47. Rogers to Morrison, September 30, 1964, in Morrison Papers.

creative depressives, he was a perfectionist who left nothing unexamined. *The Mind of the South* is a study of social interrelationships, but the manner of exposition is one seldom if ever employed for that purpose: the fictive narrative line. More than that, the writer assumes the role of what writing theorist Robyn Warhol calls "the engaging narrator."[48] By that term is meant one who seeks to inspire belief in the material presented. Rather than take a transcendent, distant pose, the author enters the text with direct address. The method is designed to play upon either the reader's sentiments, sense of logic, or, as in Cash's case, both. Interestingly, the engaging narrator reveals little of the author's own personality but only a figure with which the reader is welcome to identify.

Thus Cash's creativity cannot be arbitrarily divorced from his personal anguish. Even as an "objective" observer, he did not employ the usual approaches of the sociologist and historian, not because he was ignorant of their *modus operandi,* but because he had to speak in a voice true to his nature. Thus his generalizations and pen portraits were not merely results of his research in archives or biographies.[49] In part, they came from his voracious newspaper and book reading. He had a gift of total recall, which is often a feature that talented depressives share.[50] But with care and precision, Cash drew chiefly from personal observations of southern life and habit and, most of all, from his insight into himself and kin relations. His illustration of an ill-educated Irishman on the cotton frontier rising to wealth in upland South Carolina is well depicted: "Tall and well made, he grew whiskers after the Galway fashion—the well-kept whiteness of which contrasted very agreeably with the brick red of his complexion—donned the long-tailed coat, stovepipe hat, and string tie of the statesmen of his period, waxed innocently pompous, and, in short, became a really striking figure of a man" (17). He saw that figure in his mind's eye in terms of a patriarch on his own family tree.

Two crucial aspects of the work seem particularly appropriate for a

---

48. Robyn R. Warhol, "Toward a Theory of the Engaging Narrator: Earnest Interventions in Gaskell, Stowe, and Eliot," *PMLA,* CI (October, 1986), 811–18.

49. See Shael Herman, "W. J. Cash and Southern Culture" (Paper presented at American Studies Association convention, New Orleans, October 30, 1990), and Michael P. Dean, "W. J. Cash's *The Mind of the South:* Southern History, Southern Style," *Southern Studies,* XX (1981), 297–302.

50. Hershman and Lieb, *Key to Genius,* 23–24.

writer with depressive inclinations and rebellious heart. The first is the underscoring of southern violence and crudity. In *The Mind of the South,* Cash notes, for instance, that in 1937 "Southern cities were over five times as murderous as those of either the North Central area or the Far West, over six times as those of the Middle Atlantic country, and over eighteen times as those of New England!" (424) The writer blamed ruralism, frontier spirit, and poverty—factors often still cited— but also the very culture itself, a proposition not so pleasing to regional boosters. Although questions still arise about just how homicidal the South really was, recent studies indicate that the question was as persistent and as rooted in the mores of the populace as Cash insistently contended.[51]

Although violence was an objective fact of southern life, Cash gave it such prominence because of his own personal perspective. He knew exactly the consequences of being the object of ridicule. As a child he had experienced the ridicule of his peers. Cursed with a squint from nearsightedness, the bespectacled boy was mocked by his classmates. They called him "Sleepy," an epithet that his daydreaming and fascination with books did nothing to dispel. He hated schoolyard fighting. Once he ran home, defeated, only to be told by his father in good southern fashion to go back and "act like a man."[52] Cash seldom alluded in his work to intimate experience. Yet no doubt such mortifying encounters informed his exploration of the "savage ideal."

Even his description of the lazy southerner, numbing himself with red-eye and taking little interest in his appearance, resembled Cash himself. The hedonistic-puritan dichotomy in the southern soul had as much to do with himself as with the South as a whole. Too much reading of romantic novelists rather than personal engagement with work may have been the source of his notion. As Katherine Rogers, his shrewdly blunt friend, reminisced, the emphasis on southern laziness simply reflected "Cash's own relatively sheltered childhood and adolescence with leisure to daydream and read romantic novels . . . even the silly outputs by Augusta Jane Evans Wilson . . . and J. Phillips Oppen-

51. See Lynwood Montell, *Killings: Folk Justice in the Upper South* (Lexington, Ky., 1986); Michael S. Hindus, *Prison and Plantation: Crime, Justice, and Authority in Massachusetts and South Carolina, 1767–1878* (Chapel Hill, 1980); Edward L. Ayers, *Vengeance and Justice: Crime and Punishment in the Nineteenth-Century American South* (New York, 1984).
52. Clayton, *Cash,* 7.

heim."[53] Harried with the thought of his inefficient work habits, Cash regarded himself as lazy. He spent much time brooding—and sometimes drinking much more than he should have.

Other habits—slovenliness for instance—were further indications of depression. Cash eyed personal hygiene with indifference, slouched about in "soiled gray underwear," and often took sedatives.[54] By the time Mary Ross Northrop (later Maury) appeared on the scene, however, he had begun to bathe regularly. So unrefined a self-presentation fits well his hostile attitude toward the wealthy of his own day and in the Old South. Coupled with his criticism of southern savagery, he gleefully lambasted Virginia gentility, the venerated icon of southern refinement. The "man at the center," he argued, showed too much respect for the high and mighty, whose hand-on-the-shoulder condescension toward less powerful kinfolk and neighbors evoked deference, not fury. Can one detect in such an argument Cash's disaffection about his own problematic station in life? Certainly with regard to the Agrarians of Vanderbilt, whom he despised as arrogant defenders of the Cavalier Legend, he once took their apology for an anti-Yankee, anti-industrialist ethic as a personal affront. (Later he softened his attitude.)[55] Beneath his carefully articulated and convincingly evocative themes, as Fred Hobson astutely observes, lay a serious burden of personal insecurity.[56]

The second characteristic of *The Mind of the South* that his depressive nature elicited was its essential negativism and sense of predetermination. The South, Cash concluded, had never and would never change. To be sure, he proposed the existence of three frontiers—the agrarian advance of King Cotton, the disruptions that attended Yankee conquest, and the rise of a new industrial order before World War I. Despite these watersheds, the constancy of the stream was unaffected. The same customs and prejudices that had shaped the South's earliest history continued to exercise a baleful influence. Those on top, Cash

53. Rogers to Morrison, September 30, 1964, in Morrison Papers.

54. Quotation from Burke [?] of Colonial Williamsburg to Morrison, June 2, 1965; see also Rogers to Morrison, September 10, 1964, Maury to Morrison, May 31, 1965, and Maury to Morrison, n.d., p. 10, in Morrison Papers.

55. Morrison, *Cash,* 165–67; Maury to "Miss Milam," May 6, 1957, in Morrison Papers.

56. Fred Hobson, *Tell About the South: The Southern Rage to Explain* (Baton Rouge, 1983), 262; Louis D. Rubin, Jr., "The Mind of the South," *Sewanee Review,* LXII (Autumn, 1954), 683–95.

insisted, remained there, with occasional injections of new blood, like his renowned fictional Irishman, from below. Antebellum planters had sons who became superintendents and owners of textile and phosphate plants in the post–Civil War period. The rich, indeed the whole society, remained loyal, through thick and thin, to the old precepts about race, social order, sex, and intellectual constraints.

At the same time, the depressive mode, we must remember, reaches a level of dark reality in human affairs that is often repressed, both culturally and individually. Melancholy, Michael Ignatieff points out, "is a way of seeing, one which captures an essential aspect of human existence. As such, depression is both a personal catastrophe and a necessary stage in our encounter with life." Richard King caught this connection perfectly in titling an essay on Cash "Narcissus Grown Analytical." He observed that what Cash had to say about southerners' sense of guilt, morbid romanticism, addiction to fantasy, sensitivity to outside criticism, and impulsiveness was true for him as well as for the South he loved and hated. These were regional conditions as unchangeable as that of a single personality—a white and male one. For that reason in *The Mind of the South* Cash treated southern blacks and women as white men saw them. That was the experience he knew and could draw upon.[57]

No wonder Cash's reputation fell so precipitously in the 1960s and 1970s. What message of hope could this prophet of an unchangeable South proclaim to academic liberals, feminists, civil rights reformers, or black nationalists? Did not federal policies to dismantle Jim Crow, integrate schools, enfranchise black voters, and establish new acknowledgments of ethnic integrity refute Cash's grim interpretation?

In particular, C. Vann Woodward found *The Mind of the South* distressing because it offered no means of escaping the South's fatal weaknesses of character and ideology. As one who sought an end to the tragedy of racial antipathy and injustice, Woodward denied Cash's concept of continuity and virtually unrelieved conformity. Irony, not doom, informed his reading of the southern past. Even-tempered and sanguine, Woodward thus indicted Cash's work for being not only factually but philosophically wrong. Michael O'Brien, Dewey Grantham,

---

57. Michael Ignatieff, "Paradigm Lost," *Times Literary Supplement,* September 4, 1987, p. 939; Richard H. King, *A Southern Renaissance: The Cultural Awakening of the American South, 1930–1955* (New York, 1980), 146–72.

Joel Williamson, Paul Gaston, and many others have scored Cash's misinterpretations, many of them common to the time he wrote. Yet Woodward's challenge to Cash's rendering of a persistent southern folk ethic remains the most articulate and intense. Surely that is related to temperamental and not just intellectual differences.[58]

A final query remains. If Cash's creativity was directly related to his mental state, how valid can *The Mind of the South* be? Woodward proposed that the book was misnamed. Cash might have more accurately entitled it, the Yale scholar suggested, "The Temperament of the South,' 'The Feelings of the South,' or more literally, 'The Mindlessness of the South.'" Perhaps we can add one more alternative and christen it "The Mind of W. J. Cash." In some respects, that is what it was. The term, however, is not meant facetiously. The book has more persuasive insights and broader penetrations of what made the South distinctive than most others of its time or ours. Cash was a southerner to the marrow of his being. Unlike others, he knew its essential failings because they were, on some level, his own.

To elaborate on the last point, Cash was peculiarly in touch with what one might call a deep underself. That is, he had the depressive's special insight into his own recesses. He could draw upon that fundament to create his images, ideas, and intuitions and provide them with a synthetic framework so that no part seemed inconsistent with another. Some of those ideas were true for the South as a whole. Some were more true for Cash than for the region. His widow put it well: "What he did was arrive at inference. He heard old stories, handed down. Why some trashy lot went up in the world while the local seigneurs were going to seed. He lived as a child in a region where almost the only recreation was conversation—'visitin'. He listened and dreamed over things he heard, and understood them later."[59] Such was the method and the aim of many southern writers of fiction.

58. See Michael O'Brien, "W. J. Cash, Hegel, and the South," *Journal of Southern History,* XLIV (August, 1978), 379–98; O'Brien, *The Idea of the American South, 1920–1941* (Baltimore, 1979), 213–17; Joel Williamson, *The Crucible of Race: Black/White Relations in the American South Since Emancipation* (New York, 1984), 3; Paul Gaston, *The New South Creed: A Study in Southern Mythmaking* (New York, 1970), 11–12; C. Vann Woodward, "W. J. Cash Reconsidered," *New York Review of Books,* December 4, 1969, pp. 34–35; Woodward, "The Elusive Mind of the South," in Woodward, *American Counterpoint: Slavery and Racism in the North-South Dialogue* (Boston, 1971), 261–84.

59. Maury to "Miss Milam," May 16, 1957, in Morrison Papers.

In light of that approach, what should we expect of any imaginative rendition? Cash provides not literal truth but verisimilitude. It was derived from his own self-understanding. The struggle in his mind was his posing of paternal opposites—John Cash, on one hand, and William Poteat, on the other. In *The Mind of the South,* they were represented in the antinomies of regional folk culture and the mandates of modern intellectuality. These conflicting impulses were janusian in character, to borrow from Rothenberg once again. Cash could raise these antinomies to consciousness only as abstractions about the South. In his own mind, however, they could never be satisfactorily resolved. The result was emotional exhaustion and resort to too much alcohol. The energy devoted to such inner warfare left him little room to know exactly who he was—except as he could project a persona through the creative process.

Virginia Woolf once wrote a friend, "As an experience madness is terrific I can assure you, and not to be sniffed at; and in its lava I still find most of the things I write about." Although he wrote in a different genre, in a sense that was Cash's essential method. He was by no means a novelist, historian, autobiographer, or poet, but something *sui generis,* like the tormented South itself. If he mirrored a certain southern culture in his own volatility, pessimism and gothic inclination, desires and contradictions of love and anger, he could thank his melancholy disposition for providing the anguish that extracted so imaginative a response. Mental adversity was a tragically high price to pay. Had he not paid it, however, we would most likely not be honoring his name and achievement a half-century later. In concluding, one can only repeat the epitaph that Woodward offered in his wise if critical essay on Cash: "Peace to his troubled spirit."[60]

60. Virginia Woolf to Ethel Smyth, June 22, 1930, in Nicholson and Trautman, eds., *Letters of Woolf,* IV, 180; Woodward, "The Elusive Mind of the South," 283.

W. J. Cash in 1941. Drawing by Manuel Domecq, from a photograph.
Courtesy News Bureau, Wake Forest University, Winston-Salem, N.C., and Manuel Domecq

WILBUR JOSEPH CASH, *Eu.*

Candidate for B.A.

BOILING SPRINGS, NORTH CAROLINA

Age 22; Height 5' 10"; Weight 158.

"Go where he will, the wise man is at home."

Just because he is called "Sleepy" does not mean that this gentleman is always in a somnolent mood, for he is usually very wide-awake. "Sleepy" served two Alma Maters before he came to Wake Forest, but, having arrived, he soon distinguished himself in the literary fields of the college. As managing editor of *Old Gold and Black* and as a frequent contributor to the *Student*, both of prose and poetry, his work has been of high order. In the class room also "Sleepy" has been a fair and consistent student throughout his course, ranking high in the fields of literature and history. While not the friendliest fellow in college, "Sleepy" is important in the social life of his chums here. He will probably return next year for the study of law.

Associate Editor Old Gold and Black, '20-'21; Anniversary Marshal, '21; President Cleveland County Club, '20-'21; Member Political Science Club, '20-'21-'22; Contributor to College Wits Number "Judge," '21; Manager of Tennis, '21-'22; Member of "W" Club, '21-'22; Quill Club, '21-'22; Managing Editor Old Gold and Black, '21-'22.

Entry on Cash from *The Howler,* the Wake Forest yearbook, from 1922, Cash's senior year

Courtesy Wake Forest University Archives, Winston-Salem, N.C.

W. J. Cash and Alfred A. Knopf at the Hotel Charlotte in March, 1941
Courtesy Charles Elkins, Sr.

Mary and W. J. Cash with Cash's parents, Nannie and John Cash, and his
sister, Bertie Elkins, in 1941, shortly before W. J. and Mary left for Mexico
Courtesy Charles Elkins, Sr.

Cash's typewriter, on which he composed the original typescript of *The Mind of the South*
Courtesy Rare Books and Manuscripts Department, Z. Smith Reynolds Library, Wake Forest University, Winston-Salem, N.C. Photo by Martine Sherrill

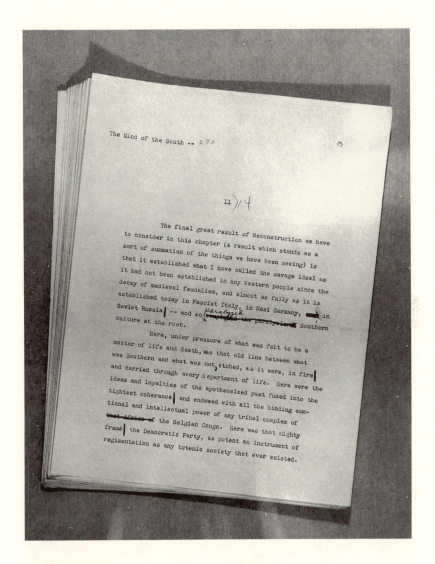

Page 270 of the final edited typescript of *The Mind of the South*, containing the passage in which Cash explains his concept of the savage ideal

Courtesy Rare Books and Manuscripts Department, Z. Smith Reynolds Library, Wake Forest University, Winston-Salem, N.C. Photo by Martine Sherrill

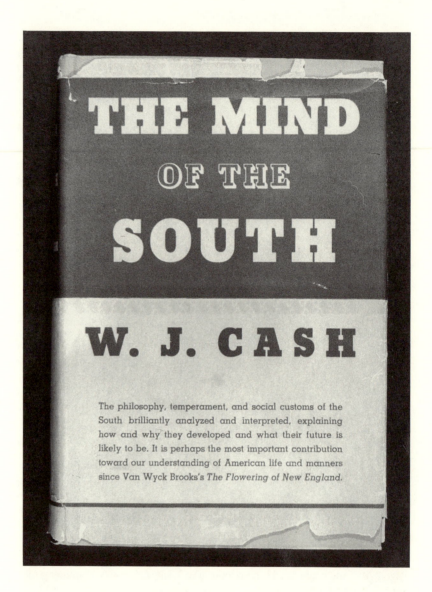

The first edition of a classic

Courtesy Rare Books and Manuscripts Department, Z. Smith Reynolds Library, Wake Forest University, Winston-Salem, N.C. Photo by Martine Sherrill

PART II

The Mind of the South Reconsidered

Cash and the Crisis of Political Modernity

RICHARD H. KING

Over the last two and a half decades, *The Mind of the South* has been subjected to considerable scrutiny. W. J. Cash has been scored as a dummy for H. L. Mencken and lacking in regional piety. He has been characterized as an essentially romantic historian. Several intellectual historians of the modern South have labeled him a modernist. Most recently, Cash has been located in a southern tradition of Machiavellian/republican discourse that seeks to rescue a patriarchal, aristocratic tradition from the depredations of commercialism and racial pollution. However different or dubious these various readings are, they all consider Cash in a specifically southern context, which is hardly surprising because his only book was *The Mind of the South*. They also tend to classify *The Mind of the South* as history, even though Cash was a journalist by trade. Like many newspapermen, he wanted to be a writer of fiction and had the proverbial unfinished novels—which all southerners are said to have—in his desk drawer to prove it.[1]

1. C. Vann Woodward, "The Elusive Mind of the South," in Woodward, *American Counterpoint: Slavery and Racism in the North-South Dialogue* (Boston, 1971), 261–84, lodged the charge of impiety, while Michael O'Brien in "A Private Passion: W. J. Cash," in O'Brien, *Rethinking the South: Essays in Intellectual History* (Baltimore, 1988), 177–89, classifies Cash as a romantic. Cash the modernist has been analyzed and largely praised by Daniel Singal, *The War Within: From Victorian to Modernist Thought in the South, 1919–1945* (Chapel Hill, 1982); Richard H. King, *A Southern Renaissance: The Cultural Awakening of the American South, 1930–1955* (New York, 1980); Fred Hobson, *Tell About the South: The Southern Rage to Explain* (Baton Rouge, 1983); and most recently Bruce Clayton, "A Southern Modernist: The Mind of W. J. Cash," in *The South Is Another Land,* ed. Bruce Clayton and John A. Salmond (New York, 1987), 171–86; Clayton, "W. J. Cash and the Creative Impulse," *Southern Review,* XXIV (Autumn, 1988),

But there are other contexts relevant to understanding the shape and substance of *The Mind of the South*. From the standpoint of American cultural and intellectual history, Cash's text is part of the quest for community through rediscovery of region and exploration of locale that observers ranging from Alfred Kazin to Warren Susman and Richard Pells have taken as one of the seminal preoccupations of American writing in the decade before World War II.[2] Susman has identified culture as the central concept of the Depression decade; and certainly Cash's "mind" is a metonymic way of talking about culture in the broadest, descriptive sense. To bring to bear such a national focus highlights some of the historical concerns that fed Cash's steady ambition and flagging resolve and helped sustain Alfred and Blanche Knopf in their eleven exasperating years of waiting for the elusive manuscript. But *contra* Pells, unlike the Vanderbilt Agrarians, Cash discovered a South that was hardly a consolation against the uncertainties of modernity or an alternative to economic depression. Rather, Cash's South suggested the perils of regional celebration, the stifling effect of community, and the patent inability of the southern tradition to accommodate the spirit of modernity.[3]

As I have suggested elsewhere, Cash was far from alone among southern intellectuals in distancing himself from regional tradition during the 1930s. Much of the writing of the Southern Renaissance took issue with the region's "authorized" way of life. But the variousness of regional reassessment in the Depression decade can be sampled when we place Cash's *Mind of the South* next to two other texts by southerners that appeared in 1941: William Alexander Percy's *Lanterns on the Levee*

777–90; Clayton, *W. J. Cash: A Life* (Baton Rouge, 1991). Finally, Richard Nelson's *Aesthetic Frontiers: The Machiavellian Tradition and the Southern Tradition* (Jackson, Miss., 1990) offers a reading of Cash as a Machiavellian/republican that I think is unconvincing, though the book is intellectually demanding and certainly worth reading.

2. Alfred Kazin, *On Native Grounds: An Interpretation of Modern American Prose Literature* (New York, 1942); Warren Susman, "The Thirties," in *The Development of American Culture*, ed. Stanley Coben and Lorman Ratner (Englewood Cliffs, N.J., 1970), 179–218; and Richard Pells, *Radical Visions and American Dreams: Cultural and Social Thought in the Depression Years* (New York, 1973).

3. The definitions of and differences between modernity, modernization, and modernism are contested to say the least. Here I will use the term *modernism* to refer to a literary and artistic movement; *modernization* to refer to the intersecting set of social, political, economic, and cultural transformations; and *modernity* ambiguously to encompass both phenomena without assuming that modernizers were modernists or vice versa.

and James Agee and Walker Evans' *Let Us Now Praise Famous Men*. Connections and affinities there are, of course, among the three works, each of which is a masterpiece of prose. All are deeply felt and argued. But their differences in structure, style, and informing sensibility are striking. These differences can perhaps be explained by the disparate provenances of their authors—piedmont, delta, and mountain South; occupations—journalist-litterateur, lawyer-poet, and avant-garde, urbanized intellectual; and genre—(very) extended essay, autobiographical memoir, and meta-documentary cum autobiography. Such differences remind us how risky large generalizations about context or shared intellectual and literary cultures or even the nature of modernism are.

It is not my brief here to assess Cash's *Mind of the South* as a work of (failed? successful if eccentric?) regional history as such. Fifty years down the road, with our perspectives refined and concerns diversified, it should scarcely be surprising that Cash seems too dismissive of southern intellectual culture, too heedless of countercurrents and oppositional forces in southern politics, and too willing to fall into easy, often slighting characterizations of black southerners. Nor do I see much point in proceeding to identify all the literary and intellectual influences Cash might have had anxieties about, a task that Bruce Clayton's reconstruction of Cash's mind has accomplished admirably.

Rather I want to read *The Mind of the South* as an oblique response to the political crisis of the interwar years, as a work of protopolitical thought in which Cash explored the question of where political modernity went wrong through an analysis of the "mind" of the South. What, I want to imagine Cash asking, are the possibilities and perversions of democratic politics? What is the nature of political authority and consent? And, encompassing all these concerns, how did the political culture of the West produce fascism, Nazism, Stalinism, in sum, totalitarianism, and make it, not democratic politics and cultural freedom, appear the wave of the future as the 1930s accelerated toward disaster?

For the most part, Cash did not ask these questions directly and in such abstract form. That is, I am making no strong or important claim about his intentions as such. Rather, his book suggests that for Cash coming to terms with the mind of the South was imperative for some of the same reasons that a reckoning with totalitarianism was. The southern version of these questions about politics and modernity might be couched in the following way: Why had Thomas Jefferson's South become Nathan Bedford Forrest's, in which pride in Enlightenment rationality was transmogrified into pride in racial superiority? Why had one of modernity's most precious achievements—the autonomy of the individual—led to mass conformity in political and cultural matters and the ruthless suppression of African-Americans during and after slavery? The cunning of history and the dialectic of the Enlightenment seemed diabolical.

To examine Cash in relation to the crisis of political modernity, it is important to set the intellectual stage of this crisis of the late 1930s, to examine Cash's central thesis and in particular his analysis of the political culture and psychology of the antebellum South, and finally to draw out the implications of this analysis by putting Cash's explanation for the origins and development of totalitarianism next to that of a southern conservative, Richard Weaver, who began writing about the South and the crisis of modernity shortly after Cash's death. I should also say that I am concerned not only with influences on Cash but with the way other American and southern intellectuals responded to this same crisis, whether Cash knew of them or they of him.

THE CRISIS OF POLITICAL MODERNITY

It should come as no surprise that there is no consensus about the origins or nature of totalitarianism. Nor, for that matter, is there agreement on how useful the term is altogether. But by the mid-1930s many American intellectuals—and European émigré intellectuals in America—had come to realize that something new and ominous, something resembling a massive historical countermovement, had appeared on the scene. In analyzing and exorcising this new phenomenon of totalitarianism, three broad positions emerged.[4]

---

4. The term *totalitarianism* was already in use in the late 1930s and had been used in a positive sense by Mussolini even earlier. This is ironic, since Hannah Arendt denied that Mussolini's regime was totalitarian and thus insisted on the distinction between fascism and totalitarianism and between both those phenomena and authoritarian regimes. Cash's main interest/obsession was with Nazism, and when I use *totalitarianism* or *fascism* here, I refer primarily to Nazism, even though he mentioned both fascist Italy and Stalin's Soviet Union as well. Writing, as he did, before the extermination policy of the Nazis or the Gulags of Stalin were generally known, Cash could not be expected to make these or similar distinctions. Overall, I do not want to argue a theory of totalitarianism but merely to chart the way Cash tried to come to terms with what were clearly examples of pathological dimensions of political modernity. See the Introduction to Stephen J. Whitfield, *Into the Dark: Hannah Arendt and Totalitarianism* (Philadelphia, 1980) for a brief history of the origins of the usage of the term *totalitarianism*.

First were those figures on the Left who viewed fascism and totalitarianism of the Right as heightened expressions of traditional conservatism in the religious, cultural, and intellectual spheres and unrestricted monopoly capitalism in the economic sphere. The problem with authoritarianism was just that—too much authority, dogma, and intolerance. Totalitarian fascism was a reversion to earlier levels of political and cultural life, a retreat into the barbarism of national, religious, and racial atavisms. A central figure in this liberal-Left tradition was philosopher John Dewey, who, according to one student of the period, had been "arguing that philosophical absolutism implied political authoritarianism for over three decades."[5] At the same time, totalitarianism created structures of social, political, and cultural domination through the use of the most sophisticated technology and advanced organizational techniques. For liberals such as Dewey or neo-Marxists such as émigré intellectuals of the Frankfurt School or figures such as Dwight Macdonald or Clement Greenberg among New York intellectuals, the ominous new political and cultural developments deployed rational, modern scientific devices and methods, especially the mass media, in the service of regressive or reactionary goals. They represented no triumph of mass communication, no triumph of the will.

Yet others thought such an analysis was inadequate, for something deeper, more serious, was at work. Robert Maynard Hutchens and Mortimer Adler at the University of Chicago contended that the symptom and cause of the new barbarism was what Edward Purcell calls "scientific naturalism," precisely the regnant liberal worldview purveyed by Dewey, the Legal Realists, including men such as Jerome Frank and Thurman Arnold, and empirical political science that denied any foundational or traditional philosophical supports to democratic institutions and values. In the 1920s Walter Lippmann's *Public Opinion* had seriously questioned the political capability of the average citizen, and in the 1930s legal thinker Thurman Arnold in his *Folklore of Capitalism* questioned the rationality of the average citizen and denied that legal principles were grounded in anything more than political self-interest. But the foundationalists contended that if the scientific naturalists were correct, or at least if their message was taken to be true, the fascist

---

5. Edward A. Purcell, *The Crisis of Democratic Theory: Scientific Naturalism and the Problem of Value* (Lexington, Ky., 1973), 200. Purcell notes that by the late 1930s, the term *totalitarianism* included Italy, Germany, and the Soviet Union (135–36).

emphasis on action, will, and energy would win by default. These critics felt that scientific naturalism's "skepticism and moral cynicism were
largely responsible for the spread of totalitarianism."[6]

Similarly, the late 1930s saw a reaction against cultural relativism
in anthropology and historical relativism in historiography. If there
were no transcultural or transhistorical values, then the West's democratic values were just one among several possibilities. What Peter Novick refers to as the "turn toward affirmation and the search for cer-
tainty" was also detectable in the salvos directed against the emotional
"objectivity and detachment" that relativism seemed to encourage, even
as fascism and Stalinism were on the march. Among historians, Charles
Beard and Carl Becker drew the most fire for their relativistic and critical views. And Van Wyck Brooks, Lewis Mumford, and Archibald
MacLeish lashed out at the "irresponsibles" of literary modernism for
being out of touch with the people and sapping their morale and will
to resist fascism.[7]

Interestingly, this quest for foundations undertaken mainly by liberals was not for alternatives to democracy but for a firmer footing from
which to defend it. Nor was the foundationalist position without self-
contradiction. Novick notes that cognitive relativism—the inability to
provide foundations for our knowledge claims—does not necessarily
entail moral relativism—the doubt that we can find foundations for our
values claims. Not to mention the often willful confusion between relativism, which refers to the existence of competing value systems, and
nihilism, which implies the lack of values altogether. Moreover, critics
sometimes pilloried the liberals for their naiveté, for an inadequate
sense of human sin and of the necessity for force in politics. Such at
least was theologian Reinhold Niebuhr's standing criticism of Dewey.
Yet the same liberal, critical temper was also savaged for cynicism about
the possibility or advisability of democratic participation or the ability
of voters to identify or act on their own interests.[8]

But there was also a conservative intellectual position pressing to

6. *Ibid.*, 65.

7. Peter Novick, *That Noble Dream: The "Objectivity Question" and the American
Historical Profession* (Cambridge, Eng., 1988), 281. See also Dwight Macdonald's response to the MacLeish-Brooks-Mumford attack on the modernists in *Memoirs of a Revo-
lutionist* (Cleveland, 1958), 203–14.

8. One reason for the latter inconsistency is that, according to Purcell, there was a
liberal-radical and a more conservative, apolitical, and cynical wing of scientific naturalism.

be heard in the 1930s. Rather than seeking transcendent support for democracy, it questioned the wisdom or possibility of democratic institutions or values altogether. Not surprisingly, such a traditionalist (as opposed to libertarian) conservatism was strong among southern writers and intellectuals, particularly the Agrarians (and second-generation figures such as Richard Weaver) and Will Percy. For them the emergence of mass society and the collapse of the structures of religious, cultural, and intellectual authority opened the way for demagogues to mobilize the masses against now discredited elites and otiose traditions of authority and hierarchy. At the root of Nazism, according to Percy, was the power of *Demos,* the mob. For Weaver it was variously "pragmatism," which he felt, like the radical Randolph Bourne, allowed means to be turned toward any pernicious ends, including total war, and "materialism" that arose from the loss of a sense of transcendent grounding for thought and action. Weaver explained southern hostility to Hitlerism by claiming that fascism was intellectually and socially a post–French Revolution phenomenon to be understood as a reaction against secular, liberal individualism and materialism. Though its goals seemed to coincide with those of traditional conservativism, fascism, according to Weaver, was actually the "kind of usurpation toward which radical democracy always tends" and a species of "extreme proletarian nihilism."[9] Weaver contended, however, that southern conservatism was a traditional rather than modern cast and thus had no affinities with the "revolution of nihilism." Only those who were most skeptical of the cult of democracy could understand the true origins of the mass psychology of fascism.

CASH AND POLITICAL MODERNITY

To read Cash's *Mind of the South* as a text that reflected and illuminated the crisis of political modernity that exercised American minds in the 1930s, a brief review of Cash's essential thesis is in order. Cash, as

9. Richard Weaver, "The Revolution of Nihilism" (1944), in *The Southern Essays of Richard M. Weaver,* ed. George M. Curtis III and James J. Thompson, Jr. (Indianapolis, 1987), 187. Several essays relevant to the topic are in this volume. Weaver also addresses the issue of fascism and the South's relation to it forthrightly in the Epilogue to *The Southern Tradition at Bay: A History of Postbellum Thought,* ed. George Core and M. E. Bradford (New Rochelle, N.Y., 1968), but as far as I can tell the Epilogue was written at the time for its publication in 1968.

C. Vann Woodward has emphasized, did present a view of southern continuity and unity over the century and a half of its existence. The material force most profoundly shaping southern history was, according to Cash, the frontier. In Frederick Jackson Turner's original conception, the frontier had been both a place and a process / experience. It was where (white European) settlement ended; more important, what happened there was the destruction of traditional institutions and values. The frontier was a place of institutional and cultural reconstruction.

For Cash the frontier was less a place than a continually recurring process in southern history. It was essential to his thesis that frontier conditions had been recreated during Reconstruction ("Thorough" or "The Frontier the Yankees Made") and then in the process of regional industrialization and urbanization ("Progress"). Generally, Cash's frontier thesis, southern style, represented his effort to explain why southern society and culture were modern rather than traditional. Whatever traditional values and institutions had been brought to or had emerged in the area below the Mason-Dixon Line were periodically weakened, even destroyed, by the effects of the frontier. During the antebellum years, in particular, the frontier created a situation of institutional underdevelopment, particularly in the areas of government and law. It brought with it grand opportunity for some but also produced two fateful traits which Cash placed at the center of the southern mind— individualism and romanticism.

By individualism, Cash meant nothing like the Transcendentalists' rarefied and intellectualized "expressive" individualism.[10] Rather, to Cash the trait amounted to a basic "simplicity," a lack of social sophistication, derived from the absence of a complex urban environment and perpetuated by the plantation system. Not only did it produce the illusion that the individual could, if he but chose, do pretty much anything he liked. It also implied a lack of class consciousness: "The Old South may be said, in truth, to have been nearly innocent of the notion of class in any rigid and complete sense" (*Mind,* 35). But "the tendency toward unreality, toward romanticism, and . . . toward hedonism" (46) was also a function of this lack of social sophistication. This romantic mentality was reinforced by the landscape and climate, a relative lack of

10. See Robert Bellah *et al., Habits of the Heart: Middle America Observed* (Berkeley, 1985), chap. II, for the concept of "expressive individualism."

want, and the presence of slavery and enslaved people of African descent in interaction with northern Europeans of Celtic stock.

Cash developed several lines of implication from these two central characteristics. But one characteristic of southern social psychology had profound political importance—the almost total identification of the individual ego of the average white southerner with the region as a whole and its upper-class leaders (the "Proto-Dorian bond"), a particularly glaring example of which was what Cash called the "savage ideal." On first glance, this "identification" thesis seems to contradict the "individualism" thesis. But it does not when we remember that Cash's point about the "man at the center" was precisely the failure of that figure to realize that social, cultural, economic, or political differences were fairly fixed rather than fluid or nonexistent. And it was this lack of class consciousness that allowed increasing attacks from the North, the vague possibility of social advancement, the fear of the black presence, more generally the "community" or "democracy of feeling" (43) among whites, deriving from intense racial and kinship ties, to solidify the Proto-Dorian bond. From "just as good as," Cash seems to be saying, it was but a short step to "just the same as." The result was a white society best characterized as a "herd of independent minds."[11]

The savage ideal—"that ideal whereunder dissent and variety are completely suppressed and men become, in all their attitudes, professions, and actions, virtual replicas of one another" (93–94)—was in turn the cultural and intellectual expression of this social and political solidarity among whites. It crystallized during the slavery crisis, re-emerged in times of crisis such as Reconstruction through the offices of the Democratic party and the Ku Klux Klan, and then played a major role in the fundamentalist Kulturkampf against the ideas of Darwin, Marx, Freud, and other modern thinkers inside and outside the beleaguered walls of southern academia in the twentieth century.

The theoretical assumptions underpinning Cash's historical and political analysis were thoroughly modern. Cash's interpretive affinities were with what Paul Ricoeur has called the "hermeneutics of suspicion." Indeed, the three figures Ricoeur cites as instances of this mod-

---

11. Harold Rosenberg uses this phrase to characterize the anticommunist temper among New York intellectuals after World War II (*The Tradition of the New* [New York, 1959], 207).

ern cast of mind—Marx, Freud, and Nietzsche—all exerted a profound effect on Cash's intellectual and psychological development.[12] Freud's influence on Cash has been often remarked. Indeed, Cash's identification thesis is the same sort of explanation of political authority and consent as Freud's analysis of mass psychology, Wilhelm Reich's explanation of the mass psychology of fascism, and Erich Fromm's attempt to explain the modern escape from freedom that led to the triumph of Nazism. Cash, like his mentor Mencken, had read his Nietzsche. Finally, though Cash was no Marxist, his fundamental explanatory move as an analyst of historical phenomena was to probe beneath the surface for the "real" cause or explanation. "It is plain," writes Cash, "that slavery was inescapably brutal and ugly. . . . The stark fact remains: It rested on force" (85). Analogously, when tracking the emergence of southern modernization, that is, "Progress," Cash had no doubt that its foundation was "cheapness of labor" (202).

Yet Cash was no vulgar psychological reductionist. If he emphasized one thing, probably too much, it was that white southerners were not hypocrites. Their behavior implied no personal mendacity or calculating dissembling: they really believed what they did and said: "There was much of Tartarin in this Southerner, but nothing of Tartufe" (60). He was never a foundationalist—liberation from the religious fundamentalism of the region was too precious to him for that—and his emphasis on intelligence and rationality suggests a general position nearer to Dewey's than to those who searched for religious and metaphysical foundations to stave off the impending totalitarian catastrophe.

Cash's normative theory of politics was also thoroughly modern. It posited the desirability of a politics organized around self-interest. Reflecting the hard-boiled tenor of contemporary liberalism,[13] which based its appeal on self-interest rather than rights, Cash believed that "in the so-called democracies of our Western world at least, one of the proper functions of politics is the resolution of essential conflict in interest in groups and classes. . . . From such a realistic content the politics of the South was in a peculiarly thorough fashion barred away" (54). Later he describes the "proper business of politics" as "the reso-

12. Paul Ricoeur, *Freud and Philosophy: An Essay on Interpretation* (New Haven, 1970), 32–36.
13. See Daniel Rodgers, *Contested Truths: Key Words in American Politics Since Independence* (New York, 1987), 176–211 ("Interest").

lution of the inevitable conflict in interest between the classes, and the securing of a reasonable degree of social equity" (132).

Ironically, considering its function in postwar American political culture as a way of defending the status quo, interest group liberalism was progressive, even radical in the southern context. This was the case because southern politics was dominated by leaders, ideas, and movements that defied common sense or the needs of the modern world, much less worked for greater social equity. Emphasis on the region as a whole and its peculiar moral position (the southern way of life) stifled open appeals to the interests of the less well-off, the excluded, or the oppressed of both races. Indeed, Cash is one of the charter members of modern southern intellectual liberalism, a position developed after World War II by V. O. Key and C. Vann Woodward, which identified the pursuit of interests with political rationality. Just as Woodward was fascinated by Tom Watson's challenge to the Proto-Dorian bond of the Democratic party and his effort to forge economic and political alliances across racial lines, Cash had kind words for Huey Long's forswearing of racial demagoguery but thought that Long's great failure lay in his unwillingness to confront the blight of tenancy and sharecropping or to deal with class divisions among the nonaristocratic southern farmers. Moreover, Cash wrote in 1935 in terms that echoed the great populist dream of southern politics: "To succeed in revolt he [the "Cracker"] must join forces with the Negro." Thus it is fair to say that increasingly Cash saw the South's entrance onto a course of political maturity and rationality as proportional to the growth of class awareness and pursuit of the politics of self-interest among the common whites and between them and southern blacks. Where identification upward and deference were, there rationality and realistic self-interest should be.[14]

Cash, like Marx and Freud, stood with the Enlightenment fraction of the modern mind. In contrast with the Agrarians, who were modernists in literature but hostile to modernity in general, Cash managed to combine a passion for modernist writing, a fascination with modern thought, a chastened liberal politics, and a humane skepticism. In describing the inadequacies of the southern mentality, he indicated his own commitment to "the complexity of mind, the knowledge, and, above all, the habit of skepticism essential to any generally realistic at-

14. Quoted in Clayton, *Cash*, 105.

titude" (47). "Skepticism," he wrote in 1938, "is, after all, the very essence of the spirit of the liberal tradition." This is not to say that Cash was Pollyannish about human nature; indeed, his assessment of human nature was decidedly mordant. The trouble with Marx, contended Cash, was that he was "one of the two or three most naive idealists who have lived on this planet . . . humanity is not only not noble inherently but also not in any other fashion. . . . It has its moments no doubt. . . . We are ruled by ego. We are out to get ours."[15] There is nothing very profound about these journalistic musings. They are the reflex of a literate, hard-bitten journalist, more cynical sounding than his book. But they flowed from Cash's larger conviction that personal and collective survival depended on realistically assessing the situation without losing one's head. Though he admired the romantic gesture and a certain extravagance of spirit, they had negative political consequences as a rule.

CASH AND TOTALITARIANISM

This brings us directly to the great perversion of political modernity—the rise of European fascism and the emergence by the late 1930s of totalitarian regimes in Germany and the Soviet Union. What stance did Cash take toward these ominous developments and how did he relate them to the mind of the South? As both of Cash's biographers emphasize, Cash became obsessed with Nazism and Hitler in the last years of his life. Friends and colleagues witnessed moments of apoplectic rage when Cash would all but lose control as he ranted about the German dictator. His editorials and analyses in the Charlotte *News* provide ample evidence of his deep concern, even if we did not know of those unbearably sad last days in Mexico City when he felt pursued by Nazi agents to the point of committing suicide. Bruce Clayton notes that already in late 1936 Cash's Guggenheim application asked for money so that he could write a novel, but he also, says Clayton, "hoped to observe fascism up close" in Italy and Germany. Cash had, he wrote in the application, a "particular interest in the Nazi regime and movement as a historical phenomenon." Clayton also reports that during his fits Cash would rage against Hitler as, in Clayton's words, "a maniac, a

15. Quoted in Joseph L. Morrison, *W. J. Cash, Southern Prophet: A Biography and a Reader* (New York, 1967), 248, 229–30.

Ku Kluxer, white trash." [16] Whatever Cash's intentions for the book, his later years were haunted by Nazism.

Still, the relevant source here is *The Mind of the South* itself. My rereading of it turned up relatively few direct mentions of contemporary European politics or of fascism. But they are significantly located in the book. There is an oft-quoted passage in which Cash waxes indignant about the fate of the South under Reconstruction, comparing it with other small nations that have been the playgrounds for imperialist powers: "Not Ireland nor Poland, not Finland nor Bohemia . . . not one of these, for all the massacres, the pillage, and the rapes to which they have so often been subjected, was ever so pointedly taken in the very core of its being as was the South" (108). Not long afterward Cash summarizes the effects of Reconstruction on the South by suggesting that it established the savage ideal "almost as truly as it is established today in Fascist Italy, in Nazi Germany, in Soviet Russia—and so paralyzed Southern culture at the root" (137) and possessed "all the binding emotional and intellectual power of any tribal complex of the Belgian Congo." In the aftermath of Reconstruction the "instrument of [regional] regimentation" was the Democratic party, which was as "potent . . . as any totemic society that ever existed" (138). This is pretty strong stuff, combining righteous indignation against political extremism and occupation with ethnocentric, even racist, analogies.

In his discussion of southern demagogues such as Coleman Blease and Ben Tillman, Cash offers a convincing analytic description of Hitler's seductive appeal to the masses who stood enthralled at Nuremberg. Perhaps Cash could have written the following without Hitler in mind. But I doubt it. "In his every word and deed precisely to render what, given all the forces at play upon them, they most secretly wanted: the making vocal and manifest of their slowly gathering melancholy for and resentment against their economic and social lot, without ever losing sight of the paramount question of race" (259).

Finally, when Cash focuses on the revival of the Klan after World War I, he comes closest to asserting an identity rather than just an analogy between Nazism and the grimmest dimensions of the southern political culture: "In its [the Klan's] essence the thing was an authentic folk movement—at least as fully such as the Nazi movement in Germany, to which it was not without kinship" (344). He continues: "And,

16. Clayton, *Cash*, 110, 156.

summing up these fears, it brought them into focus with the tradition of the past, and above all with the ancient Southern pattern of high romantic histrionics, violence, and mass coercion of the scapegoat and the heretic" (345).

No doubt the tone of such passages becomes more insistent as Cash approached the historical present and the end of his book. Their impact must have been then, and I think still is, quite powerful, particularly since the Nazi analogy bears not just on modern southern racist dema-goguery but also assumes a continuity—not a radical break—between that form of political pathology and the antebellum political culture of the South.

CASH, THE AGRARIANS, AND RICHARD WEAVER

For those traditional, organic conservatives such as Weaver and Agrari-ans such as Allen Tate, modernity itself was the *fons et origo* of all evil. Yet for all the strong exception Cash and the Agrarians took to one another, their analyses of the southern tradition sound remarkably simi-lar. One of Tate's standing complaints from the 1930s through the 1950s had to do with the lack of a consequential and rigorous intellec-tual tradition south of the Mason-Dixon Line. As a result, the South had been intellectually defenseless against the world the Yankees made after the Civil War and still largely were. Nor did the most important second-generation Agrarian, Richard Weaver, object to analyses of the South that pointed to the region's lack of a "dialectical" capability, the rigorously logical unfolding of a position from fixed abstract principles. Weaver, unlike Tate, saw no great problem with this incapacity and took it as a sign that the South had not yet been infected with the modern Cartesian spirit.[17]

Similarly, both Cash and the Agrarians, almost to a man, saw in-dividualism, including the "laissez-faire" spirit—Weaver added the "be-lief in inalienable personal rights"—as pernicious. But where Cash placed this lack of social concern or class consciousness at the very heart of the southern tradition, Weaver and the Agrarians clearly distin-guished socially responsive southern "social bond" individualism from

---

17. This was a term that Weaver used to characterize the "modern" mind as op-posed to the traditional and southern propensity for "rhetoric." See Weaver, "Two Types of American Individualism," in *Southern Essays,* ed. Curtis and Thompson, 88–91.

what Cash and later C. B. MacPherson would identify as "possessive individualism." The latter, according to the conservatives, was foreign to the essential mind of the South.[18]

Nor would Weaver and the Agrarians have had trouble accepting a certain form of Cash's identification thesis. But where to the democrat Cash the close identification of the classes and the masses seemed politically irrational, to traditional southern conservatives such a close tie was but another form of rational deference on the part of the southern common man. It was an open acknowledgment of what was the case— the political, social, and cultural superiority of the southern planter aristocracy. That was why masters were masters and captains, captains. If the democratic idea was a swindle, if the common man, white or black, needed social and political guidance, then what could be more reasonable than that the common whites should fall in line behind their betters? To do so was their true self-interest. Where the common whites fell prey to irrationality and irresponsibility was in heeding the seductive message of the political demagogues. But this was a perversion of democracy, not of a traditional aristocracy.

Indeed, for Weaver, as for most conservative analysts of totalitarianism and for a later student of the phenomenon, Hannah Arendt, the social-historical precondition for totalitarianism was a mass society in which traditional institutional structures and internal moral structures had been seriously undermined, even destroyed. "Nihilist revolutions," wrote Weaver, involve "the substitutions of the formless mass manipulated by a group of Machiavellians. . . . Against this alliance of mass and self-appointed leader, every traditional society has protested, because in its formlessness and in its insistent pressure against the usages which have the sanction of time and experience . . . it moves toward a kind of extinction."[19] Cash would have disagreed, not with the analysis but with the assumption that the political and social psychology linking the twentieth-century southern demagogue to the mob was somehow qualitatively different from that which tied the common whites to their captains in the Civil War, that the former was irrational while the latter was rational.

But Cash's analysis provides a powerful answer (before the fact) to Weaver's central contention that the South had "never entered the

18. *Ibid.,* 77–103.
19. Weaver, "Revolution," *ibid.,* 187.

French Revolution," and thus its cultural and political traditions were poles apart from Nazism and fascism. Here it should be said that, though there has always been considerable harrumphing over Cash's even hinting that the mind of the South might have had fascist tendencies or secret hankerings after total domination, Weaver was nothing if not candid on this issue. In the midst of World War II, he wrote: "The South would have been hard put to it to distinguish between some of the slogans of the New Order and the tenets of its own faith. . . . That the Southern whites considered themselves *Herrenvolk* in relation to the Negro is one . . . and belief in the influence of blood and soil is powerful with them. . . . The glorification of the martial spirit, the distrust of urban liberalism, the hatred of money economy are pages that might be found in the book of any unreconstructed Southerner."[20] This is straightforward enough, much more explicit and damning than anything Cash wrote in *The Mind of the South*. But, again, Cash challenges Weaver and southern conservatism by explicitly denying that the South was ever traditional, except for the few pockets of genuine aristocrats whose ethic had beneficial but limited effect in the region's history. That was the whole historical point of the book.

No, the South "never entered the French Revolution." But neither did the North. Nor did either section or the nation need to, because the American Revolution and the Enlightenment, the market economy and commercial expansion, and the frontier had done their work well. How telling that Weaver implies that it was the French Revolution that brought with it "inalienable personal rights" when those resonant words derived of course from Jefferson and were signed off on by southerners as well as northerners. This is not to deny that the second quarter of the nineteenth century saw a southern reaction against the Enlightenment and that many southern intellectuals and some planters rejected the liberal political culture implied by the structure of government established in the Constitution.

Put another way, Weaver was right about the revolution of nihilism—it was a reaction against the deformations of the post–French Revolution political culture of the West. But Cash was also right: the South was not born but tried to become traditional—and failed. Its conservativism was, as Tate implied in his *I'll Take My Stand* essay, con-

20. *Ibid.*, 183.

sidered and self-conscious. It was an ideology, not a tradition: in short, it was a product of modernity.

What, finally, does Cash suggest about the totalitarian potential of the southern mind? Does he help us see how the comparisons might be illuminating? First, it is important that in *The Mind of the South* Cash explicitly cleared the Agrarians of the charge of being fascists, though some of their associations were a bit dubious. Beyond that, Cash's analysis of the psychology of white southern political culture and of the appeal of the Klan, his realization of the demagogic cultural and political purposes to which the ideology of antimodernism could be turned, and his insight that the politics of self-interest could work as a powerful check on political acquiescence are suggestive and should raise questions about any claims for American or southern exceptionalism on the matter of totalitarianism. Moreover, his analysis, along with Weaver's, forces us to remember that fascism and Nazism are not simply conservatism backed into the corner or the result of the lack of foundational values for modern political institutions. For Cash, certain social conditions—the absence of cities and the lack of social density, and, most important, the social conflict between races and resulting ideology of racism—are necessary to anyone's definition of fascism or totalitarianism. But where for Weaver the ethos of modernity was fundamental to the emergence of political nihilism, for Cash the failure of cosmopolitanism and tolerance marked the rise of political pathology.

Furthermore, Cash and Weaver help us understand what vital ingredients for the totalitarian brew were missing in the South. In *The Origins of Totalitarianism* (1951), Arendt noted that a distinction should be made among totalitarian ideologies, movements, societies, and states or regimes. Clearly, if southern conservatism lacks one thing, it is a glorification of the state or of charismatic mass leaders. Here Weaver is admittedly of more help than Cash, who tends to conflate deference to aristocracy with blind submission to a demagogue. Cash does, however, raise the question southern conservatives always beg: Did southern aristocratic leaders have anything other than their own self-interest at stake? Why should common whites have accepted such a historically disastrous leadership and continued to do so down to the 1960s? Why were southern whites so easily hoodwinked by demagogues?

The Klan (and later the Citizens Councils) might qualify as quasi-totalitarian movements; and at certain times and certain places in the

Deep South in this century, most, if not all, of the institutions of civil society—the churches, private and public schools, clubs, and universities—have been dominated by the savage ideal and neutralized as sites of critical opposition. Surely Mississippi was not the only southern state that set up semiofficial organizations such as the State Sovereignty Commission to carry out illegal surveillance of its citizens, tamper with the legal system, and institute something approaching a reign of fear, even terror, during the 1950s and 1960s.

Considering where Cash located the tragedy of the South circa 1940, it was a good thing that the ideology of southern conservativism, what Weaver called the "southern philosophy," lacked mass appeal. For the gap between the intelligentsia, the politicians, and the masses of white people was not bridged in those desperate days after 1954. It is not hard to imagine what the liberal skeptic Cash would have thought of Richard Weaver's peroration "The South and the American Union" (1957). Near the end of the essay, Weaver, who in other of his writings had scorned political fanaticism, expansionist visions, and the idea of total war, revealed another, more sinister side to his thinking: "By all the standards that apply, the South has earned the moral right to lead the nation in the present and coming battle against communism, and perhaps also in the more general renascence of the human way of life. . . . It may be . . . that this unyielding Southerner will emerge as a providential instrument for saving the nation. . . . If that time should come, the nation as a whole would understand the spirit that marched with Lee and Jackson and charged with Pickett."[21] Had he been alive, Cash would have recognized the depressingly familiar southern departure from reality, the substitution of fantasy for reality, the refusal to think rather than to feel, and particularly the evocation, one more time, of that last moment before "it" became "the Lost Cause." But with one eye toward Montgomery, Cash just might have observed that Weaver was right—but about the wrong southerners.

CODA: *THE MIND OF THE SOUTH* AS TEXT

The literary effects of Cash's *Mind of the South* demand comment. What is going on with its structure and texture, its form and shape? I am par-

21. Weaver, "The South and the American Union" (1957), in *Southern Essays,* ed. Curtis and Thompson, 255–56.

ticularly concerned with this because the cadences and rhythms, style and tonalities of Cash's text stay with the reader even after the details, or the exact way Cash develops his thesis, have faded from mind.[22]

To begin: *The Mind of the South* is too long—or it seems that way. The last "book" constitutes over half of the text, and it is the section in which Cash's prose becomes most workaday, often reportorial and even occasionally pedestrian. A work that posits continuity of mentality should never allow this sameness to be reinforced by the length of the work itself. The ability to master foreshortening should be required of writers as well as visual artists and sculptors. Perhaps the circumstances under which Cash completed the book help explain this distension. Still, *The Mind of the South* could have been one hundred pages shorter without significantly affecting its thesis or its literary power.

To describe Cash's textual "voice" is in part to describe certain conscious influences on his intellectual and aesthetic development. Mencken is undeniably there. But Cash echoed, advertently or inadvertently, a tradition of specifically American prose stylists. For one also hears the distinct echoes of Thorstein Veblen with his willful obscurity and archaisms, the exaggeration in the service of satirical critique, and even something of the mannered self-distancing of Henry Adams the author from "Adams" the character in the *Autobiography*. This is writing that took the high style of nineteenth-century Victorianism, hollowed it out, and turned it to other than entirely solemn purposes. It is W. E. B. Du Bois, unbuttoned and on a night out, Thomas Wolfe with a sense of the ridiculous serving to undermine his flowery rhetoric. Indeed, the more one considers them, the more unconvincing it becomes to link Cash with Faulkner and Wolfe and Agee as exemplars of the southern propensity for rhetoric. They are all so different.

Indeed, one can detect remnants of or variations on this Cashean voice, a largely male, nonfiction narrative one, in the cynical realism of Thurman Arnold in the 1930s, the baroque self-consciousness of Norman Mailer, the sly archness of John Kenneth Galbraith, and even the dandified preening yet at times smash-mouth style of Tom Wolfe. Though its intentions are ultimately analytical and critical, it tries to avoid the pedantry and affectless irony of academic writing and to

22. See Michael Dean, "W. J. Cash's *The Mind of the South:* Southern History, Southern Style," *Southern Studies,* XX (Fall, 1981), 297–307, for an interesting analysis of Cash's syntactical devices. Dean does not, however, try to locate Cash in a tradition of rhetoric or diction except the southern one.

achieve some of the atmospheric effects of the nineteenth-century novel. This homemade American diction also includes the colloquial and the informal. Although ostensibly straining for profundity, it cannot resist mixing modes and moods. It is a collage of wisecracks and broad exaggerations, archness and the conversational, parody and occasional profundity. It seeks to penetrate beneath the surface, even as it postures.

All this is to say that it is an explicitly adopted style, and those who adopt it are always slightly at a distance from their own voices. Cash is in the analysis of the mind of the South but not entirely of the language of *The Mind of the South*. Though this style is studiedly literary, it has fallen out of favor with the modernist or postmodernist mood. It is too caught up with itself, too self-conscious in a willed way to allow fictional characters enough room to grow and develop. As everyone recognizes, Cash is a master of thumbnail sketches, set pieces, and memorable phrases. But it is hard to think of a major American writer, except perhaps Mailer or Wolfe, who writes this way now, and certainly Wolfe is better, when writing as a novelist, at creating effects than at exploring character.

Put another way, in *The Mind of the South,* the tonality is often mock-heroic, with the spotlight lighting on a distinctly nonheroic figure, "the man at the center." This means that the style itself at times becomes the center of attention as it engages in a search, as it were, for objects worthy of its intelligence and ambition. Yet it is always disappointed, for Cash's mind, style, and voice are more interesting than the one he seeks to penetrate and then represent to us. It is a debunker's style in part but one that occasionally straightens out, gathers itself together, and delivers. Still, though Cash evokes the tragic sense at the end of the book and though it might be said the South's situation was a tragic one, most of *The Mind of the South* suggests that Cash finally does not think the region's dominant sensibility is intelligent enough to achieve tragic status. The South's history never achieves the status of a story worth contemplating in itself. Rather it must serve a cautionary purpose, become an object lesson. Nor could Cash, perhaps for reasons of temperament, adopt the quietly ironic posture of C. Vann Woodward. When he makes a point, even if obliquely, he wants to make sure we get it.

Still, for all my emphasis on the parodic, the willful, and the mock-heroic, Cash does succeed where most academic historians fail: he conveys something of the joy and agony of telling a story that, despite all, he cared deeply about. And what he cared about, what it was that rankled, even angered him, what if anything did seem to him tragic, I think, was the sheer waste of talent, energy, and especially intelligence that so glaringly characterized the history of his native region. His fate was a tragic one in that his talent was expended on one rather than several things and ultimately he could not sustain or imagine life without that original obsession. Though it would perhaps be too much to claim that Cash was one of those historians who Hayden White has suggested wrote for the purpose of "avenging the people," his decision to abjure footnotes, his departure from the measured and disciplined diction of the professional historian, his willingness to cut loose occasionally, all testify to a deep dissatisfaction with just writing another book about the South or about the political dangers of his contemporary world.[23] Cash's urgency has to do with his desire to seize the narrative from the rest of them, to tell it like it really had been, to get beneath the romantic posturing and ostrichlike denial of reality. That is the reason for the urgency that breaks through and makes *The Mind of the South* still count for something, even today.

23. Hayden White, "The Politics of Historical Interpretation: Discipline and De-Sublimation," in White, *The Content of the Form: Narrative Discourse and Historical Representation* (Baltimore, 1987), 56–82.

Race, Gender, and Class in *The Mind of the South:* Cash's Maps of Sexuality and Power

NELL IRVIN PAINTER

The cultural landscape of the American South, like other cultural land-scapes, is profoundly sculpted by polyvalent relations of power, includ-ing politics, which, in turn, affect personal relations that are shaped according to conventions of race, class, and gender. Because the recent past of this region of the United States includes a cultural, political, and relational watershed—the civil rights movement—Cash's South is, in many regards, far distant from our own. To the degree that the figura-tive landscape that he surveyed between 1929 and 1940 differs signifi-cantly from the present-day South, the maps that he drew of his society and those that we take for granted do not coincide. The last part of *The Mind of the South* shows that Cash realized that things were changing, but he did not discern the advent of a civil rights movement and could not imagine the social revolution that would result. This revolution ultimately recast literate southern culture, influenced readings of his book, and permitted the enunciation of this particular critical essay.

Just as Cash did not foresee the changes that have occurred since the original publication of *The Mind of the South,* he could not have imagined my existence as a critic. Not only am I able to speak as an equal, I can deploy part of his theoretical conceptualization—that which is based on Freudian psychoanalysis—to read his work against the grain, but not without a certain sense of irony. As a mind and a body, I personify the changes that have undermined the pertinence of so much of what Cash had to say; hence my comment represents an odd clash of generations that emphasizes change that has been more dramatic than merely generational. I do not ignore the awkwardness of our historical coexistence, which is due to the continued interest in his book as history and historiography. As a current historian of his region, I can analyze Cash's South and Cash's southerners; yet it is extremely doubtful that he, who in this sense wrote and died too soon, ever supposed that he would be confronted by a critic who is educated, black, female, and feminist.

I also belong to a different world of scholarship from Cash's own. I view the Freudian concepts that he employed through lenses of feminist theories, which in the 1970s and 1980s reoriented psychoanalysis away from the popular, antifeminist manifestations of Cash's time. Cash would be astonished to behold what has become of both southern studies and psychoanalytic theory. Looking about in the 1930s, Cash described a South without women who could be other than "his women" or "complaisant" sexually and without black men who might have a capacity to reason independently. He is being reread in a world bristling with people saying and doing unfamiliar things.

As was the case with so many of his peers, it seems not to have occurred to Cash that black people (beyond, perhaps, the problematic Walter White) could or would read—never mind write—books. Cash spoke to an audience of people who more or less resembled himself, though some of them were not southerners. Addressing fellow white North Carolinians, educated white southerners, and northern book buyers, Cash never conceived of any but the most informal black or female critics. Nor, despite his acquaintance with Lillian Smith and Paula Snelling and the acquisition of his book by a woman publisher, Blanche Knopf, did Cash imagine that female persons would ever gain enough intellectual prestige or initiative to formulate and publish gendered analyses of his work. Like so much that emanated from the American intellectual tradition before the civil rights revolution, black studies, and feminism, *The Mind of the South* was not intended for eyes like mine.

My apparent unfitness as a critic of Cash is not simply a matter of Cash's personal, regional shortsightedness; changes in the marketing and reviewing of books are also implicated. In the 1930s Cash's New York publishers, Blanche and Alfred A. Knopf, acquired his book after having read his 1929 essay "The Mind of the South," which contains phrases that would have offended people like me at the time, such as my parents and grandparents. My family might have grumbled to themselves, but they lacked the ability to publish their critique in outlets that reached a national readership and that the Knopfs would have heeded. Hence Cash's language did not give the Knopfs pause when it came to assessments of audience and critical reception at the time.[1] That *The Mind of the South* is still in print would probably have surprised Cash and the Knopfs, for Alfred A. Knopf evidently had to be persuaded to reprint the book in the early 1960s.[2] But even then, it is unlikely that he and the ghosts of Blanche Knopf and Wilbur Cash would have imagined that a black feminist would influence the way in which the book is perceived. My views on Cash contrast sharply with previous appraisals, even those of recent vintage.

Cash was thoroughly criticized in the 1970s and 1980s, notably by C. Vann Woodward, Michael O'Brien, and Eugene Genovese, who yet preserve a qualified fondness for the author. Until 1990, all published Cash commentary came from white men who identify themselves, by origin or field of study, with the South.[3] Some white woman or person of color may be discovered who reads *The Mind of the South* with affection; yet I doubt that a feminist or race-conscious reader could go so far as to add, as did one of his most biting critics, C. Vann Woodward: "Peace to his troubled spirit."

Although I respect this book's persuasiveness for masses of readers

1. "The Mind of the South" appeared initially in the October, 1929, issue of the *American Mercury*. It is reprinted in Joseph L. Morrison, *W. J. Cash, Southern Prophet: A Biography and a Reader* (New York, 1967), 182–92. In this essay, Cash writes that "the slaves spent most of their lives on their backsides, as their progeny do to this day" and that "the Southerner" is in a "perpetual sweat about the nigger" (183–84). The Knopfs also published many of the writers of the Harlem Renaissance, which would indicate that they saw a market for varying, even conflicting, expressions of opinion.

2. Lillian Smith claimed to have persuaded Knopf to reprint *The Mind of the South*, which became a steady seller in paperback in the 1960s (Smith to George Brockway, July 3, 1965, in *"How Am I Going to Be Heard?": Selected Letters of Lillian Smith,* ed. Rose Gladney [Chapel Hill, forthcoming]).

3. C. Vann Woodward, "The Elusive Mind of the South," in Woodward, *American Counterpoint: Slavery and Racism in the North-South Dialogue* (Boston, 1971), 261–84; Michael O'Brien, "A Private Passion: W. J. Cash," in O'Brien, *Rethinking the South: Essays in Intellectual History* (Baltimore, 1988), 179–89; Eugene D. Genovese, *The World the Slaveholders Made* (New York, 1970), 137–50. A far too generous analysis is found in Richard King, *A Southern Renaissance: The Cultural Awakening of the American South, 1930–1955* (New York, 1980), 146–72.

and have assigned it in my southern history courses, I have never been susceptible to what some of my colleagues see as its magnetism. I cannot agree with Richard King that this book "improves with rereading," or that it is "exciting" and "audacious" and compelling, or that "at times Cash edged toward a vague, hazy sort of racism, especially when discussing black women."[4] I have always had to dissent from such analyses.

When I first encountered *The Mind of the South* as an undergraduate in the early 1960s, I found it thoroughly racist. To my graduate student eyes, rereading it in the early 1970s, the book seemed to be deeply sexist. Rereading it as a teacher in the 1980s, I noticed Cash's contempt for the poor of both races, particularly as manifested in his inability to see poor women of either race as much more than sexualized subject beings. I was struck by Cash's blindness to the ways in which slavery and racism had distorted relations of power, whether in politics or the household. Cash's characterization of the slave South—a society in which one-third of the men did not even own themselves, never mind vote, and no women, no matter how wealthy or educated, enjoyed the rights of citizens—as a region in which there existed an "old basic feeling of democracy," strikes me as narrow-minded (*Mind,* 38–41, 43).

The Mind of the South may be more clear-eyed than many on white southerners. But as Cash's contemporary Lillian Smith realized, the analysis is superficial.[5] Cash wrote out of a conservative "common sense" (in the Gramscian meaning of the term) that reflects the racism, sexism, and class prejudice of conventional, middle-class white southerners of his generation. Given all our differences, I may be an unseemly critic, but this book, because it is still in print, remains fair game. I begin at the beginning, by asking what Cash was writing about.

4. King, *Southern Renaissance,* 146, 163.
5. In his prison notebooks, Antonio Gramsci distinguishes between the fragmented, contradictory, uncritical, and unconscious way that most people perceive the world, which he terms "common sense," and the thoughtful, critical, self-conscious approach to the world that he terms "good sense." Common sense includes all of a society's unexamined prejudices. See Quintin Hoare and Geoffrey Nowell Smith, eds. and trans., *Selections from the Prison Notebooks of Antonio Gramsci* (New York, 1971), 322, 325, 396, 419, 423. See also Stuart Hall, "Gramsci's Relevance for the Study of Race and Ethnicity," *Journal of Communication Inquiry,* X (Summer, 1986), 20–21. Lillian Smith said that *The Mind of the South* lacked "in-depth probing" (Smith to George Brockway, July 3, 1965, in *"How Am I Going to Be Heard?,"* ed. Gladney).

WHAT IS "THE MIND" OF THE SOUTH?: FREUD AND CASH

The central character in *The Mind of the South* is "the South," an anthropomorphic construction that is synonymous with the "Southern psychology" and seems to stand for the thing mentioned in the title of the book (98, 112, 115, 371). Only in the last section, in which so many of the patterns that typify the preceding chapters of the book break down, does the "body" of the South make an appearance (394, 429, 435). Without his having pulled them together in so many words, Cash leaves the distinct impression that "the South," "the mind of the South," and "the Southerner" are the same thing. His verbal constructions reinforce this conclusion.

This anthropomorphism is striking in a book that presents itself as a history of the South in the nineteenth and early twentieth centuries. In the "Preview to Understanding," Cash says that the mind of the South "has actually always marched away . . . from the present toward the past" (x). He contends that "the South" has always been "natively more extravagant" and "more simple and less analytical" than the rest of the country. It has "horse-trading instincts" and a "trigger-quick dander," and it believes only what it wants to believe (265, 285, 382, 414). Can such language be employed when the subject at hand is a society? Can collectivities, as opposed to individuals, be said to have "*a*" mind? Hardly. "The South/the Southerner" has a personal identity, which wavers as the identity of the narrator fluctuates. Sometimes the narrator is upper class, sometimes he is middling, as are Cash's presumed readers; sometimes he is "the common white." Sometimes he is first-person plural—Cash plus reader. But fundamentally this is a book written in the singular about a single character of indeterminate but relatively intimate identity. This confusion of the subject's and the narrator's identity makes the speaker Cash and/or southerners and/or us and lends the book much of its attraction for readers who recognize themselves in its pages in a way they can accept.

Rather than the history of a society, Cash has written a biography of a character named "the South," in which the use of singular constructions conveys unity and continuity, as Woodward so clearly understood.[6] A singular, anthropomorphic subject also invites language that

---

6. Woodward, "The Elusive Mind of the South," 271–75.

is psychological rather than social, economic, or political. As his biographers and critics have long noted, Cash's vocabulary owes much to the popular work of Sigmund Freud.

Cash's framework features key words and phrases that are not merely psychological, but Freudian, for example, "subconsciousness," "ego," "defense mechanisms," "pleasure principle," "sublimated," "hysterical," and "taboos" (31, 40, 64, 71, 86, 129, 136, 337, 387). Such terminology declares *The Mind of the South* not only biography, but Freudian psychobiography. In this sense, the book resembles a sort of psychoanalysis of "the South"/"the Southerner."

I cannot name which, exactly, of Freud's works Cash knew, for his book lacks notes and his biographers, Joseph Morrison and Bruce Clayton, provide no citations.[7] If Cash had actually read Freud, as one of his letters would indicate—rather than absorbing general Freudian notions from American popular culture—I would expect him to have been familiar with Freud's most famous essay, *Civilization and Its Discontents*, which mentions all of the concepts that appear in *The Mind of the South*. *Civilization and Its Discontents* was first published in 1929, and the first English translation appeared in 1930.

The parallels between *The Mind of the South* and psychoanalysis run deeper than borrowed terminology. Both Cash and Freud use the singular collective. Where Cash favors "the Southerner" and "the Negro," Freud speaks of "the male" and "the child." Both Freud and Cash tend to generalize from the individual case to the social so that Cash can conflate "the Southerner" and "the South" while Freud speaks of the "cultural super-ego."[8]

Cash and Freud had something else in common that appears in Freud's writing in German and the ways in which others have interpreted Cash's concerns. Bruno Bettelheim reminds Freud's readers in translation that Freud's fundamental concern was more with the human soul than the mind—that for Freud, "psyche" meant the soul. Similarly, Richard King, one of Cash's more sympathetic critics, notes that *The*

7. Morrison, *Cash,* 44; Bruce Clayton, *W. J. Cash: A Life* (Baton Rouge, 1991), 58, 60, 66, 78, 86, 93, 198–99, 206; Bruce Clayton, "A Southern Modernist: The Mind of W. J. Cash," in *The South Is Another Land,* ed. John Salmond and Bruce Clayton (Westport, Conn., 1987), 177.

8. Sigmund Freud, *Civilization and Its Discontents,* ed. and trans. James Strachey (New York, 1961), 91.

Mind of the South represents a counterpart to W. E. B. Du Bois's *Souls of Black Folk.*[9] In light of these insights and Joel Williamson's famous University of North Carolina at Chapel Hill course on southern race relations and white soul, Cash seems as much to be peering into the soul of the (white) South as its mind, which returns him to Freud.

Considering Cash's personal experience and individual needs and taking at face value his claim to have read Freud, I would suspect that, in addition to the more famous works (*The Interpretation of Dreams, Civilization and Its Discontents*), Cash probably also encountered a less-known essay that begins by addressing one of his own most poignant disabilities and also speaks to private worries that were common in the United States South. Again, the preoccupations of Cash and of his "the South" resist partition.

This essay, the second of Freud's "Contributions to the Psychology of Love," entitled "On the Universal Tendency to Debasement in the Sphere of Love," was first published in German in 1912.[10] Both Freud and Cash knew that many educated men in their societies found it difficult to achieve sexual fulfillment with well-brought-up (Freud) or respectable white (Cash) women. Freud, of course, discussed the matter in far greater depth and with more sensitivity than Cash or his biographers even hint at, but the disparity should not obscure the relevance of Freud's essay. Despite the imbalance in rhetorical sophistication between Cash and Freud, this piece of psychoanalytic writing is worth a closer look in connection with *The Mind of the South.*[11]

Freud begins "On the Universal Tendency to Debasement in the Sphere of Love" with the prevalence of the problem of male impotence, which may stem from psychological causes. Men thus afflicted often split the two currents of their feelings so that the same love object cannot inspire in them both affection and sensuality. According to Freud, well-brought-up women who have been taught not to enjoy sex tend to be inexperienced, inhibited, and frigid, and their husbands relate to them more as judges than as joyous physical partners. At the same time,

---

9. Bruno Bettelheim, *Freud and Man's Soul* (New York, 1983), xi, 12, 73, 32–33; King, *Southern Renaissance,* 164.

10. This essay is sometimes anthologized under the title "The Most Prevalent Form of Degradation in Erotic Life."

11. Sigmund Freud, "On the Universal Tendency to Debasement in the Sphere of Love," in Freud, *Collected Papers,* authorized translation under the supervision of Joan Riviere (New York, 1959), IV, 203, 207, 210; Cash, *Mind,* 86–88.

only love objects that seem to these men to be debased—prostitutes, women of the lower class—can inspire full sensual feelings and a high degree of pleasure. In a statement that has become famous, Freud says: "Where such men love they have no desire and where they desire they cannot love." Freud sees this problem as a consequence of Western civilization and the motive behind the widespread practice of middle- and upper-class men's taking as mistresses working-class women whom they do not respect. Deep in their hearts, Freud adds, such men regard the sex act as degrading and polluting.[12]

If Cash's analysis of such themes convinced masses of his readers, his writing benefited from both its relevance to many of his fellow southerners and from the passion of autobiography. Morrison reveals that Cash suffered from impotence and that his sexual experience was limited to only two women, or, at least, to two respectable white women: a young woman identified only as Peggy Ann and Mary Ross Northrop, whom he married in December, 1940.[13] His friend Lillian Smith described Cash as a man who was very much "involved with his own taboos," and the Morrison and Clayton biographies show Cash as a prig who was obsessed by sex.[14] In *The Mind of the South,* Cash deplores the modern Western "collapse into barnyard morality," the "collapse of old standards," and the "eternal and blatant concern with the theme of sex" that followed World War I (338–39). A close reading of *The Mind of the South,* particularly of the pages on prostitutes and bellboys, suggests that Cash (as well as many respectable white southern men about and to whom he was writing) fits the pattern that Freud laid out in the second of his "Contributions to the Psychology of Love."

CASH'S WHITE PROSTITUTES AND BLACK BELLBOYS

The second chapter of Book Three, entitled "Of Returning Tensions—and the Years the Cuckoo Claimed" contains two numbered sections that deal with what other authors have termed the "New Negro"

12. Freud, "On the Universal Tendency to Debasement in the Sphere of Love," 207, 210–11. See also Cash, *Mind,* 86.

13. Morrison, *Cash,* 38–39, 42, 46, 56, 108–109.

14. Smith to George Brockway, July 3, 1965, in *"How Am I Going to Be Heard?,"* ed. Gladney. Morrison says that Cash had a "particular brand of woman worship" and that he "harbored a strong Victorian streak" (*Cash,* 46, 52).

of the post–World War I era.[15] As in other parts of *The Mind of the South,* Cash cannot begin a discussion of "the Negro" (*i.e.,* black men) without bringing in white women. In other parts of the book, where "the Negro" is discussed in relation to political activities, "the Southern woman" belongs to a more elevated moral order. But here the white women are prostitutes.

Section 20 begins with Cash's narrative of black soldiers' experiences in France during World War I, which made them prone to what he calls "insolence or provocation on the slightest pretext or sometimes none at all." Cash calls France a "topsyturvy land," in which white prostitutes entertained and sometimes even preferred "the Negro" (319). This section continues with a page-long discussion of blacks who had lived in the North and returned to the South full of citified notions; the discussion then segues into another page on black bellboys working in southern hotels. Considering where his narrative would take him, Cash is relatively dispassionate about black soldiers with French prostitutes. His indignation erupts in the discussion of black bellboys and white prostitutes back home.

During Prohibition in the South, he says, black bellboys came to monopolize the marketing and distribution of bootleg whiskey through the hotels where they worked, which respectable white men patronized for the satisfaction of unacknowledged desires. These hotels had become whorehouses as a consequence of the crackdown on red-light districts, and bellboys added the vocation of pimp to that of bootlegger. The great damage, for Cash, starts with the fact that as pimps, black bellboys take much of the earnings of the white prostitutes they control. Worse, they also enjoy the pimp's right to sexual intercourse with his prostitutes. Worse yet, bellboys wield the power that comes with knowledge, here the secret knowledge associated with Freud's essay on the tendency to debasement in love. Like France, southern hotels became a world turned upside down.

In one exasperated paragraph, Cash depicts the "horde of raffish blacks, full of secret, contemptuous knowledge" that white men who pretended to be respectable members of society have another, disreputable side. He repeats the word *contempt* as he describes the grinning

---

15. Interestingly enough, Cash uses "black" to modify the plural "bellboys," even though he usually speaks of "the Negro." This use of the plural may indicate a stepping out of abstraction and into the memory of actual people and events.

bellboys, who, beneath the thinnest veneer of subservience, are "hugging to themselves with cackling joy their knowledge of the white man's women" (321). The mortification Cash betrays in this idiosyncratic passage reinforces the pertinence of Freud's observations about "degradation in erotic life" and corroborates the suspicion that Cash wrote out of his own experience of hypocritical embarrassment.

Although the resemblance between Cash's actual and rhetorical sexual conundrums and Freud's discovery of the "tendency to debasement in the sphere of love" is noteworthy, I stress it without intimating that Freud's observations pertain to Cash alone. In her *Killers of the Dream* Lillian Smith links class and race and religion and sex perceptively. Others connected race and sexuality in political writing—Thomas Dixon springs to mind—so that race, sex, and gender together represent an important theme in white supremacy. This intertwining explains both Cash's reliance in *The Mind of the South* on terms that implicate sexuality (puritanism, hedonism, romanticism) and the book's enduring attraction to readers who consume it as fact.

More Freud does not help explicate *The Mind of the South*, for Cash seems not to have intended to take the psychoanalysis of "the South" very far. First, Cash's use of Freudian concepts is not very rigorous, so that even though he borrows the pleasure principle and the ego, he leaves aside Thanatos (the death instinct), the id, and the rule of law as an essential characteristic of civilization. He is not interested in the Oedipus complex, even though his use of southern women as the mothers of the race is central to his analysis of southern culture. Second, and just as important, Cash and Freud generalize from individuals to families to societies very differently. With a circumspection that is nowhere in Cash, Freud warns that civilizations are not individuals and that comparisons between them are no more than useful analogies.[16]

Another, less direct approach to Freudian insights will illuminate Cash's thinking, for Freud (and his more recent followers) realized, as Cash may or may not have, that sexuality is central in the formation of human identity.[17] In Cash's case, the coincidence of his preoccupations

16. Freud, *Civilization and Its Discontents,* ed. and trans. Strachey, 91.

17. See, for instance, Nell Irvin Painter, "Lily and Linda Brent: Two Doras of the Mid-Nineteenth-Century South: A Non-Exceptionalist Approach to Race, Class, and Gender in Southern Studies," *Georgia Historical Review* (forthcoming); Jane Gallop, *The Daughter's Seduction: Feminism and Psychoanalysis* (Ithaca, 1982); Elisabeth Young-Bruehl, ed., *Freud on Women: A Reader* (New York, 1990); Mary Poovey, *Uneven Devel-*

with race and gender led to his configurations of sexuality and power.

CASH'S MAPS OF SEXUALITY AND POWER

By now it is well understood that the notion of *woman* often serves men as a sign of political power. We remember, too, with Michel Foucault, that sexuality is full of power relations.[18] In southern history race functions in a similar manner so that the least powerful people in southern society, African-Americans, have always been sexualized in white-supremacist writing. This convention continues in *The Mind of the South,* in which race and women appear together in discussions that invariably end up with or pass through sex.

Cash conjoins race and sex often in *The Mind of the South*. His maps of sexuality and power overlap, but they do so in reverse. The figures who are more powerful are less sexualized, those who are powerless are very sexualized. A closer look at the book's characters begins with "the Negro woman," the figure who makes this point with maximum clarity.

Cash reduces the least powerful figure in the South, "the Negro woman," to nothing but sex. Writing about her at length, he calls her the "all-complaisant Negro woman," who was "to be had for the taking" and whom plantation boys (white, one assumes) "inevitably learned to use." As is common in gendered discussions in which men stand for reason and culture and women stand for nature, Cash's Negro woman is "natural" and can "give herself up to passion in a way impossible to wives inhibited by Puritanical training" (56, 87–89).

In comparison with his figure of the southern white woman, who is the source of physical and social reproduction and a symbol of political "mastery," "the Negro woman" is an important possession in only

---

opments: The Ideological Work of Gender in Mid-Victorian England (Chicago, 1988); Jane Flax, *Thinking Fragments: Psychoanalysis, Feminism, and Postmodernism in the Contemporary West* (Berkeley, 1990); Nancy J. Chodorow, *Feminism and Psychoanalytic Theory* (New Haven, 1989); Richard Feldstein and Judith Roof, eds. *Feminism and Psychoanalysis* (Ithaca, 1989).

18. *E.g.,* Mary Douglas, *Purity and Danger* (New York, 1966); Joan Scott, "Gender: A Useful Category of Historical Analysis," *American Historical Review,* XCI (December, 1986), 1053–75; Lynn Hunt, ed., *Eroticism and the Body Politic* (Baltimore, 1991); Michel Foucault, *The History of Sexuality: Volume 1: An Introduction,* trans. Robert Hurley (New York, 1978). Foucault speaks of sexuality as "an especially dense transfer point for relations of power" (103).

one particular aspect, the sexual. After she makes a quick appearance as mammy, "the Negro woman" is not allowed to play any role other than that of sex partner. Cash plays down her role as substitute mother to emphasize her role as a sexual partner to white men and boys. Standing for the poorest, least-educated, most-disfranchised group in his South, "the Negro woman" in *The Mind of the South* is sex, full stop, and no more.

As suits Cash's thoroughly patriarchal vision, even white women receive little attention in *The Mind of the South*. With the exception of Harriet Herring, Lucy Randolph Mason, and a few others whose names appear briefly, Cash's white southern women lack both individuality and agency. They fall under the designation of "his women" or "his womanfolk," and they serve two closely related functions: they are the mothers of the white race and signifiers of men's social standing. Cash says that as "perpetuator of white superiority in legitimate line" the white woman "inevitably became the focal center of the fundamental pattern of proto-Dorian [white supremacist] pride" (87). He sexualizes this figure in terms that the Nazis carried to extremes. In the guise of "his women," white wives and daughters mark the rising status of the male *nouveaux* or the inability of the cotton-mill worker to clothe his dependents in style (245–46, 260). Lacking other roles in society, Cash's southern white women are simply wives and mothers, the embodiment of what Cash calls legitimate sex, and they belong to white men. In life, southern white women, though wealthier than their black counterparts, seldom numbered among the entrepreneurs who brought progress to the South or who wielded political power. Cash's Southern woman represents people who had gained the vote only in 1920 and who were not considered likely to be officeholders or otherwise to wield political or economic power.

The figure of "the Southern woman" is also defined by the political dynamics of race. As the well-bred wife who is left alone while her husband pursues a "mulatto wench," she discovers that being placed upon a pedestal is her compensation as the victim of adultery (88–89). From the other side, "the Southern woman" is a trope in white supremacist political ideology, in which she figures as the forbidden counterpart to "the Negro."

A crucial character in Cash's book is "the Negro" (not the same as the less abstract black bellboys), who, paradoxically, is not part of "the South." Cash emphatically places "the Negro" apart from "the South," going so far as to identify this figure as "a special alien group," whose presence assures enduring white unity (40). Nonetheless, in the second paragraph of *The Mind of the South,* Cash mentions the presence of Negroes as an apparent but not decisive factor distinguishing the South from the North. He also cites the enormous impact of "the Negro" on "the Southerner" (and vice versa) and admits that "the Negro" has influenced the way the white man thinks, feels, speaks, and moves. Throughout the book Cash underlines the centrality of race and white supremacy in phrases such as "the hypnotic Negro-fixation" and "the ancient fixation on Negro" (vii, 38, 51, 68, 132, 171). Alien though he may be, Cash's Negro functions as a compelling notion in the mind of the South. At the same time, however, Cash is not interested in "the Negro" as an autonomous historical actor; Cash creates a potent force in the experience of white people, then denies it agency in its own. "The Negro," therefore, represents an ambiguous character, an influential cipher, whom Cash sexualizes thoroughly.

"The Negro" stands for a virtually powerless people, for only black women were more oppressed than black men. The poverty and political impotence of black men prevented Cash from imagining them in political roles. Black political action seemed so farfetched that when Cash broaches the subject, he veers off into ridicule. Cash could not imagine black men as political actors who would be a positive force in the South, although he did discern that certain black men were becoming wealthy. These tiny exceptions do not diminish the pungency of Cash's treatment of "the Negro," which deals more in sexuality than power.

A long, lurid passage portrays the Negro slums as they are glimpsed, overheard, and imagined by a white bourgeois. Although it deserves quotation in full as an illustration of Cash's hysteria over the secret lives of the black poor, this section is too long to reproduce here. In it Cash describes neighborhoods that are "dark, mysterious, and ominous." From the churches and dance halls of these "half-hidden" regions emanate "the jungle beat of drums . . . high, floating laughter; sudden screams," which the white man hears when he is at home with his family or when these noises bring him to "nightmarish awakening" in the middle of the night. At daybreak the denizens of these mysterious slums hide their secrets beneath masks of servility as they go about their work in the white man's home. He fancies he knows them, but in the back of his mind he wonders what "whispering, stealthy, fateful thing might they be framing out there in the palpitant darkness?" (325–27).

All this libidinous fantasy masquerades as a discussion of politics, as an explanation of why southern blacks would never join the Communist party, in which Cash cannot untangle the personal from the political. He is too riveted by the situation's lust and violence—his words—to analyze the South's political economy in objective language.

As is the case in other white-supremacist writing, Cash's political anxieties coalesced around the concept of Reconstruction, which he presents in the image of emancipated, enfranchised, self-confident black men, as seen through the eyes of erstwhile slaveowners. Depicting the figure of "Cuffey" in town of a Saturday, Cash shows him having a few drinks, letting his "ego a little out of its chains," and relapsing into self-confident Reconstruction manners. "Cuffey" hogs the sidewalk and swaggers about in razor-flashing, pistol-brandishing, "guffawing gangs" (232). In a discussion of politics that repeats the word *mastery,* Cash puts himself and the reader in the position of those forced to endure the sight of "their late slave strutting about full of grotesque assertions, cheap whisky, and lying dreams, feeling his elbow in their ribs, hearing his guffaw in high places" (116). However ludicrous, the image of independent black men leads Cash directly to white women, this time to the crime of lynching.

Ever since 1941, Cash has been complimented for presenting an enlightened—for a white southerner—discussion of lynching. He admits that rapes might be imaginary or trumped-up and that lynch mobs, which had been unjustly blamed on white trash, were led or manipulated by elites.[19] Although Cash deserves credit for moving past thoughtless characterization, he does not go far enough; he speaks of "the rape complex," not the rape-lynch syndrome or the phenomenon of lynching, and again, his Southern woman functions as a sign in the heavily gendered, white-supremacist political ideology. As he explains how lynching is related to politics, Cash invokes concepts such as natural laws and inevitability. Speaking of rape rather than of lynching, Cash concentrates on the sexual and the personal rather than on the public and the quasi-judicial aspects of vigilante violence. In Cash's framework, rape (sexualized assault) is the most salient cause of lynching, and lynching's function in the oppressive southern political economy recedes.

19. Morrison, *Cash,* 173; Woodward, "The Elusive Mind of the South," 261; King, *Southern Renaissance,* 159, 165–66.

The sexuality that permeates Cash's discussion of politics even spreads to the figure he presents most fully: "the Southerner" in all his various guises. Because Cash spends so many words on "the Southerner," he is less susceptible to a neat summing up; omnipresent in *The Mind of the South*, the various versions of "the Southerner" do all sorts of things. But who, for Cash, is "the Southerner"?

Several characters appear repeatedly in this book under the rubric of "the Southerner": "the Virginians," "the old Irishman," "the *nouveaux*," "the yeoman farmer," "the common white," "the mill worker." These men, rather than historical events, lend the book its distinctive character. The very ambiguity and tension in Cash's writing about his male characters enliven his arguments but make his southern white males run together. These figures more or less collapse into two classes. The Virginians, the old Irishman, and the *nouveaux* together represent the better class.

The values and way of life of "the Virginians" laid the groundwork for all succeeding southern aristocracies (5–8, 11–14, 64–66, 70–81). Without challenging the enormous prestige of "the Virginians," Cash points out that there were simply not enough of them to engender all the succeeding aristocrats who claimed to be their descendants. He introduces another source of respectability in the figure of "the old Irishman," modeled on his grandfather, who stands for the likable new rich of the antebellum era.

The transformation from hardworking yeoman farmer to aristocrat occurs within one generation, yet the family of "the old Irishman" is not to be confused with "the *nouveaux*," for whom Cash has tremendous scorn. The *nouveaux* appear at the same time as the old Irishman's generation (for instance, in the story of George Washington Groundling, modeled on the New South Duke and Reynolds families), but "the old Irishman" is exempt from Cash's repeated accusations of coarseness (15–17, 77–79, 235–40). The old Irishman achieves his standing through thrift, hard work, and high cotton prices so that he deserves the respect that comes to him in his maturity. "The *nouveaux*," by contrast, are characterized by grasping ambition and bad taste.

Three other characters meld together to form the more modest and yet greater half of "the Southerner": "the yeoman farmer," "the common white," and "the mill worker." They are the core of the book, and the muddled relations between and among them lend *The Mind of the South* its ring of truth. Renouncing the commonplace formula that in other southern writing obliterates the existence of poor whites, Cash touches upon class conflict among whites and reveals the shallowness of claims of universal aristocracy. Throughout the book, Cash calculates "the common white's" chances for economic mobility, which with the exception of the antebellum era, he sees mostly as very limited. This concern does not translate into very much sympathy, for the slaveless ancestor of these three is not an attractive character. At his worst, he is idle and shiftless and degenerate. At best, he is the unreflective prisoner of his passions (27–29). In the post–Civil War period this personage blends into "the common white," about whom Cash has a great deal to say.

Cash's late nineteenth-century "common white" is an unfortunate figure, for his shabby cultural inheritance compounds his difficulties in economic hard times. Hobbled by his physical background, which Cash depicts in Lamarckian and Social Darwinist terms, "the common white" is the victim of low cotton prices and Populism. His instincts are romantic and hedonistic; he is blind to his "real interests"; he is "perhaps the least fitted" of southerners to get ahead. "Descending from those who in the beginning had had the smallest portion of industry and thrift and acquisitive will" and losing more and more of these characteristics over the generations, "the common white" has only whiteness, the badge of his superiority over "the Negro," as a basis for his self-esteem. With so much riding on that single trait, "the common white" resorts to violence to preserve his sense of racial supremacy (160, 170–72, 175–76).

When the depression of the 1890s threatens to bring "the common white" into close competition (Cash speaks purposefully of "intimate" competition) with "the Negro," wealthy southerners, although "men of a generally coarser kind," step in with capital P "Progress" in the form of cotton mills. Employment in the mills saves "the common white" from descent into a fate worse than death—social equality with "the Negro." Such work also transforms "the common white" into "the cotton-mill worker," who retains "romantic-hedonistic impulses" and hatred of "the Negro." "The common white" and "the mill worker" are connected to aristocrats by what Cash terms the "proto-Dorian bond" of white supremacy. By the time the cotton-mill worker arrives on the scene, the closely related figure of the yeoman farmer has begun to recede.

Viewed from above, the social characteristics of Cash's yeoman farmer, the common white, and the mill worker are essentially the same (175–76, 204–205, 279, 289, 295–99). At one point Cash speaks through an expert who knows how farmers waste their money. Then, in his own voice, Cash adds that the characterization also holds for mill workers: they squander their earnings on "whiskey, gambling, indulgence in sexual pleasures, purchase of useless articles of luxury, and excursions to distant towns" (281). For all the time spent on "the common white"/"the mill worker," their actions seem somehow futile. Cash paints them as hedonistic, and one section in particular reveals the ways in which he sexualizes poor whites.

In an evocation of the mill workers' Saturday night, Cash's writing turns steamy. Discharging (and here Cash's language of "egress" echoes Freud's hydraulic theory of emotions) their "old romantic-hedonistic impulses," his cotton-mill workers indulge in drunken sex with girls they pick up in town. Left to their own devices, his mill workers concentrate on three things only: casual sex, violence, and "orgiastic religion."[20] Whatever they try to accomplish that is constructive—to strike, to organize, to get ahead—their ineptness dooms them to failure. Sex and fighting, which are unadulterated wastes of human energy, are their natural resort.

The squandered Saturday becomes the hallmark of Cash's southern poor, the means by which he ridicules their use of their own time. What he has to say about "the mill worker" on Saturday repeats images of "the Negro" on Saturday. In both cases, he sensationalizes and sexualizes the poor. Within Cash's map of power, this sexualization denotes relative powerlessness. With their minds fixed on their pitiful Saturday dissipation, neither poor whites nor poor blacks in *The Mind of the South* are able to realize their political or economic potential.

The southern poor whom Cash sexualizes were relatively (if white)

20. Cash describes the hedonistic antebellum "common white" on pages 43–48, 52, 69–70, and the hedonistic "mill worker," on pages 249–50, 281. His description of the mill workers' Saturday night is on page 296: "maybe to have a drink, maybe to get drunk, to laugh with passing girls, to pick them up if you had a car, or to go swaggering or hesitating into the hotels with their corridors saturated with the smell of bichloride of mercury, or the secret, steamy bawdy houses; maybe to have a fight, maybe with knives or guns, maybe against the cops; maybe to end whooping and singing, maybe bloody and goddamning, in the jailhouse—it was more and more in the dream and reality of such excursions that the old romantic-hedonistic impulses found egress."

or virtually (if black) powerless in the southern political economy, although he finds things for the better classes to do beyond sex and violence. As the Virginians, the old Irishman, and the *nouveaux,* they amass wealth, hold office, and build factories. Wealth and power have Cash's respect in the sense that he accords to the figures with some autonomy a regard that he cannot offer members of the working classes. As much as Cash seems to want to sympathize with the poor, he finds it hard to take them seriously. This is not an accident.

The whole labor history of the South, with its utter degradation of workers through racial slavery and its closely related contempt for anyone else engaged in manual labor, resulted in the cultural devaluation of people who do work. Cash does not recognize that very early on the legalization of racial slavery and its attendant white supremacy segmented the southern work force and made labor politics extremely difficult. Just as slavery acquired a racial character, so black workers carried a racial taint into freedom that marked them as ineligible for solidarity with white workers, no matter how useful such solidarity would have been for both in the long run. A segmented work force was the result of white supremacy among southern workers, and workers so deeply divided could forge no enduring unity based on class. With the status of laborer so closely identified with blackness during and after slavery, white supremacists succeeded again and again in preventing the formation of farmer or labor parties across the color line.[21]

No working-class republicanism appears in *The Mind of the South.* The lack of enduring labor politics in the South and the absence of a strong, countervailing worker-centered sensibility deprived Cash of images of wise and sturdy workers. So one-sided a class culture meant that, by default, Cash wrote out of class prejudice as well as white supremacy and never scrutinized his deep-running contempt for the southern poor. Rural and urban, farmer and worker, black and white, he saw them as the childish prisoners of their carnal appetites. Only toward the end of the book does he begin even tentatively to envision workers cooperating across the color line (428–29).

Until the very last chapter, Cash segregates his discussion of the

21. White supremacy defeated interracial working-class–farmer cooperation in Virginia in the early 1880s and in North Carolina in the late 1890s. Similar tactics helped disfranchise blacks in Georgia in 1906, and they succeed to this very day.

mind of the South according to race, which means that although he never concludes that southerners of both races are hedonists, he can say that "the Southerner" is hedonistic and "the Negro" is hedonistic, as though hedonism were a racial characteristic in either case (51, 56, 58). The one, like the other, is impotent politically because he misused the vote during Reconstruction, when he was the dupe of unscrupulous outsiders, or because he lacked a sense of his economic self-interest and thoughtlessly voted for demagogues. At one point Cash realizes that the southern polity is hierarchical, but he fails to understand what racial slavery and disfranchisement did to southern politics and to his own mapping of power and sexuality.

The Great Depression represents a watershed in Cash's historical reckoning. He notes that planters had called the tune in southern states before the Civil War and is willing to concede that in the late nineteenth and early twentieth centuries the white poor were never able to realize the power of their numbers; but the picture is no longer clear after southerners embrace the New Deal. Once the old political verities fail, Cash begins to write differently. Earlier in the book he draws a strict color line, even when he comes to identical conclusions about the weaknesses of the poor, black and white. Toward the end of the book, however, Cash begins to see across the racial divide.

His poor are still "laughing, sleeping, drinking cheap wine or corn whisky, or dreaming restlessly of violence" regardless of color. Again and again toward the end of the book, Cash sees that social and economic ills are not bounded by race (418–20, 424–27, 438). By extension—here Cash is not explicit—effective remedies cannot be race-specific. He speaks instead of the tragedy of his South, whose political leaders do not heed the counsel of intelligent and analytical thinkers (like W. J. Cash?). Because the politicians cannot transcend race or surmount white supremacy, they cannot even serve all southern white people effectively.

It is not clear whether Cash realizes that the southern tragedy he sees around him during the Great Depression represents the political impotence of the poor or that this impotence is directly related to the enslavement, disfranchisement, and subjugation of a large portion of the southern laboring population. I suspect not. And I suspect, too, that Cash's confusion, springing from white supremacy and characterized by the sexualization of even "the Southerner," paralyzed him intellectually.

THE TRAGEDY OF SOUTHERN POLITICS

The Mind of the South ends with a long passage on the political and economic needs of the South in 1940. Even though those needs were long-standing, Cash saw that the Great Depression exacerbated the region's poverty. Yet Cash cannot pursue his glimmerings of insight. After explaining the great tragedy of the South, which was a lack of effective political leadership, he ends his book with a return to anthropomorphism. Why does he abandon the analysis? Why does Cash ultimately move away from the vision of pages 394–439, which is social and economic, rather than psychological? Why, in the last two pages (439–40) does he fall back on the figure of "the South" as individual and write of individual traits such as pride, bravery, courtesy, personal generosity, and loyalty?

Cash realizes that economic remedies require political change, and he already knows that the region's elected officials cannot meet the challenge of the Great Depression. The problem is that envisioning solutions would mean embracing remedies too radical for a segregationist like Cash. As Radical Republicans discovered in the wake of the Confederate defeat, fundamental change would mean enfranchising all the poor. But for Cash, as for so many white southerners of his generation, the confusion of race with class precludes real consideration of the enfranchisement of the poor. Racism, therefore, led segregationists into a political cul-de-sac.

So dramatic a remedy as extending the franchise to the poor who were black lay beyond a segregationist's ken. Like so many of his time, Cash could not see past segregation, which was a system built on black disfranchisement and which, as a phrase, encapsulated black political impotence. In Cash's "common sense" reckoning of politics, extending the franchise, for whatever reason, would permit what was called "social equality"—meaning sex between "the Negro" and "the Southern woman." Social equality symbolizes everything threatening about desegregation and black enfranchisement so that a remedy for problems in the political economy entailed other dilemmas, of gender and hence of sex. Increasing the political clout of the southern poor might have remedied the economic ills that distressed Cash, but that remedy involved something that tormented him on the gut level: the sexualization—and therefore the disempowering—of the entire polity, not just of the poor and the black and the female. This peril brings us back to his sexualization of the other, richer half of Cash's figure of "the Southerner," even though he is the most effective and autonomous figure in the book.

In much of *The Mind of the South* "the Southerner" is an ambiguous amalgam of whites. Ultimately the real "Southerner" is differentiated from "the mill people" whom the poor become.[22] The poor are never able to accomplish much, but this Southerner can exercise power within certain limits. Yet even he is sexualized, if not so thoroughly as the poor. In the long discussion of Negro women's "easy complaisance," Cash admits that the rulers of the South did their share of race mixing, and race mixing means sex (88).

Southerners of the better class are fatally flawed, for they, too, betray the weakness that symbolizes powerlessness. In Cash's analysis, in which even elite white southern men are prisoners of lust, the root of the political tragedy of "the South"/"the Southerner" lies in sexuality. "The Southerner," even when wealthy, even when educated, cannot be effective in the public realm.

In *The Mind of the South* sexuality means impotence, for Cash's map of sexuality is an inverse map of power. This identification may be mainly autobiographical in its literal meaning, but it also relates to the network of power that characterized southern culture in the eras of slavery and segregation. At the same time, and without realizing it, Cash is pointing to the social and political repercussions of a hierarchal society in which only a few men held enormous, multivalent power. Having monopolized public agencies, including the legislatures, the police, and the courts, the few white men in power freely deprived everybody else of whatever they wanted, from decent wages, to the ability to organize their workplaces or vote their own interests, to sex. As Foucault remarked, sexuality expresses all sorts of power relations, and here they were private and public, actual and symbolic.

Realizing however hazily that sexuality and power are linked, Cash still backs away from the implications of his intimation that the answer to economic distress lay in the empowering of the southern poor. That last step—away from segregation into something that Cash could only see as "social equality"—is not possible to take. His South remains tragic, his southerners tainted. The only people who emerge from the

---

22. "They [the mill workers] had always met the narrow social contempt which the South visited upon them" (*Mind,* 399).

pages of *The Mind of the South* with unimpaired agency are Yankees, male and female.

POTENT YANKEES

Unlike Cash's southern figures, "the Yankee" appears only sporadically. In some places Cash seems to confound "the Yankee" with "the tariff gang," as though protective tariffs were as significant an issue in the forging of white southern identity as antislavery and Radical Reconstruction. Cash concedes enormous power to "the Yankee," who is undiminished by sexuality and plays a crucial role in Cash's (odd) version of southern history. During the antebellum era and during Reconstruction (which for Cash unaccountably covers the thirty years following the Civil War and is characterized by Yankee occupation), "the conflict with the Yankee" creates and intensifies southerness (185). As a powerful Other, "the Yankee" defines by opposition what is southern, or, in Cash's words, he "really created the concept of the South as something more than a matter of geography . . . in the minds of the Southerners" (68).

"The Yankee" is a symbol of modernity, one of the most compelling concepts in the book. More than once Cash admits that he practically uses the terms *Yankee* and *modern* interchangeably (141–42). Yankees are the originators of Progress, so that when local capitalists take it upon themselves to provide "the common white" a sanctuary, Cash says that they have decided to copy "Yankeedom." Both factories and schools are the brainchildren of Yankees (177–79).

Although she appears on only one page, "the Yankee schoolma'am," who stands for northern teachers to the southern freedpeople right after the Civil War, does something. The inspiration for the schooling of the masses comes from a figure whom Cash detests but allows considerable autonomy, which is all the more remarkable because this figure is a woman who is not sexualized. Quite to the contrary, Cash tries to desexualize her by disparaging her femininity. With the disdain of a man who more easily envisions white women as breeders and ornaments, Cash subjects "the Yankee schoolma'am" to stereotypical ridicule and blame. Judging her as a woman and gauging her success by the degree to which she appears attractive to men, he finds nothing worth admiring in her physiognomy or her mission: "Generally horsefaced, bespectacled, and spare of frame, she was, of course, no proper intellectual, but at best a comic character." This woman was "at worst a dangerous fool, playing with explosive forces which she did not understand. She had no little part in developing Southern bitterness as a whole, and [with Yankee journalists] . . . contributed much to the growth of hysterical sensibility to criticism." As much as Cash dislikes her—and to show his disdain he puts her vocation in quotation marks—the Yankee schoolma'am teaches people something. And she inspires strong emotions, even though they are negative, in the mind of the South (140–41). She is the only active, educated female type in *The Mind of the South*.

These Yankees are able to push around everyone in the South. They dupe "the Negro," outrage "the Southerner," but set an example that southerners feel impelled to follow. Standing at the edge of Cash's maps of sexuality and power and unfettered by sexuality and the weaknesses it entails, "the Yankee" and "the Yankee schoolma'am" manipulate the southern scenario from a position that is only half on the stage of *The Mind of the South*.

CONCLUSION

Wilbur Cash was more perceptive than most of his contemporary southern commentators: he saw through the moonlight and magnolias tradition of southern aristocracy and brought poor whites into his South. But his was only half-sight; he was blind to the power dynamics that led him to ridicule poor whites and define "the Negro" out of what was essentially southern. Cash recognizes hierarchy and calls it that. But he does not see that his comments on race and gender spring directly from his limited understanding of southern class relations. He can decipher the difference between "the Southerner" and "the common white," between "the South" and "the mill worker," but he does not perceive that his definition of the South reaches only as far as voters. On some level, he knows that women had only recently gained the vote and that poor people do not vote (much) in the South, but he does not recognize that their powerlessness makes them ridiculous in his eyes.

Lillian Smith saw how Cash's taboos blocked his vision and kept his discussion close to the conventions of southern life and history. But *The Mind of the South* persists as a phenomenon more than a half-century after its publication. The enduring popularity of this quirky big book bears witness to the degree to which Americans to this day share Cash's conflicts, his blindness, and his complexes. Southerners and Americans of all races still confuse race with class and political power with sex so that their maps of power and sexuality are still likely to be as misleading as Cash's. Out of fear of the disabilities of the poor as expressed as racial failings, many still balk at allowing democracy to fulfill its whole promise. If *The Mind of the South* still reaches an audience, we may yet take some comfort in knowing that the revolution separating Wilbur Cash's time from our own has, at the very least, reworked the legal and hence the political foundations of his South. His confusion of gender, class, race, and sexuality no longer represents an enlightened view of a benighted region, and we are able to envision—if not yet to shape—a landscape of power that is less booby-trapped by history and prejudice than was his.

The South's Palladium:
The Southern Woman and
the Cash Construct

ELIZABETH JACOWAY

> She was the South's Palladium, this Southern woman—the shield-bearing
> Athena gleaming whitely in the clouds, the standard for its rallying, the
> mystic symbol of its nationality in face of the foe. She was the lily-pure
> maid of Astolat and the hunting goddess of the Boeotian hill. And—she
> was the pitiful Mother of God. Merely to mention her was to send strong
> men into tears—or shouts. There was hardly a sermon that did not begin
> and end with tributes in her honor, hardly a brave speech that did not
> open and close with the clashing of shields and the flourishing of swords
> for her glory. At the last, I verily believe, the ranks of the Confederacy
> went rolling into battle in the misty conviction that it was wholly for her
> that they fought.
>
> —Cash, *The Mind of the South*

Wilbur J. Cash coined the term *gyneolatry* to refer to the South's supposed idolization of its women. In his monumental *Mind of the South*,
Cash developed an intricately woven argument that rested on a few
central premises, one of them being the following: in response to the
mounting northern assault on southern culture and the escalating (and
perhaps envious) northern charges of southern bestiality and inferiority
resulting from miscegenation, antebellum southern white males com-
pensated the southern white woman for their own sexual transgressions
by glorifying her. According to Cash, southern males answered the

I wish to thank Mary Frederickson, Elizabeth Payne, and Virginia Wray for their
care and assistance in conceptualizing this essay and Numan Bartley, Joan Curtner, Donald Mathews, and Joel Williamson for their generous and helpful critiques.

Yankee by "proclaiming from the housetops that Southern Virtue, so far from being inferior, was superior, not alone to the North's but to any on earth, and adducing Southern Womanhood in proof" (89). More important, identification of southern virtue with the protection of white womanhood became tantamount to preservation of the South, its culture, and its cause. In Cash's view, therefore, the white southern woman functioned primarily in the southern mind as a symbol of southern virtue, and ultimate maintenance of southern culture—both before the Civil War and after—depended on her remaining racially undefiled; by extension, her patriotism became tied in the southern mind to her willingness to function in that role, and her inaccessibility to black males became the overriding concern of every true southern patriot.[1]

In casting the southern woman as a statue, a Palladium, Wilbur Cash made her passive as well as cold and unresponsive. Even her mystical powers to preserve southern culture and her centrality in resisting the foe derived their force and power only from male action. It is significant, therefore, that Cash chose first of all in his pantheon of southern womanhood the image of Athena—the warrior goddess, potentially frightening and threatening, an amazon. It is significant as well that he mixed with this warrior image Tennyson's lovely and pure Elaine of Astolat, who chose death by her own hand to life without her beloved, the chivalrous Lancelot. Cash also blended into his formula the hunting goddess of a race of men whose very name has become a byword for stupidity and boorishness; and certainly not least, the Virgin Mary, the Madonna, the ultimate and only true intercessor between God and man—in Cash's rendering, a mother. What is one to make of this bewildering array of images, this range of possibilities from the powerful warrior to the fainting maiden, from the overseer of the mindless and irrelevant gaiety of the hunt to the arbiter of life's deepest yearnings and needs? Was Wilbur Cash trying to say that woman played all these roles in southern thought, or was he simply very confused?

---

1. *Webster's* defines Palladium as follows: "Any statue of the goddess Pallas Athena; esp., the famous statue on the preservation of which was supposed to depend the safety of Troy, which fell only after Odysseus and Diomedes had carried the statue off" (*Webster's New International Dictionary*, 2nd ed., Unabridged [Springfield, Mass., 1960], 1758). For a devastating critique of the process and the consequences of the South's perverted chivalry see Lillian Smith, "The Women," in Smith, *Killers of the Dream* (Garden City, N.Y., 1963), 120–35; see also Jacqueline Hall, *Revolt Against Chivalry: Jesse Daniel Ames and the Women's Campaign Against Lynching* (New York, 1979).

Cash was, in fact, employing bitter irony, as he did so often throughout his book, to reveal the unreflective, highly romantic, and emotional "habits of thought" that he argued had led the South into its many dilemmas. Cash was also revealing his own very tortured relationships with womanhood, manhood, sexuality, failure, and romanticism, as well as his tendency to read into the southern mind a projection of his own perceptions.[2]

Much of Cash's critique of southern life was encoded in his tribute to southern woman, as well as much of his own personal anguish about his inability to relate to women effectively. Ultimately Cash's verdict on the South was that its deeply ingrained capacity for self-deception held it in thrall to an ignoble ideal. In the final analysis, that ideal called for little more than maintaining power in the hands of unworthy men—horse traders, captains, mill barons, Babbitts—men that Cash acknowledged collectively as "the ruling class." Throughout his book Cash referred disparagingly and despairingly to the latter-day Boeotians whose incapacity for analysis caused them to pay deference to such "charlatans" and led them time and again into such ridiculous positions as "the misty conviction that it was wholly for her that they fought." Similarly, Cash scoffed at the notion of gyneolatry, using it only to reveal once more the South's limitless capacity for muddle-headed romanticism.

Although Wilbur Cash might scoff, the phenomenon that he named gyneolatry had a long and impressive pedigree in southern life and thought. The virtuous and adored white woman was standard fare in the southern mythology slaveowning patriarchs had created, zealous apostles of the Lost Cause had adopted, and southern politicians and demagogues had used shamelessly for a variety of purposes long before this mythology was captured as historical "fact" by the upstart intellectual from North Carolina.

Other variations abound throughout southern letters, such as

2. For an illuminating account of the role of the code of chivalry in the socializing environment of nineteenth-century southern white girls, see Cita Cook, "The Knight's Fair Lady as a Model for White Genteel Young Women of the New South" (Paper presented at the Second Southern Conference on Women's History, June 8, 1991). *Webster's New International Dictionary* defines Boeotian as "noted for its moist atmosphere and the dullness of its inhabitants. Of or pertaining to Boeotia; hence, stupid; dull; obtuse" (301). William Rose Benet defines Boeotian as "a rude, unlettered person; a dull blockhead. The ancient Boeotians loved agricultural and pastoral pursuits, so the Athenians used to say they were as dull and thick as their own atmosphere" (*The Reader's Encylopedia* [2nd ed.; New York, 1965], 117).

George W. Bagby's characterization of the southern belle in his 1885 novel *The Old Virginia Gentleman:* "More grace, more elegance, more refinement, more guileless purity, were never found in the whole world over, in any age . . . a complete, immaculate world of womanly virtue and home purity was [hers], the like of which . . . was . . . never excelled, since the Almighty made man in his own image. . . . Young gentlemen, hold off. . . . Lay not so much as a finger-tip lightly upon her, for she is sacred."[3] Charming as this mythology may have been in some circles and efficacious as it may have been in serving a variety of purposes, the burgeoning literature in southern women's history has demonstrated that it was a gross oversimplification and distortion of past reality. This growing literature amply documents a multiplicity of roles, forms of expression, and ways of being for both black and white women that until the emergence of women's history in the 1970s remained largely unrecovered. Although contemporaries of Cash such as Katharine Du Pre Lumpkin, Lillian Smith, and Pauli Murray were just beginning to describe a different reality from the one he saw, Cash did have available to him (if he had been interested) the pioneering studies by Julia Cherry Spruill and Guion Griffis Johnson, both of which challenged the very circumscribed roles Cash postulated for southern women. In light of these studies and the recent proliferation of information about the diversity of roles and contributions of southern women, two intriguing questions press for answers: Why did W. J. Cash view the past of southern women in terms of white Madonnas and black whores (with a sprinkling of archetypal steel magnolias), and why have southern historians been content to leave his characterizations of southern women unchallenged?[4]

3. Bagby quoted in Kathryn Lee Seidel, *The Southern Belle in the American Novel* (Tampa, 1985), xi.

4. Jacqueline Dowd Hall and Anne Firor Scott, "Women in the South," in *Interpreting Southern History: Historiographical Essays in Honor of Sanford W. Higginbotham,* ed. John B. Boles and Evelyn Thomas Nolen (Baton Rouge, 1987), 454–510; Nancy A. Hewitt, "Beyond the Search for Sisterhood: American Women's History in the 1980s," *Social History,* X (October, 1985), 299–321; Elizabeth Fox-Genovese, "Socialist-Feminist American Women's History: A Review Essay," *Journal of Women's History,* I (Winter, 1990), 181–210. Katherine Du Pre Lumpkin, *The Making of a Southerner* (New York, 1947); Smith, *Killers of the Dream;* Pauli Murray, *Proud Shoes: The Story of an American Family* (New York, 1956); Julia Cherry Spruill, *Women's Life and Work in the Southern Colonies* (Chapel Hill, 1938); Guion Griffis Johnson, *Ante-Bellum North Carolina: A Social History* (Chapel Hill, 1937).

Although Cash's *Mind* was a very personal re-creation of the reality he perceived around him, surely he spoke for a larger constituency, re-flecting values and attitudes that were prevalent in his culture. But whereas much of the power and appeal of Cash's book lay in its chal-lenge to many of the South's long-cherished myths, the central myth of the maid of Astolat—what Cash called gyneolatry—he left intact, even seemed to enshrine. Why? Elements for framing an answer to this ques-tion undoubtedly lurk in Cash's life experience and in his work.[5]

Though a journalist and therefore freed of some of the constraints of the historian, W. J. Cash fell heir to one of the historian's central dilem-mas when he undertook his foray into the past: he viewed the past through the lens of his own perspective, and he crafted an interpreta-tion of that past that was shaped by his own very personal perceptions. William R. Taylor has written, "In general it has always been men with the ardent but tortured Southern loyalties of a . . . Wilbur Cash or a William Faulkner . . . who have possessed the vision required to look into the deepest recesses of the Southern character and, if only fleet-ingly, see it in all of its complexity." But Taylor acknowledged that Cash and Faulkner and others who have written as insiders worked "from a construct compounded out of memories, artifacts and other fragments of an evasive social past . . . further transformed by their own wishes and fears into something even more synthetic." In particular, Cash's interpretation of southern women, black and white, was as much a product of his own peculiar experience as it was a reflection of the larger culture of which he was a part.[6]

Cash's biographers craft a picture of a brief and tortured life, staged entirely in the Carolina piedmont. The firstborn son of a taciturn textile mill superintendent and a plump church organist, Wilbur Joseph Cash grew up in a "drab, sooty mill town" where he was "shy, retiring, moody, scrawny, awkward, and unathletic." Life in the Cash household revolved around family, church, mill, and the Democratic party; as Jack Cash described those years for H. L. Mencken: "The keening of the five-o'clock whistles in the morning drilled me in sorrow. And for years,

5. Cash's most recent biographer, Bruce Clayton, concurs: "Thus did Cash, so daring and emancipated on many issues . . . reaffirm the prevailing myths" (*W. J. Cash: A Life* [Baton Rouge, 1991], 211).
6. William R. Taylor, *Cavalier and Yankee: The Old South and American National Character* (Garden City, N.Y., 1963), 303.

under the influence of the Baptist preacher's too graphic account of the Second Coming, I watched the West take fire from the sunset with a sort of ecstatic dread."[7]

As a boy, young "Sleepy" Cash (as he was called because of a life-long tendency to squint) had few playmates, but he did have "a little black nurse-maid . . . who filled me with preposterous notions, particularly in regard to sex." Undoubtedly Cash's later analysis of a "psychic split" in the southern mind between twin tendencies toward puritanism and hedonism found its genesis in his own childhood introduction in the same time and place to both a terrifying religion and the first stirrings of interest not only in sex, but—that ultimate of southern taboos—interracial sex.[8]

Always a romantic at heart, Cash believed, according to his biographer, that "mankind is inherently romantic and insists on finding beauty and love." And yet, as so many things do, even Cash's tendency toward romanticism seemed to stem from his childhood environment. As he recalled it:

> All of us who grew up in the first two decades of the 1900's—in that south with its heroic rhetoric, its gyneolatry, its continual flourishing of the word noble, and its constant glorification of the past—were foreordained to the thing [romanticism]. All of us learned to read on "The Three Little Confederates," all of us framed our hero-ideal on Stuart and Pickett and Forrest—on the dragoon and the lancer—ten thousand times, in our dreams, rammed home the flag in the cannon's mouth after the manner of the heroes of the Rev. Tom Dixon, ten thousand times stepped into the breach at the critical moment on that reeking slope at Gettysburg, and with our tremendous swords, and in defiance of chronology, then and there won the Civil War; all of us learned to choke for "The Conquered Banner" and southern womanhood—to think of women in terms of some enhaloed vision compounded out of the fair-haired Helen, the lily-white maid of Astolat, and the hunting goddess of the Boeotian hill; all of us, in a word, lived absolutely under the sway of what Cabell calls "Domnei [woman worship]," of glory, and of patriotic worship of the idea of the south.[9]

Wilbur Cash graduated from Boiling Springs High School, having made a good record there, and then went on to five years at a small Baptist college near Raleigh, Wake Forest. While at Wake Forest, Cash

7. Clayton, *Cash*, 6, 7, 12; Joseph L. Morrison, *W. J. Cash, Southern Prophet: A Biography and a Reader* (New York, 1967), 8.

8. Clayton, *Cash*, 7.

9. Clayton, *Cash*, 58; Morrison, *Cash*, 12–13.

was an indifferent student, but he developed something of a reputation as a writer for the school newspaper and a campus character. As Bruce Clayton describes him, "To his friends, the owlish, bookish Sleepy Cash was a lovable oddball, usually disheveled and distracted, known for his chaw of tobacco and prodigious spitting—traits and skills that impressed his male friends but severely limited his love life, which was all but nonexistent during his Wake Forest days."[10]

As so many college students do, Sleepy Cash rebelled against his puritanical father while he was an undergraduate. He wrote editorials railing against the fundamentalists who opposed the teaching of evolution, smoked cigarettes, drank beer and corn whiskey, and even joined "in an occasional foray into Raleigh's notorious vice district." In all ways, as Joseph Morrison concludes, Wilbur Cash was "a long way from Boiling Springs, North Carolina."[11]

Although Sleepy Cash was indolent as a student, outside the classrooms bull sessions flourished, and often at these "Cash held forth with great eloquence, but never more so than in speaking of something he called 'the mind of the South.'" According to Morrison, by the time he graduated from Wake Forest,

> Cash was already suffering from the hyperthyroid condition that was to plague him throughout his adult life. Even in high school he had been known to suffer from spasms of choking that suggested hyperthyroidism, but at Wake Forest he had to wear his collar open because of an incipient goiter. Cash was more touchy now, more emotional, more a trial to his few friends, apt on occasion to burst into tears. Out of his physical difficulty arose a fear that also plagued him throughout his adult life and that he voiced that year to a college mate: that he was becoming sexually impotent.[12]

After a year of law school, Cash tried his hand at college teaching and failed miserably. The most important result of that year was a nervous breakdown, suffered apparently because he wooed and won a pretty little freshman named Peggy Ann but then "could not perform the manly deed." Cash next tried his hand at writing fiction and at

10. Clayton, *Cash*, 28.

11. Morrison, *Cash*, 26–27, 30.

12. *Ibid.*, 30, 35. Morrison (27) claims that Cash used the title "The Mind of the South" well before Vernon L. Parrington used it to open Volume II of *Main Currents in American Thought* in 1927.

working for various newspapers, but again success eluded him. Always a "sensitive" boy, Cash was "a frequently irritable adult, battling physical problems and psychological demons," and after a series of emotional breakdowns and a variety of treatments for his "neurasthenia," he moved back home with his parents.[13]

In time Cash recovered sufficiently to resume his writing; he planned a series of articles in the style of his idol, H. L. Mencken of the *American Mercury,* and to his delight, Mencken liked them and published them. Emboldened by his success, and with Mencken's encouragement, Cash approached the prestigious publisher Alfred A. Knopf with his plans for a book to be titled *The Mind of the South.* Before he could proceed very far with this project, however, he got sick again, and on the advice of his doctors he abandoned all attempts to write for several years.[14]

Through the next years, Cash continued his lifelong pattern of prodigious reading—especially in Freud, Voltaire, and Mill, Conrad and Dreiser, Shakespeare and Cervantes—and eventually he resumed his writing, tinkering with several projects. By early 1936 he had recovered sufficiently to mail the Knopfs 306 manuscript pages, with more promised shortly. Knopf mailed a contract in early March, but little new manuscript copy would be forthcoming from North Carolina for the next four years. Throughout this period Cash demonstrated markedly erratic behavior, promising repeatedly that he would complete the book and then delaying, starting new projects, dreaming new dreams.[15]

As Cash described his project to the Knopfs, "ultimately the book is one man's view—a sort of personal report—which must rest in large part on . . . a pattern into which I was born and which I have lived

13. Clayton, *Cash,* 46, 49.

14. *Ibid.,* 96.

15. *Ibid.,* 60. Clayton refers to Cash's "seeming lack of interest in works of southern history" and argues that "his dream of becoming a 'real writer' was at least partially responsible for his failure to buckle down to finish his book." Clayton also refers to Cash's "intense reading of European masters, notably Conrad. Couple that with his early acceptance of Darwin, his absorption in Freud and Nietzsche, and his familiarity with Marx, and one sees his literary journalism as an amalgamation of traditional and modernist assumptions. . . . But Cash's literary journalism also reveals that his feelings often collided with his intellect as he sorted out his thought and came to understand that for all his rebelliousness, for all his emancipation, he and his generation were, as Lillian Smith said, 'forever southerners'" (115, 116).

most of my life." No objective history was intended. The book was to be a very personal probing of what Bruce Clayton has called "an engulfing emotional entity, an ever-present reality, a folk mind."[16]

About this time Jack Cash went to work for the Charlotte *News.* He enjoyed the camaraderie of the newsroom, and in time his friendships there would lead to an introduction to Mary Bagley Ross Northrop and love at last. By all accounts, Cash idolized women, but he was "more than a little afraid of them and generally uncomfortable in their presence, particularly if he did not know them well." An early colleague recalled for Joseph Morrison that Cash "let down his reserve with a woman only if she was someone who worked for the *Star* [an early job] and was regarded as 'one of the boys.'" But Mary was different. Even though she was an Episcopalian, and thus potentially "snooty," she was "uncomfortable with the conventional notions of southern womanhood and wanted to break free. . . . As a divorcee with a vivacious, perhaps boisterous personality, she would have had little success pretending to be a southern lady." In short, she was perfect for Wilbur Cash. They fell in love, and they talked of marriage.[17]

Cash wanted to delay the marriage until after publication of *The Mind of the South,* but he had great difficulty bringing that project to completion. He told Mary about Peggy Ann "and confessed that his youthful failure had left him afraid that he would never know true happiness with a woman. He was sure that his earlier sexual fiasco had contributed markedly to his recurring neurasthenia."[18]

In time, he did begin to write again, but now the threat of war hung over Europe and "intensified Cash's long-standing alarm at fascist aggression in Europe into an ominous, obsessive rage against Hitler."

16. *Ibid.,* 109, 92. As Bruce Clayton writes: "Cash had to draw upon himself, upon his own perceptions. His task required that he plunge deeply into his own feelings for an understanding of his people. He was, in short, his own authority. He had no notecards to fall back on, no graphs or charts or statistics to fill up pages and 'prove' that this or that was true. For a writer of Cash's tender psyche, this was a herculean task, made all the more excruciating because he had undertaken a sweeping critique of his own people" (114).

17. Morrison, *Cash,* 65; Clayton, *Cash,* 120, 147. Clayton continues: "She smoked cigarettes, enjoyed a drink or two, wisecracked (sometimes in a loud voice), and had no intention of being an empty-headed southern 'belle'" (147). Morrison writes that Cash's "plain country upbringing—of which he was proud, because he was not one to 'go back on his raising'—nevertheless made him admittedly uncomfortable and self-conscious in the presence of 'the country clubbers,' as he called them" (Morrison, *Cash,* 42).

18. Clayton, *Cash,* 150.

Increasingly, Cash began to suffer episodes of anger and outrage directed toward Hitler, and his friends and compatriots at the newspaper viewed these "fits" with pity and horror, as Cash would rail and scream at the Nazi aggressor. According to Joseph Morrison, "This wholly rational fear of Hitler's evil intentions became, whenever Cash had been drinking, a mortal fear of Hitler the man." Cash resumed his friendship with the Charlotte doctor who had treated his hyperthyroidism years earlier, and "invariably the author would question his ability ever to marry because of his supposed impotence and, as he took a few drinks, express his fear of Hitler."[19]

And Cash was drinking more and more. Somehow, however, in 1938 he sent extensive revisions and some new manuscript to the Knopfs, promising the remainder very shortly. Excuse followed excuse until finally in 1940 the publisher threw up his hands in desperation. Then, without fanfare, in July, 1940, Cash forwarded the completed manuscript to Knopf with the explanation, "I have never been able to approach the task of continuing it without extreme depression and dislike."[20]

The task at last completed, Wilbur and Mary were married. Clayton reports that "according to Mary, Cash's sexual anxieties proved to be groundless, and they knew true marital happiness." The book reviews rolled in and they were good, Cash was awarded a Guggenheim Foundation grant to pursue his lifelong ambition and write a novel, and the Cashes set out for a year in Mexico. But, according to Clayton, "even with a novel in mind, a Guggenheim in hand, and a year free for writing, there were signs of stress, and depression dogged his steps in the spring of 1941. . . . He was also anxiety-ridden and unable to shake the feeling of being completely worn out." On the train trip to Mexico, Cash had one of his nervous episodes, a "violent fit of anger, stomping a newspaper on the floor and biting his hands," and the couple arrived in Mexico City "hot, tired, and with ragged nerves."[21]

Cash's biographer writes that from that point on, "nothing went right for the two provincials far from home. The altitude made them dizzy; the food made then nauseous; diarrhea attacked both of them. Neither felt like doing much sightseeing. Cash tried to work. He

19. Morrison, *Cash*, 80; Clayton, *Cash*, 154, 156. For a description of Cash's agitation about Hitler, see *ibid.*, 156–57.
20. Clayton, *Cash*, 159–61, 162.
21. *Ibid.*, 165, 179, 182, 183.

pecked out a straightforward piece of journalism about the city on his damnable portable, piercing the air with periodic oaths and obscenities and gnawing nervously at his hand. Serious writing seemed out of the question for the moment. Clearly, Cash was depressed and disturbed."[22] After three weeks of these depressing conditions, Cash lapsed into a terrifying paranoid episode in which he was certain that Nazis were plotting against him in the hallway outside his door. While a frightened and distraught Mary was out seeking help, Wilbur Cash fled from their room, checked into another hotel, and hanged himself by his necktie from the bathroom door.[23]

What had gone wrong? Cash had at last achieved the status of successful and acclaimed author. He was happily married. He was embarked on an adventure to write the great American novel, a novel of the piedmont that would be "a historical saga, a family romance that explored the world of patriarchs, fathers and sons." Cash's biographers have suggested that his suicide stemmed either from a degenerative brain disorder or the onset of delirium tremens. Undoubtedly the full truth will forever remain shrouded in mystery.[24]

Out of the diverse elements of a lifetime of study and his own experience, Wilbur J. Cash constructed an interpretation of the southern past that has been challenged in many of its particulars—and especially on the larger issue of continuity versus change—but has endured as a classic in southern thought. Contributing to the continuing appeal of *The Mind of the South* are its very southern eloquence, its monumental scope, its agonized love-hate relationship with the South that strikes the heart of so many southerners' experience with their region, and its availability as a deceptively easy one-volume explanation of the South's peculiarities during a time when the attention of the world was focused on that troubled region. Cash constructed an exceedingly intricate argument, but he wove his tale with such spellbinding eloquence that it is easy to miss the connections he forged in his masterful conceptual scheme. In the final analysis, it was his purpose to outline the creation and maintenance of a hegemonic patriarchal *mentalité* (not truly an ide-

---

22. *Ibid.*, 183.
23. *Ibid.*, 184–87.
24. *Ibid.*, 178; Morrison, *Cash*, 127–30.

ology), and this is ultimately the source of Cash's enduring appeal, for he touched on much that continues to resonate in southern life.[25]

At the heart of Cash's argument is the construct he calls the "ancient pattern," the particular "habits of thought" that were held in place by the operation of recurrent "frontiers." Central to this pattern is domination by a ruling elite that changes outwardly over time—from the large plantation owners of the Old South, to the industrial barons of the New, to the Babbitts of the twentieth century—but that remains constant in its greed, selfishness, and general unworthiness.[26]

Cash argues that domination by the "ruling class" bears lightly on the average southerner, however, because this "man at the center" is an intense individualist, and under the conditions of opportunity presented by the recurring frontiers, he always believes that he could rise in the world if that were truly his desire. Given his predisposition to view the world as an "aggregation of self-contained and self-sufficient monads, each of whom was ultimately and completely responsible for himself," the average southerner is not much given to thinking of rectifying his grievances by banding together with other like-minded people; in other words, he never develops class consciousness (113).

The real explanation for the South's lack of class consciousness lies in what Cash calls the "Proto-Dorian bond" among all white men. As a result of this convention, no matter how bad his condition or impaired his status, the white man will always have his white skin, and this guarantees his equality to all who are white and his superiority to all who are black. This racial solidarity provides a floor under the white man's status anxieties, and precludes a need for class consciousness. The ruling elite maintains itself in power because no opposition to its control develops.

Fantastic as all of the above may sound at first blush, Cash argues that the southerner's predisposition for romanticism deflects any tend-

25. The most relentless critique of Cash's interpretation is to be found in C. Vann Woodward, "The Elusive Mind of the South," in Woodward, *American Counterpoint: Slavery and Racism in the North-South Dialogue* (New York, 1971), 261–84.

26. One assumes that these "Babbitts" were the selfsame "country-clubbers" for whom Cash felt such disdain and in whose presence he felt so very intimidated. Clayton writes that "'Country clubbers' and their private retreats normally gave Cash the willies" (Clayton, *Cash*, 176). Morrison says that Cash "later admitted that he had settled on Wake Forest precisely because . . . 'country-club' skills would not be required of him there" (Morrison, *Cash*, 34).

encies toward clear-headed analysis, thereby further obscuring the control of the elite and the true interests of the man at the center. Furthermore, as southern patriotism becomes tied increasingly to what Cash calls the "savage ideal," all criticism and dissent are stifled, and the southern psyche becomes split between twin impulses toward puritanism and hedonism. In short, Cash outlines an ideal environment for the development of mythology.

Perhaps the most celebrated element of Cash's work is the psychosexual dimension, the nexus between race and sex that he perceives in southern thought. Steeped in Freud, Cash is intensely attuned to the functioning of the irrational and the unconscious, and he holds as a constant throughout his work the Negro as a threatening element in southern life. As many others before and since have done, Cash argues that the ultimate concern of white men in this biracial society is for "the right of their sons in the legitimate line, through all the generations to come, to be born to the great heritage of white men." Central to the preservation of this white heritage—as well as to the maintenance of racial solidarity, the absence of class consciousness, and thus the continuation of control by the ruling elite—is the southern woman, black and white (119).

Beginning with his explanation that the black woman was "natural" in a puritanical world and therefore increasingly desirable to white men ("Torn from her tribal restraints and taught an easy complaisance for commercial reasons" [87]), Cash argues that the resultant disingenuous tendency to glorify the white woman led to her being used as a Palladium in the fight with the Yankee, as the very symbol of the South itself. "With this in view," he wrote, "it is obvious that the assault on the South would be felt as, in some true sense, an assault on her also, and that the South would inevitably translate its whole battle into terms of her defense" (89, 118).[27]

What was really going on, of course, was that the purity of the white woman was the ultimate safeguard for the preservation of the white race and, in turn, white dominance. Take away that purity, that "absolute taboo on any sexual approach to her by the Negro," and "the great heritage of white men" could not be guaranteed. Thus the aboli-

27. For a fascinating account of the "moral economy of gender," the trade-off of submission in return for reverence required of Confederate women, see Drew Gilpin Faust, "Altars of Sacrifice: Confederate Women and the Narratives of War," *Journal of American History,* LXXVI (March, 1990), 1200–1228.

tion of slavery "had inevitably opened up to the mind of every Southerner a vista at the end of which stood the overthrow of this taboo." In
these circumstances, "any assertion of any kind on the part of the Negro
constituted in a perfectly real manner an attack on the Southern [white]
woman," and so the conditions of Reconstruction represented for her
a condition "as degrading . . . as rape itself." Such, Cash concludes,
"was the ultimate content of the Southerners' rape complex," and such
was the justification of violence toward the Negro "as demanded in
defense of woman . . . though the offenses of by far the greater number of victims had nothing immediately to do with sex" (119). As
miscegenation continued after the Civil War, Cash claims that the resulting tension "served to intensify the old interest in gyneolatry, and
to produce yet more florid notions about Southern Womanhood and
Southern Virtue, and so to foster yet more precious notions of modesty
and decorous behavior for the Southern female to live up to" (131).

Clearly, the role of woman as symbol is absolutely central to the
entire construct that Cash has erected, and yet in a book that runs to
440 pages, Cash gives the southern woman 50. In his construct she
is passive, faceless, undifferentiated, merely an instrumentality of his
larger purposes, which are to discern the mechanisms of maintaining
male power. One can only conclude that Cash is not really interested in
the wider roles that southern women (or blacks, or workers, or any
other subgroup) may have played in the life of the region, as indeed he
was not interested in writing an intellectual or even a social history of
the South. In fact, he was not writing history at all but instead a very
special kind of essay, a literary artifact in itself, and one that was filtered
through the lens of one man's unusual and depressed and passionate
experience. "My thesis," Cash wrote to Blanche Knopf, "is that the
Southern mind represents a very definite culture, or attitude towards
life, a heritage, from the Old South, but greatly modified and extended
by conscious and unconscious efforts over the last hundred years to
protect itself from the encroachments of three hostile factors: the Yankee Mind, the Modern Mind, and the Negro." In the end, he thought,
leadership would, "in the very nature of things, continue in the hands
of the charlatans." [28]

Cash's biographer claims that Cash never intended his book to be
an "ordinary history," a "scholarly compendium of facts marshaled to

28. Clayton, *Cash*, 93.

buttress impersonal arguments." Bruce Clayton writes that Cash was "an intellectual, a critic, a prober, a thinker passionately absorbed in his subject. In truth, he never wanted to be detached." In truth, he never was. In truth, Cash's book was largely an exercise in therapy, for it allowed him to explore and work through the major forces and issues that had shaped and scarred his own life.[29]

Joseph Morrison notes that the old Irishman in *The Mind of the South* was modeled on Cash's great-great-grandfather, that the cotton mill crusade he described was based on a project developed in his home-town of Gaffney, South Carolina, and that his "later criticism of the South's romantic self-delusion grew directly out of his own back-ground." Numerous other examples of autobiographical material could be suggested, so many that one can hardly escape the conclusion that in much of Cash's analysis he was projecting.[30]

As Cash himself knew, projections are "ways an individual or a group attributes to others what it secretly fears (or believes) to be true about itself." For a person struggling with as many internal contradic-tions and ambiguities as burdened Wilbur Cash, projection can become a necessary means of protecting the ego, one of Freud's cardinal defense mechanisms. Take, for example, the romantic who disparaged roman-ticism, the woman worshiper who scoffed at gyneolatry, the agnostic who cried at Chartres, the idealist who disparaged the southern quest for honor, the fiercely proud plebeian who longed for recognition, the modernist who yearned for tradition. Cash's scoffing Menckenesque tone could not hide the gentle soul inside; he could not bully himself out of his idealism, his romanticism, his spirituality, his need to belong.[31]

What was the source of these contradictions? Of course, that is a question for the gods, but based on the evidence available, a few specu-lations seem at least plausible, if not entirely in order. When one recon-structs Cash's childhood home environment, there emerges a picture of a father who had "escaped an unloving stepmother" into the mill as a

29. *Ibid.*, 108, 105.
30. Morrison, *Cash*, 10, 12.
31. As Clayton writes: "Fortified by Freud and a keen introspective intelligence, Cash sensed that most of the labels and negative things racist whites said about blacks were 'projections' of a master race not entirely convinced in its psyche of its superiority" (*Cash*, 206).

boy, who later called his wife Mama, and who may well have heaped excessive adoration on her for providing him the female love and devotion he had needed as a child.[32] Could this be the origin of Cash's surmise that in the Old South "there grew up an unusually intense affection and respect for the women of the family—for the wife and mother upon whose activities the comfort and well-being of everyone greatly depended" (88) or of his contention that Yankee charges of southern inferiority were "answered by proclaiming . . . that Southern virtue . . . was superior . . . and adducing Southern Womanhood in proof" (89)? If this was the standard of womanly virtue Cash believed he must seek, is it any wonder that he thought women unattainable or that he found himself uncomfortable in their presence? The other side of this intense idolatry is misogyny, or as Cash expressed it in *The Mind of the South,* "the exasperated hate of a lover who cannot persuade the object of his affections to his desire" (386–87).

Is it possible that in his frustration Wilbur Cash broke through southern cultural taboos and turned to miscegenation, as many others had done before him? "For she was natural," Cash described the Negro woman, "and could give herself up to passion in a way impossible to wives inhibited by Puritanical training" (87). For a boy steeped in a puritanical Baptist background, this could have explained his increasing illnesses at Wake Forest as well as his trips "into Raleigh's notorious vice district," his fears of "becoming impotent," and his strange, unexplained college poem "Yes—old Sakyamuni—I can understand / Why you should care to believe / That Heaven could but be / In ceaselessly forgetting."[33] If it were true, then he was no doubt describing himself when he wrote of the faithless husband in the Old South: "The guilty man, supposing he possessed any shadow of decency, must inexorably writhe in shame and an intolerable sense of impurity in her eyes" (88).

Guilt over miscegenation could also be a plausible explanation for Cash's failure with Peggy Ann, for his recurring depressions, for his compelling need to understand the southern past (Clayton says that Cash's "need to understand the southern past ran far deeper than the historian's usual interest in what happened"). It could also explain his own psychic split (demonstrated by his uncontrolled weeping at the

32. *Ibid.,* 5, 6.
33. *Ibid.,* 30.

great cathedral at Chartres—the grandest physical representation of the ideas he had rejected) and his projection of that onto the South. It could explain his growing fear of Hitler (who demanded racial purity); and if, in an unguarded moment he confessed to Mary (family lore has it that they "quarreled violently" the night before they left for Mexico), it could explain his final descent into despair.[34] It could even explain his identification of miscegenation as the heart of the southern dilemma and then his hasty abandonment of the subject.

Consider, for a moment, Cash's reflections on the Celtic settlers of the Old South (Cash always trumpeted his own Celtic origins):

> Even when he was a sort of native pagan . . . hooting contemptuously at parsons, he was nevertheless at bottom religious. Ancestral phobias grappled him toward the old center, and immemorial awes, drawn in with his mother's milk, whispered imperative warnings in his ears. . . . If he was a hedonist, then, and however paradoxical it may sound, he was also likely to be a Puritan. The sense of sin, if obscured, continued to move darkly in him at every time. . . . The world he knew, the hot sting of the sun in his blood, the sidelong glance of the all-complaisant Negro woman—all these impelled him irresistibly to joy. But even as he danced, and even though he had sloughed off all formal religion, his thoughts were with the piper and his fee. (56)

Phobias, awes, warnings, sin, shame, and guilt—these are the stuff of which Cash the writer, Cash the depressive, frames his analysis of the southern mind. These are the dark underside of the lyrical beauty with which Cash describes the southern countryside; these are the awful truths that inform his every approach to the southern mind. Similar examples abound throughout *The Mind of the South;* projection would seem to be the key to understanding Wilbur Cash's book.

Whether in fact Wilbur J. Cash was a misogynous miscegenist can probably never be known, but what is known is that his book and his formulations have had a profound effect on southerners' thinking about themselves for fifty years. Cash's biographer has gone so far as to say that the book "would help shape the southern mind for decades," and certainly his terms and categories have become commonplace in southern discourse. One of the many who have reviewed *The Mind of the South* suggested that it was autobiographical, that it was an exploration of Cash's own mind. Perhaps it would come closer to the mark to say

34. *Ibid.,* 94, 182.

that Cash's book grew out of a construct that he projected onto the region.[35]

Bruce Clayton has written in an eloquent passage that Cash's true lover was the South. "The South was his great love, but it was a tempestuous, tormented love. His South was a possessive lover, who would not—cannot, it seems—tolerate being neglected. The troubled, sensitive Jack Cash hardly knew a moment's peace from the second he discovered that the South was his love."[36]

If Clayton is right, it would seem that Jack Cash was unable to consummate his love affair even with the South. His work is incomplete because he was unable to hear the many voices in which his lover spoke—the voices that could have moved him beyond his view of woman as mere symbol in an ongoing power struggle among elite males. His work is incomplete because he was blinded to his lover's many faces by his own fear and limitations—blinded, therefore, to the roles that women and blacks and workers played in shaping and being shaped by the mind of the South. Cash's work is incomplete, finally, because his depressive's view of the South showed him little of joy, or striving, or triumph, but only delusion, deception, and greed.

Fearing impotence, Wilbur J. Cash used his massive intellect to prove his prowess and to strike a blow at the lies and pretensions of the elite. Having crafted an analysis that left little room for human agency in the southern past, posing instead a deterministic "mind" that left "no way out," Wilbur Cash with characteristic contradiction and romantic flourish attempted nonetheless to save his beloved South. Son of a mill worker, born to exclusion, torn between evangelistic terrors and hedonistic yearnings, drawn to the glory of the southern past out of the drab reality of his piedmont present, Cash was a romantic soul in search of a stage grand enough for his aspirations and yearnings, an angry rebel confined by temperament and circumstance to the written word. Ultimately he created for himself a prison from which there was no escape—no place in which he could feel whole, validated, proud, safe, at peace. Ultimately there was indeed, for Wilbur Cash, "no way out."[37]

Wilbur Cash did not invent the phenomenon that he named gyneolatry. The practice of placing the southern woman on a pedestal was

---

35. *Ibid.*, 192; Neill Herring, "The Constancy of Change," *Southern Exposure*, I, nos. 3–4 (1974), 211.

36. Clayton, *Cash*, 220.

37. Morrison, *Cash*, 163.

real and widely remarked, and it is a central cultural phenomenon rich in possibilities for interpreting the southern past. But Cash's own personal experiences, perceptions, and preconceptions caused him to focus on miscegenation as the causative agent in the creation of gyneolatry—and to intertwine elements of race and gender as the bedrock underlying all other southern behavior. How fascinating it is that Cash based his byzantine, intricately woven thesis on speculations about blacks and women and then left both groups out of his book. Although Cash succeeded in unwinding the tangled skein of southern mythology, his deep personal involvement in the object of his study precluded the weaving of a clear and consistent pattern.

Cash's construct mirrored his society, but only as that image was filtered through the lens of his own experience; Cash's analysis was a product of his interaction with his world. A different surveyor of the terrain of the past might well have identified different causative elements or even reversed the order that Cash imposed. Lillian Smith seems to suggest the obverse of Cash's idea, arguing that because the southern woman was on a pedestal and therefore cold and unapproachable, southern men indulged increasingly in "the back-yard temptation" of miscegenation, with dire consequences for the health of relationships all around.[38]

There can be little doubt but that a pervasive patriarchal *mentalité* has controlled southern life through much of the region's history and that efforts to maintain this hegemony have shaped southern behavior in areas of race, class, and gender. But because this *mentalité* has been so pervasive—really a given in southern thought—it has often been difficult to identify or even to see. Cash may have been ahead of his time in groping toward such a gender-based reality in his construct, but of course his interests lay elsewhere, and so despite his dalliance with gyneolatry he failed to forge a truly useful interpretive tool with which to uncover the secrets of the southern past. Perhaps a more rigorous historian can build on Cash's promising beginnings.

W. J. Cash's biographers paint a portrait of a very human, tortured soul. Both of them are partisan, as perhaps all biographers are, but Bruce Clayton is more eloquent and passionate in his effort to assess Wilbur Cash's contribution. His concluding thoughts on his subject are sensitive, touching, and filled with gratitude for what Cash attempted:

38. Smith, *Killers of the Dream*, 99.

"His effort was heroic. He tried to write southern history on a grand scale and succeeded. No one has come close to matching him. No historian has had the courage or audacity or ability even to try what Cash did. He tried because he was, in his soul, an artist."[39]

There can be little doubt that Clayton is right, that Wilbur J. Cash was an artist. But it is doubtful that what Cash wrote can rightly be called history. This is not to detract from Cash's great achievement. One stands in awe before his accomplishment; in the words of one of his reviewers, "Cash's work came like light to a darkened room in which I had stumbled and felt and known but never seen." But the tools Cash employed to conduct his study were those of the journalist or the essayist, not the historian.[40]

The Mind of the South has been treated as history, and it has shaped much of the writing of southern history. As C. Vann Woodward noted at the time of the book's twenty-fifth anniversary: "The book is quoted, paraphrased, and plagiarized so regularly as to have practically entered the public domain. . . . It would be impossible to prove, but I would venture to guess that no other book on Southern history rivals Cash's in influence among laymen and few among professional historians."[41]

W. J. Cash did not employ the tools of the historian, and the tale he wove—however compelling and satisfying as critique, seductive, even intoxicating—does not pass muster as history. Cash read deeply, mostly in literature and psychology, and he was a keen observer of his people. (One suspects that those "lazy" afternoons on the courthouse square should more rightly be regarded as fieldwork, during which he attuned his remarkably sensitive ear to the concerns and the peculiarities of his piedmont neighbors.) But he made no effort to remove himself from his own limited perspective and capture the voices of other players. The only voice one hears in Cash's book is that of W. J. Cash.

As Cash's book reveals, we are all bound by our own experiences and worldviews, but as historians we attempt to counterbalance this human limitation by seeking out a multiplicity of diverse perspectives. The past yields up its stories in many voices, and as archaeologists of the archives our primary tool is our ear for those voices—voices that await our invitation to emerge once again and be heard. Listening to

39. Clayton, *Cash*, 222.
40. Herring, "Constancy of Change," 211.
41. Woodward, "The Elusive Mind of the South," 263.

those voices, analyzing them, just finding them, requires massive effort and time and so we as historians content ourselves with smaller goals than the "history on a grand scale" that Wilbur Cash attempted.

One of the most promising recent advances in the quest to find multiple voices—and one from which Wilbur Cash could have bene-fited—has been in the field of women's history. Southern historians have let the Cash construct stand, lo these many years, because for most of them, women have been invisible in the southern past—indeed, in Western civilization. Increasingly, women's history is challenging the intellectual constructs that have kept women invisible, and it holds great promise for enriching our understanding of the human condition. In broadening the dialogue, in asking new questions, in finding new voices and new pasts, explorations from a feminist perspective enrich the common store of the "partial truths" from which a richer, more textured, more humanizing past may be reconstructed.[42]

Although the Cash construct profoundly influenced a generation of journalists and historians, new work in southern women's history is now breaking out of that mold—first, by finding the women in the South's past, and second, by questioning the traditional constructions of gender that have informed the work of Cash and so many others. Whereas in the 1960s Cash's popularity surged—largely because he seemed to provide so many answers to the disturbing questions sur-rounding southern race relations—in the 1990s Cash has little to offer to those who are seeking answers to questions of gender.

In seeking out the infinitely varied voices of the past, we come ever closer to reconstructing a past that approaches the real. We can no more expect to find truth in the past than we can find it in the present, but the past does have its own stories to tell, its own secrets to yield. Al-though our quest into the past undoubtedly follows questions that arise from our individual experiences, concerns, and political agendas, we must guard against the errors that led Wilbur Cash astray in his venture into that alien land. Rather than being guided by our own perceptions

---

42. See Gerda Lerner, *The Creation of Patriarchy* (New York, 1986); see also Joan Wallach Scott, *Gender and the Politics of History* (New York, 1988), 17; Anne Firor Scott, *Making the Invisible Woman Visible* (Chicago, 1984), and Elizabeth Fox-Genovese, *Femi-nism Without Illusions: A Critique of Individualism* (Chapel Hill, 1991). Joan Scott makes the argument for "partial truths" (*Gender and the Politics of History,* 10); see also Jacque-line Dowd Hall, "Partial Truths," *Signs,* XIV (Summer, 1989), 902–11.

of reality, our forays into the past must be guided by a respect for the truths and the surprises that lie shrouded in the mystery of another time. Only then can we hope to make of the past a source of growth and wisdom and a light for the journey into tomorrow.

Two Minds of the South: Ideas of Southern History in W. J. Cash and James McBride Dabbs

DAVID HACKETT FISCHER

W. J. Cash's *Mind of the South* approaches its fiftieth anniversary still in print and selling briskly, still as fresh and lively on the page as when it first appeared. Since 1960, the paperbound edition of the book has sold 210,000 copies.[1] Academic commentary on the book now bulks larger than the book itself—strong evidence of an enduring classic.[2]

I wish to thank Charles Joyner, who first suggested this topic and offered much wise advice on its development; Bertram Wyatt-Brown for sharing his work on the Percys and many suggestions on the study of regional culture; Samuel Hill for his generous critique at the Wake Forest symposium; Paul Escott for very helpful editorial criticism; and Susanna Fischer for her rigorous but fair-minded critique of her father's manuscript.

1. New York *Times,* February 6, 1991.

2. Two indispensable works are Bruce Clayton, *W. J. Cash: A Life* (Baton Rouge, 1991), an excellent biography; and Joseph L. Morrison, *W. J. Cash, Southern Prophet: A Biography and a Reader* (New York, 1967), which is valuable both as a secondary work and as a collection of primary materials. Morrison has also contributed two important essays, "Found: The Missing Editorship of W. J. Cash," *North Carolina Historical Review,* XLVII (Winter, 1990), 40–50; and "The Summing Up," *South Atlantic Quarterly,* LXX (Autumn, 1971), 477–86. Also helpful are Dewey Grantham, "Mr. Cash Writes a Book," *Progressive,* XXV (December, 1961), 40–42; Bertram Wyatt-Brown, "W. J. Cash and Southern Culture," in Wyatt-Brown, *Yankee Saints and Southern Sinners* (Baton Rouge, 1985), 131–54; Michael P. Dean, "W. J. Cash's *The Mind of the South:* Southern History, Southern Style," *Southern Studies,* XX (1981), 297–302; Edwin M. Yoder, Jr., "W. J. Cash After a Quarter Century," in *The South Today: 100 Years After Appomattox,* ed. Willie Morris (New York, 1965), 89–99; Richard King, *A Southern Renaissance: The Cultural Awakening of the American South* (New York, 1980), 146–72; and Fred Hob-

Much discussion of Cash's book treats it as *sui generis*—the solitary act of a literary loner, the unique production of a dark and troubled spirit.[3] It was those things, but it was also the leading representative of a regional genre that flourished during Cash's generation in many parts of America and especially in the South.

How and why this genre developed is a problem that cannot be explored at length here. Suffice to say that during the 1920s and 1930s, regional differences became highly visible in the United States. In quantitative studies Richard Bensel and Kenneth Martis found that this was the period when congressional voting patterns were more strongly regional than at any other time in American history and nowhere more so than in the "Solid South."[4]

This was also the era when Howard Odum invented an academic subdiscipline called the "new science of the region" and put it to work mainly in his studies of the South. It was the time when followers of G. Stanley Hall (who had trained Odum) created a field called "regional psychology" and applied it primarily to the South.[5]

In the 1920s and 1930s, foreign visitors to the United States stressed regionalism in their discussions of American culture. Sir William Beveridge, for example, organized his understanding of the United States primarily in regional terms. "If I had to sum up my impressions," he wrote, "I should think in terms of drama; I should choose a parody from Pirandello: 'Six Americas in search of a faith.'" Beveridge believed that America was a constellation of regional cultures marked by "pro-

---

son, *Tell About the South: The Southern Rage to Explain* (Baton Rouge, 1983), 244–94.

Hostile to Cash are C. Vann Woodward, "The Elusive Mind of the South," in Woodward, *American Counterpoint: Slavery and Racism in the North-South Dialogue* (Boston, 1971), 261–84; Eugene D. Genovese, *The World the Slaveholders Made: Two Essays in Interpretation* (New York, 1969), 137–50; Louis D. Rubin, Jr. "The Mind of the South," *Sewanee Review,* LXII (Autumn, 1954), 683–95; Michael O'Brien, "W. J. Cash, Hegel, and the South," *Journal of Southern History,* XLIV (August, 1978), 379–98; and O'Brien, "A Private Passion: W. J. Cash," in O'Brien, *Rethinking the South: Essays in Intellectual History* (Baltimore, 1988), 179–89.

3. For example, Woodward, "The Elusive Mind of the South"; Wyatt-Brown, "W. J. Cash and Southern Culture."

4. Richard F. Bensel, *Sectionalism and American Political Development, 1880–1980* (Madison, 1984), 375; Kenneth C. Martis, *The Historical Atlas of Political Parties in the United States Congress, 1789–1989* (New York, 1989), 173–83.

5. Howard Odum and Harry Estill Moore, *American Regionalism: A Cultural Historical Approach to National Integration* (New York, 1938), 1–34.

found divisions of race and history, with opposed economic interests, with different ways of life and thought."[6]

Why regional thinking became so strong in this period is an interesting question. One answer might be found in different rates and patterns of social change in the entire nation. A second might involve other disparities: as the community of discourse became increasingly national, cultural patterns remained strongly regional—a combination that fostered the growth of a high degree of regional consciousness.

In any case, this was the context within which Cash wrote. The organizing idea of a "mind of the South" was not his own invention. The title was borrowed from Vernon Louis Parrington, who had used it in *Main Currents of American Thought* two years before Cash published his first essay of the same name in H. L. Mencken's *American Mercury*. While Cash was toiling at his book, Perry Miller was hard at work on his great project *The New England Mind,* the first volume of which appeared in 1939. After the war, Arthur Moore brought out *The Frontier Mind,* one of many similar publications.[7]

The idea of "mind" took on different meanings in these various works. Perry Miller's treatise on New England celebrated Mind with a capital M in an appropriately solemn and humorless exploration of the most exalted realms of serious thought. Arthur Moore's book on the frontier mind, by contrast, was an irreverent *jeu d'esprit* about buckskin heroes, playful savages, and other literary conceits, approached in a puckish spirit suggesting that the very idea of a frontier mind was an oxymoron, a contradiction in terms.

Cash took a third approach. It is something of an irony that he chose to call his book *The Mind of the South,* for he quoted with approval Henry Adams' canard that "strictly the southerner had no mind; he had temperament" (*Mind,* 102). Cash's interest in his subject was less cerebral and more visceral than that of Perry Miller. It was less literary and more existential than those of Parrington or Arthur Moore. In contrast to these works, he organized his book around a primitive,

6. Quoted in Katherine Jocher *et al.,* eds., *Folk, Religion, and Society* (Chapel Hill, 1964), 153.

7. Vernon Louis Parrington, *Main Currents in American Thought* (3 vols.; New York, 1927–30), II, 3, 183, 271; Perry Miller, *The New England Mind: The Seventeenth Century* (Cambridge, Mass., 1939); Arthur K. Moore, *The Frontier Mind: A Cultural Analysis of the Kentucky Frontiersman* (Lexington, Ky., 1957).

even atavistic concept of mind, which referred to a set of inherited and semiconscious folk beliefs. These folkways were understood by Cash to be at once the product of history and one of its most powerful determinants.

By yet another irony, Cash was not behind but half a century ahead of academic fashion, among historians at least. The persistent power of his book in our own time derives in part from the fact that social and cultural historiography has been moving in Cash's direction. Historians today are increasingly coming to share Cash's interest in culture as a historical process and history as a cultural product, both operating primarily within and through the mind. In his own time, academic interests were different in many parts of the United States. Cash's understanding of a regional mind-set as a system of semiconscious folkways set him apart from professional scholars such as Miller, Moore, and Parrington. But it is important that his approach (if not his specific interpretation) was shared by writers below the Mason-Dixon Line.

In this connection it might be instructive to compare *The Mind of the South* with another specimen of the same genre: James McBride Dabbs's *Who Speaks for the South?*[8] When these two books are read side by side, a curious paradox appears. Both authors undertook to write a history of southern culture, and both conceived of that culture as a set of inherited folkways. Both began by positing the existence of, in Dabbs's words, a "predominant southern type," which was a product of its history. Both believed, in Cash's words, that though there are many Souths, "the fact remains that there is also one South," which has a fairly definite mental pattern, associated with a fairly definite social pattern" and rooted in its past. Both asserted that, despite internal differences, this "southern type" or "southern mind" exhibited in Cash's phrase a "remarkable homogeneity" (viii, vii).[9]

But here a paradox appears. Even as both authors agreed that the South is, in Cash's phrase, both "singular" and "solid," they described it in terms so different that a stranger to their subject might wonder if they had the same region in mind. We might ask how and why those differences developed.

8. James McBride Dabbs, *Who Speaks for the South?* (1964; paperback ed. New York, 1967); citations are from the 1967 edition.
9. *Ibid.*, vii–viii.

THE FACTOR OF PLACE

The differences between Cash and Dabbs derived partly from their places of origin within the South. Only about one hundred miles of South Carolina soil separated their birthplaces, but culturally their homes were worlds apart.

Wilbur Joseph Cash was born in the small village of Gaffney, high in the piedmont on the northern boundary of South Carolina. Gaffney was a cotton mill town, but in Cash's childhood it was also part of a rural world. Cash remembered that he "literally played with the wind and ran with Pan, spending whole days in the tops of maple trees. . . . The keening of the five o'clock whistles in the morning drilled me in sorrow." [10]

This was the heartland of the old southern backcountry. A few miles east of his home was the revolutionary battlefield of Kings Mountain. Not far to the west lay the field of Cowpens. To the north were that great seat of backcountry culture, Mecklenberg County in North Carolina and the regional metropolis of Charlotte. Cash's ancestors had lived in this area since it was settled by Europeans in the early eighteenth century. Most were British borderers from Scotland, Ireland, and the north of England, with a few Germans on his mother's side. All his life, Cash identified strongly with his Scotch-Irish forebears.

The population of this region was predominantly white. Blacks were a smaller minority than in many parts of the North during the twentieth century. Cash himself wrote, "Since no Negroes lived in the cotton-mill villages and few even passed in and out of them, the whites there lived almost completely removed and insulated from the black man, save as they encountered him briefly in the streets on their Saturday excursions" (317).

James McBride Dabbs came from a very different part of South Carolina. He was a native of Mayesville in Sumter County. His birthplace lay in what geographers call the inner coastal plain, between the Sand Hills and the sea. To the west was the state capital of Columbia, with its beautiful old campus of the University of South Carolina and its graceful Mills Library. To the east were the old low-country parishes of Berkeley, Williamsburg, Georgetown, and Charleston.

The population of this area was and is predominantly black. In

---

10. W. J. Cash to H. L. Mencken, n.d., quoted in Morrison, *Cash,* 8.

1980, the inner coastal plain accounted for nine of thirteen South Carolina counties in which African-Americans were more than 50 percent of the population.[11] Dabbs wrote: "I remember wrestling with Negro boys at noon sometimes as we lay in the shade far down by the swamp, and playing with them from time to time. . . . I remember no feeling against Negroes; but that I had the usual sense of white privilege."[12]

Sumter was very rural even by southern standards. Today the expanding urban centers of Columbia, Florence, and Charleston are creeping ever closer, but Sumter still preserves its rural character. The countryside shaped Dabbs's attitudes toward life. "From the farm we learned that life has meaning," he wrote. "What we did belonged to the farm pattern." He dedicated one of his books to farmers, "who in this fruitful land still trust God," and to hunters and fishermen, "who as Izaak Walton says, are friendly men."[13]

Dabbs's roots, like those of Cash, ran deep in the soil of South Carolina. His ancestors on both sides had lived in the state for two centuries before he was born. In 1958, he wrote from his home in Sumter County, "Sitting by this window, looking down the avenue along which I hurried as a boy and down which I have seen my children and grandchildren walking with their dogs running beside them, I feel the throb of this land in my blood."[14]

In sharing this strong sense of place, Cash and Dabbs were one. Both men expressed similar feelings for the land. But it was not the same land that they had in mind.

THE FACTOR OF CLASS

Another important factor in differentiating these two southern minds was social class. More even than was actually the case, Cash and Dabbs thought of themselves as coming from two distant strata of southern society.

Cash identified strongly with the class that he called the southern yeomanry. To his publisher Alfred Knopf he wrote that "we were never

11. Charles F. Kovacik and John J. Winberry, *South Carolina: The Making of a Landscape* (Columbia, S.C., 1987), 15.
12. James McBride Dabbs, *The Southern Heritage* (New York, 1958), 12.
13. *Ibid.*, 5.
14. *Ibid.*, 3.

rich or aristocratic, certainly, but good upcountry farmers with land and niggers in proportion to most of our neighbors." [15] Always he described his origins as "plain" and "humble." Cash's father was manager of the company store in Gaffney, and his uncle was superintendent of the town's cotton mill—they were two of the most powerful and prosperous men in a very small village. His family was upwardly mobile in the New South. But Cash had the sense that even the owners and managers of this piedmont community came from the same class of yeoman farmers—neither rich nor poor but all of the same rural middle class (23–24, 41–42, 69, 72, 149–51, 161–89, 279–93).

Dabbs understood his origins in different terms. He was raised in his father's modest four-room farmhouse in Mayesville, but only a mile away was the mansion of his mother's family—a great house that Dabbs eventually inherited. "My father's background was farm, my mother's plantation." Of the two, he came to identify more with his mother's side of the family. "Down a wooded avenue," Dabbs wrote in 1958, "stood the plantation home where my mother had grown up and where I'm living now: a house weather-beaten in my boyhood, unpainted since 1860, looming gray among the trees, with tall columns and long halls, bitter cold in winter but deliciously cool in summer days. This was my second home: between farmhouse and plantation dwelling my boyhood swung. Life was no richer at the plantation—we were all land-poor—but there was a certain spaciousness there, partly physical, as of broad piazzas and halls, partly spiritual, as of people who, if they wore the cares of life, to a small boy seemed to wear them lightly." [16]

Dabbs's maternal grandfather had owned an estate of 10,000 acres, but his property dwindled after the Civil War. While the Cashes became modestly affluent in Gaffney, Dabbs's maternal forebears joined the ranks of the *nouveau pauvre*. When James McBride Dabbs inherited the great house, only 175 acres remained of his grandfather's 10,000. But if the family lost much of its property, it preserved its pride. Dabbs was raised as a gentleman and bred to what he called "gentle manners." [17] All his life he thought of himself in those terms.

Dabbs and Cash were the same in forming strong class identities,

15. Morrison, *Cash*, 10.
16. Dabbs, *Southern Heritage*, 4.
17. *Ibid.*, 6.

but they identified with different social classes. Cash thought of himself as descended from yeoman stock in the Carolina backcountry and never lost touch with his roots. Dabbs was raised to regard himself as a gentleman and actually came to live that role in his grandfather's great plantation house on the coastal plain of South Carolina.

THE FACTOR OF TIME

Time was also a factor in shaping these southern minds. W. J. Cash was born in 1900 and grew up with the New South. He graduated from high school in the same month that the United States entered World War I, came of age in the 1920s, wrote his book during the Great Depression, and died by his own hand in the desperate summer of 1941. He thought of the 1930s as a "great blight" (366), a bleak and desolate era of poverty and unemployment, and a time of mortal challenge to ideas of freedom and democracy. Cash witnessed the rise of what his generation was the first to call totalitarianism (a word that often appears in Cash's writing). He watched with horror the collapse of democracy throughout the Western world, when the number of free governments in Europe shrank from twenty-five in 1931 to merely four in 1941. Cash lived his adult life in the dark shadow of these events. He intimately shared the terrible anxiety that those who experienced the early years of the war will never forget and those who have been born since its triumphant end can scarcely imagine. When he ended his life, he was as much a casualty of that great struggle as if he had been shot down in battle.

But Cash also participated in the early stages of a great revival of democratic values which that titanic struggle engendered. He shared an attitude of deep concern and passionate commitment to liberal ideals with many thoughtful Americans of his generation. Cash's book was in many ways an artifact of that great world movement. Much of the special character of *The Mind of the South* derives from the moment of its birth.

The temporal context of Dabbs's major writing was different. To those who know their most important books, it comes as something of a shock to discover that Dabbs was a few years older than Cash but lived many years beyond him and did his major writing from a longer run of historical experience. Dabbs was born in 1896, four years before

Cash. In 1918 he was a lieutenant of artillery serving in France when Cash was still a schoolboy. After the war, Dabbs embarked upon an academic career, teaching English at Coker College and becoming department chairman by the age of twenty-nine. In 1937 he moved back to Mayesville, living in his grandfather's great house, and in 1942 he retired from his academic career. For the rest of his life he was a country gentleman. His land was cultivated by tenants, while Dabbs devoted his time to the management of his farm, his books, and many public causes.

Dabbs's most important book, *Who Speaks for the South?*, was written between 1960 and 1963, a psychological moment very different from the era when Cash published *The Mind of the South*. In the early 1960s, American liberals such as Dabbs experienced a moment of euphoria during the happy years that followed the election of John Kennedy. This halcyon time had a heavy impact on Dabbs's thinking. Earlier in his career, he had cultivated a fashionable mood of darkness and despair. During the 1940s and 1950s he read José Ortega y Gasset and other Jeremiahs of that generation and, in his own words, "viewed life with Ortega's 'tragic, ruthless glance.'"[18] When Dabbs drafted *Who Speaks for the South?* that attitude changed without entirely disappearing. As a good southern intellectual, he struggled to preserve a tragic sense of history in the face of mounting evidence of prosperity and progress, but the zeitgeist took its toll. The mood of the two works differed in ways that reflected the moment of their creation.

THE FACTOR OF EDUCATION

Both Cash and Dabbs were beneficiaries of the South's educational renaissance in the early twentieth century, but they experienced it in different ways. Cash was very much a product of local schools. He learned to read at home and remembered that through his childhood he "read, read, read and ruined his eyes reading."[19] In his youth Cash devoured every book he could find in Gaffney, then was sent to Boiling Springs High School and was reputed to have read every book in the school library. He went on to Wofford College and then to Wake Forest College.

James McBride Dabbs attended the University of South Carolina

18. *Ibid.*, 14.
19. Quoted in Morrison, *Cash,* 15.

for his undergraduate education. After World War I he traveled north to do graduate study at Clark University, where he experienced his epiphany in the unlikely setting of Worcester, Massachusetts. "Absent for the first time from the South," he wrote, "I had realized intensely my southern identity."[20] He continued his graduate training at Columbia University and joined the faculty of Coker College in Hartsville, South Carolina, teaching there for eighteen years.

Both Cash and Dabbs read widely, deeply, and compulsively—but not in the same books. As a child Cash devoured Scott and Henty and Kipling. In his youth he was exposed to Thomas Dixon and the hagiography of the Lost Cause. In adulthood, he read more specifically around his interest in southern culture. Augustus Longstreet's *Georgia Scenes* and especially Joseph Baldwin's *Flush Times of Alabama* had a major impact on his thinking about the Old South. He read the books of Yankee and British travelers—Frederick Law Olmsted, Joseph Ingraham, and Fanny Kemble—and was much influenced by Daniel Hundley and Hinton Rowan Helper. He also studied historical monographs, works of southern literature, and literary criticism. Cash was particularly interested in the writings of the debunking historians such as Thomas J. Wertenbaker and H. J. Eckenrode and social scientists such as Howard Odum and Broadus Mitchell. His style of writing and thinking was deeply influenced by Henry Mencken and the smart set of the old *American Mercury*.

Cash was familiar with the modern classics, but they appear to have had little impact on his thought. In 1937 he wrote a revealing piece about Karl Marx, whom he read with amused contempt. "Old Karl," he thought, was "one of the most naive idealists who have lived on the planet."[21] Always his most important reading was in the books that one might find in any literate up-country southern household during Cash's generation: Scott, Kipling, Bunyan, Milton, and especially the Bible. He kept the Bible by his bedside, often open to his favorite book of Ecclesiastes. The dark vision of the Prophets had a powerful effect on Cash's thinking—more so than Marx or Freud or Max Weber. The rich cadences of King James prose entered deep into his soul.

Dabbs was also a voracious reader, but his reading was more schol-

20. Dabbs, *Who Speaks for the South?*, 321.
21. W. J. Cash, "Old Karl's Idealism," Charlotte *News,* February 14, 1937, reprinted in Morrison, *Cash*, 228–31.

arly and more disciplined, the reading of a man who had access to large libraries and the time to explore them in a systematic way. He read academic history and kept up with the field, especially the latest essays by David Potter, C. Vann Woodward, and other southern historians. He was specially interested in the eighteenth century and read the works of the founders, Jefferson and Madison in particular. Dabbs read not only history but historiography and was much interested in Thomas Pressly's book on historians of the Civil War. In company with many male southerners he loved to read military history, working his way through Douglas Southall Freeman's biography of Robert E. Lee and studying Lee's papers and manuscripts. He became interested in the academic literature on American civilization and culture and read Sidney Mead's *Lively Experiment,* Perry Miller's *Errand into the Wilderness,* Henry Nash Smith's *Virgin Land,* Max Weber's *Protestant Ethic,* and William R. Taylor's *Cavalier and Yankee.* He also read Booker T. Washington, W. E. B. Du Bois, and much other work in black history. For eighteen years a college teacher, Dabbs systematically studied works of southern fiction, poetry, and autobiography. He read the literary journals and book reviews and kept up with the latest Manhattan fashions, reading Erik Erikson, Simone Weil, and Hannah Arendt. These interests reflect a conventional pattern of academic reading. But Dabbs differed from his secular colleagues and from Cash in his deep interest in spiritual questions. He read and wrote widely on religious themes.

Particularly important to Dabbs was the work of Walker Percy and William Alexander Percy, whose writings he profoundly admired and whose values he deeply shared. Dabbs and the Percys expressed one "mind of the south" that was to be found among literate descendants of planter elites in the low country and levee.

Cash represented another South altogether: the southern backcountry. C. Vann Woodward observes that "in the harsh depression climate of the thirties, this subregion of plain folk and small-town industries came to flower. Thomas Wolfe of Asheville was its poet, Paul Green of Chapel Hill its playwright, James Agee of Knoxville its reporter, and Jack Cash of Charlotte its historian."[22]

That these two southern mind-sets differed will come as no surprise to an informed reader. But the differences between them are very deep

22. Woodward, "The Elusive Mind of the South," 270.

and broad, even though they shared qualities in common that set them apart from other regions in the United States.

HISTORICAL APPROACHES TO THE MIND OF THE SOUTH

When Cash and Dabbs came to write about the South, it seemed natural and even inevitable for them to think of their subject in historical terms. Cash's *Mind of the South* is organized as a work of history, divided into three chronological periods on the development of the southern mind: its origin in the Old South, its "curious career in the middle years," and "its survival, modifications and its operation in our own time."

Dabbs's *Who Speaks for the South?* is also organized historically and divided into three parts. Part I follows his story from the earliest settlement through the Civil War. Part II is about a middle period, which for Dabbs was a time of "bitter testing," military defeat in war, political disaster in Reconstruction, and social injustice in the era of racial segregation. Part III finds evidence of a new beginning in the years after the outbreak of World War II.

The two books are similar in their historical architecture. They are also alike in other ways. Both authors were devoted to the South but deeply critical of its folkways. Both wrote from the heart about their common subject, with a passion rarely found in professional historiography. Both were moralists who wished to preserve the virtues of southern culture and to correct its vices. In these purposes they were much the same. At the same time, they differed profoundly in their substantive understandings of southern culture and history.

THE PROTAGONISTS OF SOUTHERN HISTORY: THE MAN AT THE CENTER

Cash and Dabbs both generalized broadly about the "mind of the South" from the culture of a different subregion. But they did so in different ways. Cash's "man at the center" was a yeoman farmer in the piedmont where he grew up: a "simple rustic figure" whose "chief blood-strain was likely to be the Celtic," whose Christian religion was an outpouring of "primitive frenzy" and "apocalyptic rhetoric," whose social attitudes were marked by "the most intense individualism the

world has seen since the Italian Renaissance," whose comity was a
world in which "no man felt or acknowledged any primary dependence
on his fellows," and whose politics was characterized by "intense distrust" and "downright aversion" to "any actual exercise of authority
beyond the barest minimum" (30, 32, 56, 58, 34, 35).

Cash thought of this man at the center as distinct from poor whites
and from the aristocracy, whose numbers and importance he believed
to have been much exaggerated in myth and legend. His quintessential
southerner was a man of middling status. He was also a man of the
frontier, secure in a system of values which Cash called "the tradition
of the old backcountry" (34), a tradition he believed had grown
stronger rather than weaker through time and had been reinforced by
events of the late nineteenth and twentieth centuries (196). Cash celebrated the virtues of this southern yeoman-pioneer while condemning
his vices—"proud, brave, honorable by its lights, courteous, personally
generous, swift to act" (439), "a primitive uprightness . . . a cleanness
and decency . . . a wholly admirable rectitude . . . one of the most pleas-
ant things that ever grew up on American soil," but at the same time
flawed by "violence, intolerance, aversion and suspicion toward new
ideas, an incapacity for analysis, an inclination to act from feeling rather
than from thought, an exaggerated individualism and a too narrow
sense of social responsibility" (439; see also 32, 34, 35, 56, 78).

On the outer fringes of southern culture, as Cash understood it,
were other groups that he deemed to be of less historical importance.
Chief among these marginal figures were a set of distant and alien figures whom he impersonally called "the Virginians." By this term he
meant to include "all those little clumps of colonial aristocracy in the
lowlands" (5).[23] His Virginians included the gentry of South Carolina
and Louisiana. Cash was not entirely consistent on this subject. He
believed that the "Virginians and all their allied aristocracies" (14) had
never been centrally important in southern culture, but he also thought
that their "decay" and persistence were powerful themes of southern
history (198). These propositions were not easily reconciled, but on
one cardinal point Cash was very clear—the "aristocrats" of Virginia,
South Carolina, and Louisiana were not the men at the center of southern history. He followed the debunking historians Wertenbaker and

---

23. In this usage Cash closely followed Joseph G. Baldwin, *The Flush Times of Alabama and Mississippi* (1853; rpr. New York, 1957), 52–76.

Eckenrode in arguing that the pedigrees of the Virginians were largely bogus and their Cavalier culture mostly a myth. Cash claimed that even in Virginia only one governor of eight who served from 1841 to 1861 was born a gentleman and that in the South as a whole, nine-tenths of the men who directed the Confederacy and nine-tenths of Confederate officers were "not colonial aristocrats" but "new people" who had risen from the ranks of the southern yeomanry (39, 61).

James McBride Dabbs had very different ideas on this subject. For him, the heart of southern culture was to be found not in the backcountry but on the Atlantic coast. He believed that southern culture was seated in the tidewater and the low country and was "as distinctive as the balmy air blowing inland across the sea-islands of South Carolina." Dabbs explained to his readers that his thinking was "probably influenced by the fact that I was born and have lived in a seaboard state, part of the original South, and not in one of the later Southern states."[24]

Cash indulged his resentment against "the Virginians"; Dabbs's book celebrates the contributions of the tidewater elite and contains many expressions of thinly veiled hostility toward "the Scotch Irish." Even though he traced his own descent partly from Scotch-Irish ancestors, he variously described them as "the Puritans of the South" and the "Yankees of the South" and thought of them as profoundly different from "the predominantly English settlers of the seaboard." Dabbs did not like the Scotch-Irish. He portrayed them as "notoriously land hungry," with a "weak aesthetic sense," a "hard dogmatic character," "wild and impulsive," a tendency to become "violent and corrupt," destructively individualist, hard, narrow, cruel, and violent. Dabbs perceived their culture as personified in Andrew Jackson, in his "provincialism, self-confidence, energy, persistency, belligerency, insubordination, individualism, honesty, simplicity, ignorance of books, loyalty to friends, and hatred of enemies." He understood their thinking as represented in John C. Calhoun, "aggressive, individualistic and logical to a fault." He believed that their temperament was exposed in the cruel blood lust of Stonewall Jackson, urging his men to "kill them, Sir! kill them all."[25]

For Dabbs, the mind of the South was deeply riven by its double inheritance of Scotch-Irish culture in the backcountry and English culture of the tidewater. But he believed that the true seat of southern

24. Dabbs, *Who Speaks for the South?*, viii, x.
25. *Ibid.*, 84, 91, 93, 98, 152.

culture and many of its redeeming virtues were to be found in the English folkways of what he called the seaboard South. In these assumptions Dabbs and Cash were fundamentally opposed.

THE PERIODIZATION OF SOUTHERN HISTORY

Closely related to these differences were the ways Cash and Dabbs understood the temporal structure of southern history. For Dabbs the vital period was the eighteenth century. "The seaboard south," he wrote, "experienced the liberal eighteenth century, and though it fell from grace as it took its place in the Cotton kingdom about 1800, it has never entirely forgotten its early history. The Old Southwest, never having had this history, succumbed more completely to the violence inherent in the slave system."[26]

Cash had little interest in the first two centuries of southern history. In company with other backcountry southerners his memory showed a good deal of temporal foreshortening. He wrote, "The South, one might say, is a tree with many age rings, with its limbs and trunk bent and twisted by all the winds of the years, but with its tap root in the Old South." By the Old South, or "great South" as he called it, Cash meant a period of about four decades before the Civil War. "From 1820 to 1860," he wrote, "is but forty years—a little more than the span of a single generation. The whole period from the invention of the cotton gin to the outbreak of the Civil War is less than seventy years—the lifetime of a single man. Yet it was wholly within the longer of these periods, and mainly within the shorter, that the development and growth of the great South took place" (x, 10).

Cash's "great South" was created when the backcountry culture expanded into the great Southwest—a process in which the effete Virginians faded away and his "man at the center" came to dominate the culture of an entire region. He understood much of southern culture as formed by the frontier experience. In *The Mind of the South* he interpreted all of southern history as a sequence of three frontier experiences—first the classical frontier, next "the frontier the Yankees made," and then "the third frontier" in the twentieth century (26–33, 105, 148, 262).

---

26. *Ibid.*, x–xi.

Dabbs was also interested in the frontier, but in a different way, a comparison of northern and southern frontiers. He understood the North's new West in Turnerian terms but thought that southern history worked very differently. A central theme of southern history, he argued, was "the rather complete transference of Old World culture to the New." He believed that the structure of southern culture "bound the frontier and the old settlements more closely together than they were bound in the North." Further, "the economic system of the South encouraged that sense of life as rooted in the past and growing into the future that Englishmen originally brought to Southern shores." Here were two profoundly different readings of southern and American history.[27]

Neither Cash nor Dabbs showed the slightest trace of nostalgia for the peculiar institution. Both condemned slavery in the strongest terms. They also believed that slavery had always been perceived in the South as a moral wrong and that guilt had long been a part of southern culture. Cash, in one of his most frequently quoted phrases, insisted that the South "in its secret heart always carried a powerful and uneasy sense of the essential rightness of the nineteenth century's position on slavery" (63). Dabbs also asserted that "the southerner was fighting not only against the North but also against himself."[28]

Cash was not very much interested in the history of slavery. He acknowledged that the "foundation stone" of southern culture had been torn away by the abolition of slavery, but the peculiar institution was not a subject of high importance to him. His book is a history of the South without any extended discussion of the history of slavery. Cash mocked what he called the "legend of the Old South" in the twentieth century when "Southerners themselves fully got around to adorning every knoll in the Old South with a great white manor-house, and to populating the land with more black slaves than China has Chinese" (105, 242).

Dabbs saw things differently. From the windows of his grandfather's old plantation house, the "legend of the Old South" appeared to be firmly grounded in historical reality. Dabbs discussed slavery at length in his book and explained it not merely as a system of labor but

27. *Ibid.*, 39, 40, 44.
28. *Ibid.*, 7. On guilt in Cash's writing see Genovese, *World the Slaveholders Made*, 143–47.

as a cultural artifact introduced by "non-Puritan settlers" who "cared little about the holiness of work, and not everything about the profits that might accrue." He believed that his ancestors had "accepted slavery as a way to obtain leisure for themselves—and indeed prestige and power also"—and added in their defense that "it is only fair to say that over the years they handled slavery more humanely, than with a different attitude, they might have." But in all of this he found a fatal contradiction. "The basic error," he wrote, "was that in adopting slavery the South adopted a means which was so sharply opposed to the ends it sought that it would finally make the attainment of those ends impossible." He repeated that "this was the Southerner's basic error. He tried to do what neither he himself nor his times permitted."[29]

Dabbs and Cash showed more in common when they discussed the Civil War and Reconstruction. Both accepted large parts (not all parts) of conventional southern interpretations of those events, however strongly they challenged other customs and beliefs. Both went out of their way to praise the courage and sacrifice of southern soldiers, the brilliance of southern generals, the prowess of southern armies. Both acknowledged somewhat grudgingly that the South lost the war, but neither seemed entirely to accept that painful fact. Both wrote of the war in language that combined lament and celebration—a "tragic glory" in Dabbs's phrase.[30]

Cash wrote that "every boy growing up in this land now had continually before his eyes the vision, and heard in his ears the clamorous hoofbeats, of a glorious swashbuckler, compounded of Jeb Stuart, the golden-locked Pickett, and the sudden and terrible Forrest" (124). Dabbs wrote in a similar vein: "The essential picture in the history of the South is Pickett's splendid but futile charge at Gettysburg. . . . And still in our memories they advance. The mind of the South, always poetic, always seeking images, found, unfortunately at sundown, an image it cannot forget." These men were both critics and captives of this powerful folk memory.[31]

Both authors also remembered Reconstruction with unalloyed horror. Cash wrote that the effect of Reconstruction was to establish "the savage ideal as it had not been established in any Western people since

29. Dabbs, *Who Speaks for the South?*, 49, 52; see also 53–78.
30. *Ibid.*, 183.
31. *Ibid.*, 253.

the decay of medieval feudalism . . . and so paralyzed Southern culture at the root" (137). He believed that "so far from having reconstructed the Southern mind . . . in its essential character, it was this Yankee's fate to have strengthened it almost beyond reckoning, and to have made it one of the most solidly established, one of the least *reconstructible* ever developed" (109). For Dabbs, Reconstruction destroyed the best of the Old South. He believed that "those who succeeded in the postwar South often did so by actions contrary to their code," first by supporting the Ku Klux Klan, then by encouraging race conflict and aligning themselves with the mass of poor whites against their former slaves.[32]

Their interpretations of the period after Reconstruction diverged. Dabbs followed C. Vann Woodward's idea that "the redeemers tried by invoking the past to avert the future . . . emphasizing race and tradition." He remembered with admiration the attempt of Tom Watson to unite poor whites and blacks and recorded its failure with regret. "The over-all purpose of Southern politics for the last hundred years has been to create, out of a sadly divided South, a solid South." This for him was in many ways the saddest and darkest period in southern history.[33]

Cash remembered the late nineteenth and especially the early twentieth century as a period when things got a little better, particularly for the people at the center of his idea of the South—the southern yeomen. But he was conscious of another great declension that began in the 1920s and grew much worse in the Great Depression. A large part of *The Mind of the South* is devoted to a discussion of the sufferings of southern mill workers, to a history of strikes, low wages, and cruel unemployment. These subjects interested Dabbs comparatively little. He was much more deeply concerned about problems of race. Both men were southern liberals, but their thoughts centered on different problems.

Both men deeply disliked the New South, but for different reasons. Cash believed that the values formed in the Old South persisted into the New—aristocracy revived, old myths renewed, old errors repeated. Dabbs, however, felt that the southerner in the twentieth century had learned Yankee vices and forgotten southern virtues. He searched for another way forward, neither that of the "rabid Southerner . . . lost in the past," nor the "driving Southern American, interested only in the

32. *Ibid.*, 300.
33. *Ibid.*, 302.

future." He hoped a *via media* would lead to the recovery of the "happy balance between past and future revealed in the early South," producing the harmony that had existed in the age of Jefferson and Madison.[34]

MODELS OF HISTORICAL CHANGE AND CONTINUITY

In the twentieth century, American historical scholarship has tended to be dominated by an orthodoxy that defines history as the study of change. With a few exceptions, published works of academic historiography in the United States today center mostly on themes of discontinuity. So strong has this orthodoxy become that deviant works are condemned in learned journals as unhistorical and even unprofessional.

This bias toward discontinuity does not appear in the historiography of other nations. It is also often absent from popular thinking in the American South and did not appear in the thought of Cash and Dabbs. Both men, in company with many other southerners, had a stronger sense of kinship with the past than do most academic historians in America today. Their books were attempts to integrate elements of persistence and change.

Cash was explicit on this point. His book was an extended argument that "the extent of the change and of the break between the Old South that was and the South of our time has been vastly exaggerated" (x). He did not ignore change and stressed particularly the revolutions wrought by "industrialization and commercialization." But the central theme of the book was the persistence of southern culture in the face of material change.

Cash's change model was highly complex—more so than the rhetoric in which it was expressed. It operated on at least three levels: first, a sequence of three dynamic change regimes; second, deeper discontinuities that set those change regimes in motion and brought them to an end; and third, a pattern of cultural persistence in southern folkways and beliefs. The theme of persistence was in many ways the strongest element.

Dabbs's model of change and continuity was much the same. In his book we also find a similar sequence of change regimes—the first called "the formation of southern character," the second titled "its bitter test-

34. *Ibid.*, 380.

ing," and the third conceived as "its present possibility." Each of these processes was conceived in dynamic terms and punctuated by more profound discontinuities. But through them all ran a strong theme of persistence in the identity of "the essential southerner" and the structure of his character and culture.

Dabbs and Cash were similar in their models of change and especially in the heavy stress they placed on themes of cultural persistence. In this respect, both writers departed from the prevailing change model of academic historiography. (The academic convention is more primitive, less accurate, and also less rhetorically effective.) The stress on elements of cultural persistence in Cash and Dabbs gives their writings their unity, power, meaning, balance, and especially an enduring relevance—qualities too often lacking in academic historiography.

MODES OF EXPERIENCE: SOUTHERN HISTORY AS TRAGEDY

Few professional historians in America think of history as a form of tragedy. Our national experience encourages other attitudes. Both Cash and Dabbs understood the history of the South in tragic terms, but in different ways.

For Cash, the tragedy of southern history appeared as an inexorable chain of disastrous happenings whose causes were far beyond the power of any individual to direct. Each of his three periods in the history of the South was a fresh chapter of disasters—first in the rise of King Cotton and the descent into the Civil War, then the dark time of Reconstruction. The early twentieth century was an intermission, but disaster struck again in the 1920s and 1930s.

These tragic events were for Cash the inexorable result of cultural and social forces that southerners could neither master nor control. In his understanding, the tragedy of southern history rose in part from the constraining power of folk myths and illusions. Ironically, when Cash tried to explain the power of these cultural constraints he became a materialist. He put heavy stress on both economic and ecological determinism, asserting that "the mind of the section" in "its primary form is determined . . . by the purely agricultural conditions of that past" (x). He observed that the people of the South were captives of their history and had little power over the events of their lives.

Dabbs also thought of southern history in tragic terms, but in a very different way. He believed that the South's disasters were self-inflicted wounds, caused largely by failure of leadership. In his understanding, southern history was a complex dialectical process in which the response of leaders to each disastrous turn of events created a new catastrophe. He thought that southern "Hotspurs" in the 1850s behaved like "true tragic characters" when they "rode fast, proudly, even insolently into the darkening future. This was true tragic *hybris*." Of the years after the Civil War, he wrote that "attempting to heal the traumatic division of the Civil War, the political leaders helped to increase the trauma." In the twentieth century, the behavior of segregationists and demagogues (whom he specially despised) provided yet another example.[35]

In these differences between Cash and Dabbs one finds two ideas that often appear in historical writing. Alexis de Tocqueville observes that "historians who wrote in aristocratic ages are inclined to refer all occurrences to the particular will and character of certain important individuals," while "historians who live in democratic ages exhibit precisely the opposite characteristics. Most of them attribute hardly any influence to the individual over the destiny of the race, or to citizens over the fate of a people; but, on the other hand, they assign great and general causes to all petty incidents. These contrary tendencies explain each other."[36]

Something related to these "contrary tendencies" appears in our two authors. Cash thought of people as the objects of historical processes, whereas Dabbs saw them as agents and even the authors of history. The result was two different tragic interpretations of southern history.

It is interesting that neither Cash nor Dabbs was able to sustain a tragic theme to the bitter end. In the last few pages of their books, both men softened their interpretations. For Dabbs, especially, writing in the early 1960s, the present and the future seemed bright with hopeful possibilities. Cash's outlook in 1941 was much more bleak. He made no predictions and shared many of his dark fears with the reader, but his last paragraph contained an expression of hope for better things to come.

35. *Ibid.*, 211, 212, 303.

36. Alexis de Tocqueville, *Democracy in America,* trans. Henry Reeve, ed. Phillips Bradley (2 vols.; New York, 1945), II, 85.

SOCIAL PROBLEMS IN SOUTHERN HISTORY: RACE

Both Cash and Dabbs were deeply concerned about the question of race. Both strongly supported civil rights and racial justice at a time when it was not merely unpopular but dangerous to do so. Cash repeatedly attacked lynching and the Ku Klux Klan in print. He published angry attacks on racial inequality in southern institutions and was honored for his courage by the NAACP and other black organizations. He shared some of the race prejudices of his era even as he struggled against them; but current condemnations of him as racist are anachronistic and inaccurate.[37]

Dabbs also worked tirelessly for civil rights and from 1942 onward described the "race situation" in the South as his "chief interest."[38] He served that cause in many ways, and his services were recognized by honorary degrees from many black colleges and universities such as Morehouse and Tuskegee.

But in many ways these two men thought very differently on the subject of race in southern history. For Cash, blacks were not so much people as a problem. He was concerned about the race problem mainly as an abstract question of social justice and for its effect on southern whites. Also, he tended to think of black southerners as not really participating in the regional culture but as a race apart.

Dabbs thought of the race question in more personal and intimate terms. Black men and women were his neighbors and friends and colleagues in the many institutions and movements that he joined. He deeply believed that blacks were very much a part of southern culture and were contributing more to its constructive development than did whites in his own time. The central theme of his book was that "the negro has been a clear and public force in the shaping of Southern life" in the 1950s and 1960s. Dabbs gloried in the struggle for civil rights and understood it not as an alien movement introduced from outside the region and inspired by the teachings of Thoreau and Gandhi. For

37. See, for example, Cash's exposé of racial inequalities in a North Carolina tuberculosis sanatorium published in the Charlotte *News,* June 11, 1939. Cash often used the racist language of his generation, but his biographer Bruce Clayton notes that "the word *nigger* could be used, as Cash did regularly, for effect, often in a way intended to expose racism" (Clayton, *Cash,* 143).

38. "My chief interest for some fifteen years has been the race situation in the South" (Dabbs, "Biographical Notes" [Typescript appended to copy of *Who Speaks for the South?* in Brandeis University Library, Waltham, Mass., n.d., *ca.* 1967]).

Dabbs the civil rights movement was quintessentially southern in its culture and both its ends and means were "drawn from the deep reservoir of Southern history." In that way and others, Dabbs believed that "the South finds its most creative expression today among Negroes." He agreed with David Potter that Negroes in his own time may have "embodied the distinctive qualities of the Southern character even more than the whites." [39] Dabbs organized his book around a single question, "Who speaks for the South?" His answer in the early 1960s was that many of the best and strongest and most noble voices were those of southern Negroes.

SOCIAL PROBLEMS IN SOUTHERN HISTORY: GENDER

Nothing so provoked Cash to sarcastic fury as did the ideal of southern womanhood—which he took to be contrived, hypocritical, and fraudulent—a cult of "gyneolatry," as he called it. His pen dripped with venom when he wrote of "the South's Palladium, this Southern woman—the shield-bearing Athena. . . . She was the lily-pure maid of Astolat and the hunting goddess of the Boeotian hill. . . . And—she was the pitiful Mother of God" (89).

For Cash this cult of southern womanhood was cruelly mocked by the harsh reality that he remembered from his childhood and witnessed all his life, especially in the great blight of the 1930s. He described with pity and horror the women of southern mill towns, "characteristically stringy-haired and limp of breast at twenty, and shrunken hags at thirty or forty" (204). That reality in his thinking utterly destroyed the myth of gyneolatry in southern culture.

Dabbs cast a similar thought in different terms. He also despised the false deification of womanhood in the South and wrote acidly of "the divine Athena," who was prevented from raising unhappy questions about the practical surrounding world, the core of which was the slave system. He believed that "the willingness to let the white woman rule in the home, but to deny her authority in the world, is an indicator of the corrupting influence of slavery. It was one of the main forces that split the South." [40]

Like Cash, Dabbs juxtaposed the cult of womanhood against the

39. Dabbs, *Who Speaks for the South?*, x, 376, 380.
40. *Ibid.*, 106; see also 166–68.

reality that he observed in the South. But whereas Cash contrasted the cult of southern womanhood with the pitiful and helpless plight of female millworkers, Dabbs compared it with the condition of black women who by their own efforts triumphed over misery and exploitation—women of strength, majesty, and courage. For Dabbs this was the sharpest contradiction of gender in the South. "The Negro woman," he wrote, "was an integral part of this native land the Southerner was fighting for, but alas, she was divorced from Yahweh, the fighting God of a chosen people."[41]

Cash and Dabbs differed in several ways on this issue. Each drew up a different indictment of the same cultural idea and took his evidence from personal experience. Both despised the hypocrisy of conventional attitudes toward women and hated the cruelties those attitudes engendered. But they did so with reference to two different groups of southern women. Another difference is the contrast between Cash's pity for the helpless misery of white mill women and Dabbs's respect for the power and strength of black women. The two men returned yet again to their very different understandings of history and the human condition, with Cash stressing the condition of poor white women as objects and Dabbs emphasizing the role of black women as agents.

In some ways, both men shared assumptions of gender inequality that were widely held in their generation. But to condemn them in a unitary way as sexist, as some scholars have done, is to miss their sympathy and sensitivity to the condition of southern women in their time and their outspoken condemnation of the conventional gender roles in southern culture. If historians must function as judges, their judgments should recognize the complexity of their subjects and of the standards by which they are to be assessed.

SOCIAL PROBLEMS IN SOUTHERN HISTORY: CLASS

Cash and Dabbs also thought differently about social class, reflecting their attitudes toward gender and race. A case in point was their response to the writings of William Alexander Percy and Walker Percy. Cash reviewed William Alexander Percy's *Lanterns on the Levee* sympathetically, observing that "Percy is that exceedingly rare thing, a surviving authentic

41. *Ibid.*, 105; see also 104, 166–68.

Southern aristocrat, as distinguished from pretenders to the title." Cash
found much to admire in Percy's book. He especially praised its attitudes on race. "It is profoundly moving to hear him talk of the Negro,"
he wrote. "There is in him no trace of that hatred and spleen toward
the black man which has always disgraced so many southern whites."
But Cash complained that Percy had one "blind spot," that he "hates
and excoriates the poor-whites." Cash conceded that "the southern
poor-white is a debased creature, yes, but who would not be debased
after a century of despair." He protested that Percy "fails to see his
philosophy adds up at last to precisely the same philosophy of violence
which he so resents and despises in the poor whites."[42]

Dabbs's admiration for Percy's work was unalloyed—"one of the
best expressions of the aristocratic *credo*," he called it. Unlike Cash, he
was interested in the internal operation of that credo on those who
shared it. Dabbs especially admired the words of advice that William
Alexander Percy's father had for his son: "I guess a man's job is to make
the world a better place to live in, so far as he is able—always remembering that the results will be infinitesimal—and to attend to his own
soul."[43] Here was merely one instance of two different approaches to
questions of class in Cash and Dabbs—differences that rose from their
own experiences.

ETHICAL QUESTIONS: SOUTHERN HONOR

Similar patterns also appeared in their discussions of southern honor.
Both men believed that honor was a central part of southern culture,
but they had very different ideas of its meaning and effect. For Cash,
honor was an empty expression of pride and egoism—"narrow and
egotistic" was the way he repeatedly described it. Southern honor, he
wrote, was far from the true spirit of noblesse oblige and chivalry and
without any "tender concern for the welfare and happiness of the weak
and powerless" (77).

For Dabbs, honor had a different meaning. It was the creed of a
Christian gentleman. Its paragon was Robert E. Lee. Dabbs quoted
with approval Douglas Southall Freeman's thought that Lee "could not

---

42. W. J. Cash, review of William Alexander Percy's *Lanterns on the Levee*, Charlotte
News, May 10, 1941, in Morrison, *Cash*, 290–94.
43. Dabbs, *Who Speaks for the South?*, 121.

have conceived of a Christian who was not a gentleman." For Dabbs the heart of this idea was precisely that concern for others which Cash believed to be missing from the southern mind. Dabbs quoted a manuscript found in the papers of Robert E. Lee: "A true man of honor feels humbled himself when he cannot help humbling others." Here was an idea that had no meaning for most Americans. But it was central to those who believed in it.[44] Dabbs believed; Cash did not. Dabbs wrote about southern honor from within that moral tradition; Cash observed it from without.

ETHICAL QUESTIONS: SOUTHERN MANNERS

Yet another difference in social thinking concerned southern manners. Both men commented with approval on what Cash called "the Southern tradition of good manners" (289). But here again their thoughts diverged. Cash identified two distinct traditions—the aristocratic manners of the Virginians and "the old backcountry kindliness and easiness in personal relations" (70). He preferred the latter. Mainly he thought of manners as "a kindly courtesy, a level-eyed pride, an easy quietness, a barely perceptible flourish, of bearing, which, for all its obvious angularity and fundamental plainness, was one of the finest things the Old South produced" (72). But he believed that these manners decayed in Reconstruction and that what remained of them in the New South tended to function as an instrument of social exploitation.

Dabbs agreed that the South "stressed" manners more than other regions, but he understood them differently, as "accepted ways of doing and saying things." He believed that manners were important to southerners because they "always felt a strong tie with the past, and one way to hold on to the past is through the use of customary words and feelings." He also thought that "all etiquette partly exists to enable people to live together closely without rubbing one another raw." As such, he believed that manners were becoming more important, even urgent, in the South during his own time as an instrument of unity and social peace.[45] When Dabbs wrote against racial discrimination, he condemned it as "bad manners."[46]

44. *Ibid.*, 123–25.
45. *Ibid.*, 110, 111, 159–60, 375–79
46. Dabbs, *Southern Heritage,* 14, 124, 159–61.

For Cash, the "kindly courtesy" and "easy quiet" of southern manners were a folkway that joined people of the same blood and kin in almost tribal unity. For Dabbs, southern manners were devices by which different people had learned to live in peace with one another. Here were two radically different visions of southern culture.

ONTOLOGICAL PROBLEMS IN SOUTHERN HISTORY: STOICISM AND HEDONISM

For Dabbs, the ethical center of secular culture in the South was a Stoic tradition, a subject in which he became deeply interested. He followed Walker Percy and William Alexander Percy on this subject and was much influenced by their writings. Dabbs summarized the Stoic idea in a sentence: "Realize your small place in the total order; within that, do your work and guard your soul." Stoicism, he believed, was an ethical creed that allows a man to live virtuously in the presence of evil. Dabbs was conscious of its uses and also of its limits. "Is it any wonder that in this uneasy world many Southerners became Stoics? It was a way of enduring the storm; it was not a way of bringing the ship into port."[47]

Nothing like this Stoic idea appeared in Cash's description of the southern mind. Cash thought of his southerners as riven in their philosophy: in his words, part puritan, part hedonist. One of the most surprising parts of his book was its heavy stress on "Southern hedonism," by which he meant the indulgence of the self and the senses. He juxtaposed this theme against its opposite, which for lack of a better word he called puritanism. Cash believed that in every major period of southern history, events and conditions caused "the further widening of the old split in the Southern psyche between Puritanism and hedonism" (233). These disjunctive terms framed Cash's conception of southern values. His ideas of hedonism and puritanism were very different from the Stoic tradition that was identified by Dabbs and the Percys. Where Dabbs admired the Stoic tradition with some reservations, Cash condemned both hedonism and puritanism outright (59; see also 46–55, 137, 233, 321).

These were not purely personal choices. Cash and Dabbs were describing ethical traditions that were deeply embedded in different southern cultures.

47. Dabbs, *Who Speaks for the South?*, 121, 129.

RELIGION AND SOUTHERN HISTORY

Cash and Dabbs discussed religion at many points in their books, sometimes at great length. Their attitudes were complex and are not easily summarized. But in general, one may say that some of the deepest differences between them appeared on this subject. Cash had been raised in the Baptist faith of the backcountry and turned strongly against it. He detested the religion of the South. Before the Civil War, he wrote, the God of the South became a tribal God, "stern, simple, direct," the God of battles, a God of wrath (82). In the New South, religion became an instrument of intolerance (227, 231, 342), primitivism (296–99), inequality and exploitation (205, 359–60).

Dabbs was a believing Christian, an active member of the Presbyterian church, and a holder of many high offices in that denomination. He also served in many liberal Christian organizations and wrote on religious as well as secular subjects. Dabbs shared many of Cash's critical opinions on the role of religion in southern culture. He also believed that the God of the South became a "tribal God" before the Civil War and that "to the normal Southern love of place was added the religious love of a sacred place."[48] Like Cash, he regretted that religious institutions in the New South had served conservative and unchristian purposes. Cash thought of religion as an instrument of oppression against southern whites, whereas Dabbs protested against its role in legitimating segregation and racial injustice.

But Dabbs's judgments were very different in their spirit. His was a criticism of southern churches by a believing Christian. Dabbs believed not in Cash's God of wrath but in a God of grace and love and mercy. He deeply felt that Christian faith and the doctrines of the church could help southerners understand their historical condition and lead them forward to a world of justice, unity, and spiritual peace. In the conclusion of his book he quoted Aeschylus: "Against our will and in our own despite, wisdom comes to us by the awful grace of God." And he ended with the thought that "Southern history was God's way of leading two originally opposed peoples into a richer life than either could have found alone."[49]

48. *Ibid.*, 254.
49. *Ibid.*, 337, 44, 381.

THE POLITICS OF SOUTHERN HISTORY: VARIETIES OF
LIBERALISM IN THE NEW SOUTH

Cash and Dabbs were both staunch southern liberals, but their ideas of liberalism were profoundly different. Cash once wrote that "skepticism is after all the very essence of the spirit of the liberal tradition." For Dabbs, liberalism was primarily a matter of belief, commitment, faith, and devotion. Cash defined liberalism primarily by what it opposed and thought of himself as the inveterate enemy of "totalitarianism."[50] Dabbs thought of himself more positively as supporting free institutions and ideas. Cash asserted that liberalism was always biased in favor of the underdog. Dabbs thought more of uniting people of every race and class: Both men identified themselves with a liberal tradition in the South, but they had different people and processes in mind. For Dabbs, southern liberals began with the great revolutionary leaders, especially Jefferson and Madison—men who built a free republic. Cash thought of southern liberals as fighters against tyranny and injustice. Many of the figures who appear in Clement Eaton's *Freedom of Thought Struggle in the Old South* also appear in Cash's *Mind of the South*. Cash celebrated the southern critics of slavery in the nineteenth century: Cassius Clay, B. S. Hedrick, and especially the antislavery minister John G. Fee of Kentucky, who was said to have been assaulted by twenty-two southern mobs, twice left for dead, and yet kept on fighting. Cash identified with southern editors and journalists who courageously spoke out for freedom, often at the cost of their lives. He was especially impressed by the record of the Vicksburg *Journal,* which had five editors killed in thirteen years (93). That was Cash's idea of journalism! He celebrated militant scholars who fought for the freedom to teach Darwin—especially his own beloved teacher at Wake Forest Dr. William Louis Poteat.

Dabbs looked to a different set of southern liberals—the builders, healers, sages, and saints—to the sage of Monticello and the master of Montpelier, to Woodrow Wilson and Franklin Roosevelt, and especially to Martin Luther King and the black leaders of nonviolent civil rights, which Dabbs thought to be quintessentially southern in its methods and manners.

Here were two different sets of role models for a southern liberal and two ideas of southern liberalism.

50. W. J. Cash, "What Is a Liberal?" Charlotte *News,* November 6, 1938, reprinted in Morrison, *Cash,* 248.

THE MEANING OF SOUTHERN HISTORY

One of the most profound differences between Dabbs and Cash appeared in their ideas on the meaning and purpose of history. For both men the purpose of history was to bring people to a true understanding of their condition. But they pursued that common purpose in opposite ways.

Cash thought of the historian as a warrior against error. The role of history as he understood it was to explode myths, shatter illusions, destroy error in the world, and by those means to liberate humanity from the mind-forged manacles of the past. *The Mind of the South* attacked one southern myth after another. With relentless fury, Cash instructed his fellow southerners that their cultural pretensions were empty of substance—not "a true culture at all." He insisted that their ideas of honor were merely narrow and corrupt egotism, and their religion was a system of savagery and superstition. At the same time, he celebrated what he perceived to be the virtues of southern culture—a warrior's virtues: "proud, brave, honorable by its lights, courteous, personally generous, loyal, swift to act, often too swift, but signally effective, sometimes terrible in its action—such was the South at its best." But he hated and condemned its "violence, intolerance, aversion and suspicion toward new ideas, an incapacity for analysis, an inclination to act from feeling rather than from thought, an exaggerated individualism and a too narrow concept of social responsibility, attachment to fictions and false values, above all too great attachment to racial values" (439–40).

Cash apparently hoped that the South could be educated out its vices through a process of historical self-discovery, which was the object of his book. For Cash, one studied history to be free of the shackles of the past. The truth of history was for him a kind of antitoxin. He believed that historical knowledge is valuable mainly as an antidote against the tyranny of history itself and that knowledge could heal the wounded heart of his beloved land.

Dabbs thought differently of history. For him, historical myths were grounded in reality. "Myths do not grow, like Spanish moss, on trees," he wrote, "they are rooted in earth." He believed that the object of history was not merely to demolish error but to proclaim a larger truth. For him the South had been riven by its history. Like Cash, he hoped that the growth of historical knowledge might heal those wounds, but he also had something more in mind—a more positive idea of history as an instrument of unity between the past and the future, region and nation, black and white. For him, there was much that was good and right in the past, and he believed that the people of the South could illuminate the darkness of the present by the light of the past.[51]

In these authors one finds two very different minds of the South and two versions of southern history. On one hand we meet the gentle South of James McBride Dabbs—gentle in every sense—the South of Jefferson and Madison, Washington and Lee, Pinckneys, Rutledges, and Percys. This was the South that respected chivalrous ideas of honor and old-fashioned manners. It was also a place where liberals such as Dabbs believed blacks and whites could live together in harmony and justice. It was the South of the tidewater, levee, and low country.

On the other hand we meet the militant South of W. J. Cash, the backcountry, up-country South. This was the South of British borderers and Andrew Jackson and John C. Calhoun, of piedmont farmers and cotton-mill workers. It was the South of primal honor and down-home manners, a hard-hearted, brave, and angry South.

How are we to pass judgment on these two minds of the South? Perhaps we should not attempt to judge them at all, but try to understand. Maybe we should find guidance in the graceful and generous words of Walker Percy. In the introduction to a paperback edition of *Lanterns on the Levee,* Percy wrote: "I cannot help but think of another book about the South, W. J. Cash's *The Mind of the South,* published oddly enough the same year by the same publisher as *Lanterns on the Levee.* . . . Both books are classics in their own right, yet they couldn't be more different; their separate validities surely testify to the diversity and complexity of this mysterious region."[52]

51. Dabbs, *Who Speaks for the South?,* vii, 380.
52. He added: "Yet in this case, I would suppose that Will Percy would today find himself closer to Cash in sorting out his heroes and villains, that far from setting aristocrat against poor white and both against the new Negro, he might well choose his present-day heroes—and villains—from the ranks of all three. He'd surely have as little use for black lawlessness as for white copping out. I may be wrong but I can't see him happy as the patron saint of Hilton Head or Paradise Estates-around-the-Country-Club" (Walker Percy, Introduction to William Alexander Percy, *Lanterns on the Levee: Recollections of a Planter's Son* [1941; rpr. Baton Rouge, 1977], xvii–xviii).

PART III

Southern Studies
Since Cash

The Politics of the Modern South

MERLE BLACK

W. J. Cash's *Mind of the South,* a convoluted masterpiece, is a work of brilliant paragraphs and wretched chapters, energized by the haunting images and provocative ideas of an obsessed, "extra-smart" native white southerner. Cash spent more than a decade writing and rewriting the manuscript. Often retreating to the family home in Shelby, North Carolina, during the Great Depression, he would discuss the themes of the book with anyone he could corner. "One would see him talking to a high-schooler," Joseph L. Morrison wrote, "gravely trying out some of his ideas on the lad with the same courteous concentration he would give a judge." The locals were mightily unimpressed. To them, he seemed to be "a grown man, and a skeptic at that, sponging on the unremitting toil of his indulgent and Christian parents."[1] The ultimate product of his travails, however, was an imaginative analysis of qualities that characterized many white southerners. Although much of the work is outdated, some of its themes continue to illuminate persisting features of the region's political life.

Cash's portrait of white southerners was hardly flattering. The title of the book was ironic, as C. Vann Woodward has pointed out, for the book was "based on the hypothesis that the South has no mind."[2] Cash believed that many southern whites did not possess a sustained and developed ability to distance themselves from their immediate cultural environment and to ask dispassionately about causes (the "why" questions) and consequences (the "so what?" questions). Instead, many southern whites had an abundance of predispositions, emotionalized

1. Joseph L. Morrison, *W. J. Cash, Southern Prophet: A Biography and a Reader* (New York, 1967), 62, 64.
2. C. Vann Woodward, "The Elusive Mind of the South," in Woodward, *American Counterpoint: Slavery and Racism in the North-South Dialogues* (Boston, 1971), 264.

likes and dislikes, which interfered with dispassionate, realistic analysis. Among these defects in temperament, Cash thought, were an "aversion and suspicion toward new ideas, an incapacity for analysis, an inclination to act from feeling rather than from thought . . . attachment to fictions and false values . . . sentimentality and a lack of realism" (*Mind,* 439–40).

Substantively, white southerners were passionately attached to the South and to other white southerners as God's chosen people and were distrustful of and hostile toward the hated Yankees. Southerners accepted "violence and intolerance" toward individuals and groups thought hostile to their way of life. In politics, these attitudes were expressed in streaks of meanness toward opponents and campaign techniques that tarred and feathered rivals. Southerners possessed "an exaggerated individualism and a too narrow concept of social responsibility," a dog-eat-dog, root-hog-or-die ethic of frontier survival that was compatible with vast inequalities in wealth. For them, the Democratic party was virtually a sacred institution, and the Republicans epitomized everything orthodox white southerners loathed. Finally, "above all," wrote Cash, southern whites had "too great attachment to racial values and a tendency to justify cruelty and injustice in the name of those values" (439–40). Cash himself was hardly exempt from these criticisms; some of his characterizations of blacks are garden-variety racist stereotypes.

This "complex of fears and hates," Cash argued, "greatly absorbed the energies of the Southern people, high and low" (341). Many white southerners were so consumed with their immediate likes and dislikes that they did not clearly understand their own long-term interests. Nowhere was this more apparent than in the attitudes of most southern whites toward blacks, who constituted at midcentury 25 percent of the region's population. In 1940, virtually all southern whites supported racial segregation in the public schools. The South's dual school system provided a poor education for most whites and an even worse one for the vast majority of blacks. The costs of such meager investment in the region's human resources were visible in the millions of uneducated, poorly skilled workers. This waste of human potential made little sense to V. O. Key, Jr., who conjectured in *Southern Politics in State and Nation* that "the only possible long-run outcome of increasing the productivity of the Negro would be to make rich whites richer and more whites rich." Yet Key was sufficiently realistic to stress that "the almost overwhelming temptation, especially in areas with many Negroes, is to take advantage of the short-run opportunity to maintain the status quo by using, or tolerating the use of, the race issue to blot up the discontents of the lesser whites."[3]

The primacy of segregationist values over long-term progress was not surprising to Cash, who was acutely sensitive to the hierarchy of values among most southern whites in the 1940s, as well as to the emotional and psychological motivations that can influence behavior. Cash's emphasis on the array of beliefs and prejudices commonplace among southern whites underscored the difficulties of creating a biracial alliance to redistribute goods and services from the "haves" to the "have-littles" and "have-nots" of southern society. A biracial alliance seemed utter fantasy in 1941 because 97 percent of the region's adult blacks were not even registered to vote.[4] Cash believed that such a political coalition was "improbable, since it involves the abandonment of the most solidly established tradition and the notion of superiority which the common white himself has always valued most" (428). The politics of white supremacy extracted an incalculable toll on blacks, but it also held back the entire society. Native southern whites offered no solution. Cash accurately analyzed a society so tied in racial knots that it could not free itself.

THE POLITICAL INSTITUTIONS OF CASH'S SOUTH

Yet if politics was reserved for whites, many of them did not vote. In most southern states well less than half of the adult white population took part in the Democratic party gubernatorial primaries. Nonvoters were concentrated among the least-educated and poorest whites, especially women. Only about one in four of the region's adults voted in either contested gubernatorial primaries or presidential elections. Power in the traditional South was held by the more established males of the small towns and rural areas. In 1940, more than two-thirds of the vote cast in the presidential contest came from rural counties, and

---

3. V. O. Key, Jr., *Southern Politics in State and Nation* (New York, 1949), 662.
4. David J. Garrow, *Protest at Selma: Martin Luther King, Jr., and the Voting Rights Act of 1965* (New Haven, 1978), 7.

less than one in five votes were cast by citizens living in counties of 250,000 or more.[5]

Unlike other parts of the nation, where both Democratic and Republican politicians competed for major offices, in most of the South one-party politics prevailed. Cash vividly explained the cultural meaning of the Democracy for southern whites in the 1940s:

> The world knows the story of the Democratic Party in the South; how, once violence had opened the way to political action, this party became the institutionalized incarnation of the will to White Supremacy. How, indeed, it ceased to be a party *in* the South and became the party *of* the South, a kind of confraternity having in its keeping the whole corpus of Southern loyalties, and so irresistibly commanding the allegiance of faithful whites that to doubt it, to question it in any detail, was *ipso facto* to stand branded as a renegade to race, to country, to God, and to Southern Womanhood. (131–32)

The single-party monopoly of political activity in the nominating primaries banished genuine issues from public debate and led to an overemphasis on the personalities of rival candidates. "Was this candidate or that one more showy and satisfying? Did Jack or Jock offer the more thrilling representation of the South in action against the Yankee and the black man? Here, and here almost alone," Cash argued, "would there be a field for choice" (133).

With the Democratic party so firmly embedded in the region's white culture, Republicans could make no headway. Some Republicans survived in the mountains of North Carolina, Virginia, and Tennessee, but elsewhere Democrats monopolized officeholding. Republicans sometimes challenged Democrats for major statewide offices in those three states, but in the majority of states in the 1940s no Democratic candidate for statewide office gave a moment's thought to serious Republican opposition in a general election.

Finally, the great fixed assumption was that the Solid South was "in the bag" for the Democratic party in presidential elections. From 1880 to 1944, the South provided an assured base for the Democratic party in the electoral college. Tennessee, with its large group of eastern Republicans, had twice bolted from partisan orthodoxy (1920 and 1928). The only other defections had occurred in 1928, when the

5. Earl Black and Merle Black, *Politics and Society in the South* (Cambridge, Mass., 1987), 175–86.

Democratic party nominated Governor Al Smith, a wet, Catholic Irish politician from New York. So concerned were national Democratic leaders about the outcry from the Protestant South that, for the first time since the Civil War, they put a southerner—Arkansas senator Joseph Robinson—on the ticket in an attempt to hold the South. It was not completely successful. North Carolina, Virginia, Florida, and Texas joined Tennessee in voting for Hoover. Four years later, though, after the Great Depression had reduced President Hoover and the Republican party to the status of despised objects of contempt, the South joined the rest of the nation in massive support for Franklin Roosevelt.

These were the political consequences of the southern white mind as Cash saw it. Although many of the South's political institutions seemed immutable and strange to whites in other parts of the nation, to many southerners they were natural, proper, and right. As Cash says of white southerners, "the peculiar history of the South has so greatly modified it [the mental pattern] from the general American norm that, when viewed as a whole, it decisively justifies the notion that the country is—not quite a nation within a nation, but the next thing to it" (viii).

POLITICS IN THE MODERN SOUTH

The last half-century has witnessed extraordinary changes in the society and politics of the South.[6] As a consequence of black protest within the region and federal legislation that abolished many Jim Crow practices, a completely segregated social order gave way to new patterns of race relations. As the South became more like the rest of the nation, it began to attract more migrants from other parts of the country, and fewer southerners left the region in search of opportunities elsewhere. Within the region, a massive redistribution occurred in which the population of the large cities and suburbs began to outnumber that of the small towns and rural areas. In 1988, about three of every five votes cast in the presidential election came from southerners residing in metropolitan areas of more than 250,000 people.

6. For overviews, see Black and Black, *Politics and Society;* Dewey W. Grantham, *The Life and Death of the Solid South: A Political History* (Lexington, Ky., 1988); Jack Bass and Walter DeVries, *The Transformation of Southern Politics: Social Change and Political Consequences Since 1945* (New York, 1976); and Alexander P. Lamis, *The Two-Party South* (New York, 1984).

Turnout in presidential elections nearly doubled, increasing from about one in four southerners in the first half of the century to the present rate of slightly less than half of the region's eligible voters. In presidential elections, the South still lags behind the rest of the nation in turnout, but the difference is the smallest since antebellum days. In southern gubernatorial elections, however, which largely occur in years when the president is not being chosen, massive nonvoting is still the rule. Only about 35 percent of eligible southerners have voted in modern gubernatorial contests, not much different from the past.

Changes in the size of the electorate have been accompanied by changes in its composition. Once it consisted almost totally of white males born and raised in the South, but diversity characterizes southern voters in the 1990s. They are whites and blacks, men and women, native southerners and those raised elsewhere. Most southerners with some college education, whether white or black, vote in presidential elections; most southerners, white or black, who never attended college do not vote in presidential elections. The southern electorate, like that of the rest of the nation, is much more affluent, educated, and middle class than the population as a whole.[7]

According to Dewey W. Grantham, these changes have caused the "death of the Solid South." Earl Black and I have shown that the majority of white southerners no longer think of themselves as Democrats, although in most southern states Democrats still outnumber Republicans.[8] The greatest change has occurred in presidential politics; the Republicans have carried the region in four of the past five elections. In major races for governorships and Senate seats, Democrats have been increasingly challenged by Republicans. The old one-party system is giving way, in piecemeal fashion, to a more competitive, two-party politics.

THE PREDISPOSITIONS OF WHITE AND BLACK SOUTHERNERS

The results of surveys exploring the likes and dislikes of whites and blacks about specific groups and symbols give some sense of the political lay of the land in the modern South. For comparison, relevant responses from northern whites are included. Instead of the traits of a

7. Black and Black, *Politics and Society,* 186–94.
8. Black and Black, *Politics and Society,* 232–56.

supposed "average" southern white, southern black, or nonsouthern white, Table 1 shows what percentage of each group is favorably disposed ("warm") or unfavorably disposed ("cold") toward a particular symbol. The data are drawn from election year surveys conducted as part of the National Election Study by the Center for Political Studies at the University of Michigan.

The table shows the percentages of each group that were warm or cold toward a series of symbols in the 1980s. The symbols are ordered

Table 1. Evaluations of Political Symbols and Groups by Nonsouthern Whites, Southern Whites, and Southern Blacks, 1980–1988 (in percentages)

	Nonsouthern whites		Southern whites		Southern blacks	
	Warm	Cold	Warm	Cold	Warm	Cold
Southerners	56	10	85	2	89	6
Whites	78	1	83	1	82	3
Environmentalists	83	8	80	8	87	4
Military	70	12	79	10	79	7
Conservatives	60	13	65	10	53	16
Republicans	58	22	60	17	38	31
Blacks	55	12	58	14	87	3
Democrats	56	22	56	22	82	4
Big business	43	33	51	24	67	13
Women's liberation	52	36	45	31	73	9
Unions	47	32	44	35	68	8
People on welfare	35	36	40	32	67	12
Liberals	42	28	39	33	59	11
Civil rights leaders	45	27	38	35	83	5
Evangelicals	26	48	32	40	55	17
Black militants	10	72	10	73	43	30
Gays	13	61	8	70	13	63
Radical students	9	74	6	78	33	40

SOURCE: Computed by the author from appropriate National Election Study Surveys, 1980, 1984, and 1988.

NOTE: Each number is the average percentage of respondents in a particular group who expressed either "warm" or "cold" reactions to selected political symbols. Scores of less than 50 are considered to be unfavorable and are classified as "cold"; scores greater than 50 are considered to be favorable and are classified as "warm." For example, 56 percent of nonsouthern whites had a warm response to the symbol of southerners, while 10 percent of nonsouthern whites were cold toward the symbol. Percentages usually do not add to 100 because a segment of each group is indifferent or neutral toward a symbol.

according to the percentage of southern whites who were favorably disposed toward them. As readers of George Tindall's *Ethnic Southerners* and John Shelton Reed's *Enduring South* would have expected, the symbols most favored by southern whites were southerners and whites.[9] The near universal warmth toward these symbols suggests the continuity of regional patriotism and the importance of a regional identity for members of the South's dominant racial group. "Love it or leave it," as they once said, and would say again if they thought it necessary. Also in this exclusive circle were two very different symbols, environmentalists and the military. Southern attachment to the land and place of birth or raising has long been a part of the culture, however much that professed attachment may have been subordinated to economic development in recent decades, and it is a value that elicits favorable responses from conservatives as well as liberals. The status of the military has long been exalted in southern life, so it is hardly surprising that it ranks as a virtually sacred symbol.

Considerably more southern whites were warm rather than cold toward the symbols of conservatives, Republicans, blacks, and Democrats. Sixty-five percent, on the average, were favorably disposed toward conservatives, and only one in ten was hostile. By comparison, only 39 percent were warm toward liberals, and 33 percent were cold. Given this stark advantage in predispositions, it is no surprise that virtually all Republicans promote themselves as conservatives and most successful Democratic officeholders emphasize, as at least part of their appeal, their conservative credentials in some areas of public policy that voters care about.

The similar evaluations of Republicans and Democrats represent an enormous sea change in the political attitudes of southern whites. Had group symbols been evaluated in 1941, Democrats would surely have ranked alongside southerners and whites as sacred symbols in the white political culture, and far more southerners would have been cold than warm toward Republicans. Indeed, it would have taken a mind even more imaginative than Cash's to conjure a situation in which the Republican party would occupy the same high ground as the Democrats.

9. George Brown Tindall, *The Ethnic Southerners* (Baton Rouge, 1976); and John Shelton Reed, *The Enduring South: Subcultural Persistence in Mass Society* (Chapel Hill, 1986).

Most southern whites viewed blacks favorably, but more than one-fourth were indifferent and about one in seven outright hostile. Politically, the feelings of whites toward blacks as a symbol may be less important than their responses to the symbols of civil rights leaders and black militants. On the average, only 38 percent of southern whites were warm toward civil rights leaders, the rest either indifferent or hostile. And toward individuals they perceived as black militants, only 10 percent of whites were warm, while 73 percent were hostile. These predispositions sharply constrain the image that black politicians can present to whites and still find acceptance.

At the far extreme, three groups stood out in the lack of warmth and extent of antipathy toward them: black militants, gays, and radical students. Each of these groups constitutes a threat to the beliefs and values of the vast majority of southern whites. Association with these groups is a potential political liability, as numerous campaigns in the South, including Senator Jesse Helms's latest version of "Wake Up, White People!" have amply demonstrated.

Situated between the symbols almost universally liked and those overwhelmingly abhorred are groups that have drawn mixed reactions from southern whites. Generally these groups were associated closely with political liberalism, such as the women's liberation movement, unions, people on welfare, liberals, and civil rights leaders. Such conservative symbols as big business and evangelicals, however, also fell into the gray zone of split evaluations. White southerners were divided: substantial minorities liked these groups, but sizable minorities were cold to them.

The predispositions of southern whites toward these various symbols suggest strong consensus toward some positive and some negative symbols but also considerable division and conflict regarding many symbols. Large numbers of southerners are warmly disposed toward many indicators of cultural conservatism, and they overwhelmingly reject symbols that smack of cultural radicalism. Yet when viewed as a whole, the predispositions of these southern whites do not amount to a portrait of Jesse Helms writ large. Most southerners do not view the political world from the perspective of right-wing extremism. If that were the case, such symbols as blacks, people on welfare, unions, civil rights leaders, and the women's liberation movement would be as universally rejected as are black militants, gays, and radical students. It is precisely because Helms does not mirror southern white opinion in key respects that he has always had to decimate his opponents. Yet if white southerners are not consistent right-wing conservatives, far more of them are favorably predisposed toward conservative than liberal symbols. In particular, the absence of positive symbols associated with political liberalism hurts liberal politicians, as does the ability of conservatives to put them on the defensive by associating them with radical symbols. In short, the symbolic likes and dislikes show a world in which political conservatives have many symbols they can use to unite whites, while liberals have few universally admired symbols.[10]

Compared with that of southern whites, the landscape of black southerners shows some important similarities as well as some profound differences. Overwhelming majorities of southern blacks were also warmly disposed toward southerners, whites, the military, and environmentalists. Unlike their white counterparts, though, most black southerners were warmly disposed toward civil rights leaders, blacks, Democrats, the women's liberation movement, unions, and people on welfare.

In the past, the term *southerner* usually carried the implicit meaning *white southerner*. Both whites and blacks viewed it that way. As a result of the changes in the Jim Crow system in the South, blacks became much warmer toward the symbol of southerners. The available evidence does not allow a definitive interpretation, but when John Shelton Reed and I examined this transformation in black attitudes several years ago, we concluded that blacks had become more comfortable thinking of themselves as southerners as well as more favorably disposed toward white southerners. It is certainly a different day in the South when blacks are as warmly disposed toward the symbol of southerners as whites are.[11] The symbolic landscapes of all whites are remarkably similar. Typically, slightly more southern than nonsouthern whites warmly evaluated conservative symbols and were a bit more hostile toward liberal symbols, but these regional differences were small. Only one symbol—southerners—elicited considerably different evaluations from southern and nonsouthern whites. A small majority of nonsoutherners were warm to the symbol, but only a few were hostile.

10. These points are further developed in Black and Black, *Politics and Society*, 57–72.

11. Merle Black and John Shelton Reed, "Blacks and Southerners: A Research Note," *Journal of Politics*, XLIV (February, 1982), 165–71.

RACIAL ATTITUDES IN THE MODERN SOUTH

Cash believed that an obsession with maintaining the racial status quo was at the heart of the mentality of southern whites in the 1940s. How have these attitudes changed over time? When participants in a sample of white southerners were asked in 1961 whether they preferred "strict segregation, integration, or something in between," two-thirds of them opted for strict segregation, while less than 10 percent preferred integration, and about one-quarter chose something in between.[12] Although most whites clearly preferred the racial status quo, the responses indicated a reduction of strict segregationist sentiment from the monolithic levels of 1940. Over the next turbulent decade, the civil rights movement and new federal legislation and court decrees desegregated many of the region's public institutions. By 1976, the last time this question was asked of regional samples, only 25 percent of whites favored strict segregation, a startling collapse of one of the pillars of the traditional white southern "mind." The strict segregationist position had become yet another lost cause.[13]

As a result of these changes, white southerners no longer differed so starkly from blacks in the South and from whites in the rest of the nation. Some regional differences remained, of course. Relatively fewer southern whites preferred integration, and relatively more wanted segregation than did their northern counterparts, but majorities of whites in both regions preferred some form of race relations that was neither the old Jim Crow system nor a thoroughly integrated society. Within the South, the changes in white attitudes had reduced but not eliminated the traditional polarization between the races. Whatever it was, the new pattern of race relations in the modern South was a far cry from the completely segregated society Cash had known and analyzed.

Many unresolved controversies remained about schools, jobs, housing, and representation that still separated whites from blacks in the South, as in the rest of the nation. Majorities of both races were in disagreement, for example, about public policies concerning preferential racial treatment in jobs and the use of racial quotas in hiring. On

12. Donald R. Matthews and James W. Prothro, *Negroes and the New Southern Politics* (New York, 1966), 331–66.
13. See Black and Black, *Politics and Society,* 195–231, for discussion of the racial attitudes reported in this chapter.

these issues, there is no consensus between whites, whether northern or southern, and southern blacks. The vast majority of whites opposed preferential treatment and the use of quotas, while majorities of blacks took opposing positions.

Blacks now make up about one-sixth of the region's voters. White politicians cannot campaign in ways that are patently offensive to blacks without risking loss of a sizable portion of the electorate. Yet whites still constitute about four of every five voters in the region. They are the majority group in every southern state, as well as in over 90 percent of the region's counties and cities. The continuing numerical advantage of whites in most electoral constituencies is a powerful continuity between the South of the 1940s and the South of the 1990s.

The emergence of a biracial electorate has made it possible for black politicians to seek and win elective office in the South. In 1989, 4,264 blacks held elective offices in the region, accounting for 59 percent of all the black elected officials in the United States.[14] Although blacks have made gains, the vast majority of officeholders in the South continue to be white politicians. Black votes do count, but white votes count also, and in most electoral constituencies there are far more white than black voters. To date, most of the black candidates elected to office have represented majority black constituencies.

Black politicians have recently begun to attempt—and sometimes win—statewide races. To win, biracial coalitions are essential, as was demonstrated in the victory of Douglas Wilder in Virginia. A black candidate who takes positions on a wide range of issues that are far to the left of the preferences of the white majority can expect to harvest few votes from whites, as the experiences of Jesse Jackson in Democratic primaries and Theo Mitchell in the 1990 South Carolina gubernatorial contest illustrate. At the other end of the continuum are black candidates who have tried to seek office by emphasizing policies and goals thought to be acceptable to a substantial minority of whites. Whether successful—as in the case of Wilder—or unsuccessful—as in the cases of Andrew Young in Georgia and Harvey Gantt in North Carolina—black candidates who have made serious efforts to win a third or more of the necessary white vote have used themes and appeals calculated to attract sufficient support among whites while retaining their

14. U.S. Bureau of the Census, *Statistical Abstract of the United States, 1990*, Table 436.

core support among blacks. As Governor Wilder tells audiences, "I want to make one thing clear: I'm a governor who happens to be black, not a black who happens to be governor."[15]

THE PERSISTENCE OF THE INDIVIDUALISTIC ETHIC

Cash thought southern whites relied too much on an ethic of individual achievement and had little sense of government responsibility. Indeed, they preached individualism while relying on the programs of work and relief sponsored by the New Deal. More recently, Reed has emphasized the importance of the individualistic ethic of success for southern whites. "I believe an individualistic ethic has been more common in the South than elsewhere," he has written, "an ethic that says: in the last analysis, you (or at best you and your neighbors) are on your own."[16]

The National Election Studies have often included a standard question about the individualistic ethic in their surveys, and it is worth examination. Respondents are asked: "Some people feel that the government in Washington should see to it that every person has a job and a good standard of living. Suppose that these people are at one end of this scale—at point number 1. Others think that the government should just let each person get ahead on his own. Suppose that these people are at the other end—at point number 7. And, of course some other people have opinions in between. Where would you place yourself on this scale, or haven't you thought much about this?"[17] Setting aside those who had no opinions, those with responses 1, 2, and 3 have been grouped as favoring government responsibility, those with responses 5, 6, and 7 as favoring individual effort, and those picking the middle position as middle-of-the-roaders.

Of those with opinions, more than half of southern and nonsouthern whites preferred reliance on individual efforts to provide economic well-being, and about one-quarter placed primary responsibility on the government in Washington. This two-to-one advantage for the more conservative option indicates the persistence of the cultural strand of individualism so well identified by Cash. Southern whites do not seem

15. New York *Times,* October 14, 1990.

16. Reed, *Enduring South,* 101.

17. See 1988 National Election Study Codebook, at Center for Political Studies, University of Michigan.

to be distinctive in comparison to whites in the rest of the nation. The individualistic ethic unites middle-class and working-class whites. In its most acquisitive form, it provides the guiding ideology for suburban, middle-class whites and takes the expression of making and keeping money.

Quite different were the beliefs about individual and government responsibility among southern blacks. Sixty-three percent stressed the primacy of government rather than individual responsibility for economic well-being. The attitudes of these southern blacks are understandable in light of the long history of racial discrimination in the South and the efforts in the 1960s by the federal government to change employment practices. But this fundamental difference between majorities of the races in the importance of individual efforts to provide for a good standard of living constitutes a huge barrier to the creation of a progressive biracial coalition. It has been expressed in political movements against paying for welfare costs and adds to the perception of many whites that they are being unfairly taxed to pay for persons who will not provide for themselves. It lends itself to a powerful combination of white economic frustration and racial resentment and helped to fuel George Wallace's movement in the 1960s and 1970s and the politics of Ronald Reagan and George Bush in the 1980s. In its most recent expressions, it has contributed to the vote for former Klansman David Duke in Louisiana and Senator Helms in North Carolina.

THE CHANGING PARTY SYSTEM IN THE SOUTH

In 1988, for the first time in the history of the South, a majority of whites (53 percent) considered themselves Republicans or independents leaning toward the Republican party. Only 41 percent of white southerners held similar attachments to the Democratic party. By contrast, 87 percent of black southerners were Democrats or independents leaning toward that party, and merely 10 percent were similarly disposed toward the GOP. The different partisan tendencies among the region's two major racial groups produced a virtual dead heat in the party system: 48 percent of southerners were favorably disposed toward the Democrats, while 47 percent expressed similar predispositions toward the Republicans.[18]

18. Martin P. Wattenberg, "The Building of a Republican Regional Base in the

The shifting party balance is largely the result of the realignment of white conservatives. They once dominated the Democratic party, but increasingly during the 1980s conservatives found a more comfortable home in the Republican party. According to the CBS News/New York *Times* exit poll of voters in the 1988 presidential election, 60 percent of southern white conservatives were Republicans, 24 percent thought of themselves as independents, and only 16 percent still called themselves Democrats. Southern white moderates split three different ways in 1988: 35 percent remained with the Democrats, 31 percent were independents, and 34 percent thought of themselves as Republicans. The Democratic party retained the loyalty of 65 percent of the small group of white liberals, but 23 percent of them thought of themselves as independents, and 12 percent identified with the Republicans.

By the 1990s, the South was moving in the direction of racially and ideologically distinct political parties. The Republican party, drawing from a majority of whites and a small percentage of blacks, was overwhelmingly white in its racial composition, its activists, and its candidates. Although the Republicans differed strongly in the issues to which they gave greatest priority, self-described conservatives constituted the largest wing of the party. The southern Democratic party, based on about two-fifths of the whites and the vast majority of blacks, was a biracial party in its mass base, its activists, and, increasingly, its candidates. Most of the whites who remained Democratic were moderates or liberals. In combination with blacks, the southern Democratic parties were increasingly dominated by moderate to progressive politicians. The modern southern party system had begun to offer voters more distinct choices in the general elections between conservative Republicans and centrist to progressive Democrats.

Whites still constitute the vast majority of voters in the South, but winning a majority of the white vote no longer assures victory. The rival parties have developed alternative strategies for winning elections in the diverse, biracial electorate of the modern South. The Democrats have evolved a biracial strategy for winning elections, while the Republicans have usually tried to win by attracting huge support from whites.[19]

South: The Elephant Crosses the Mason-Dixon Line" (Unpublished manuscript in my possession).

19. Black and Black, *Politics and Society*, 286–91, 312–16.

The strategy of the Democrats has been to combine virtually all of the black vote with a sufficiently large minority of the white vote to produce a majority of the total vote. The candidates best suited to construct successful biracial coalitions have been centrist, moderate Democrats. These candidates have mixed progressive stands on some issues (increased social security payments, support for Medicare, pro–civil rights, and environmental protection, for example) with conservative positions on other issues (strong national defense, pro–death penalty, for example). A skillful mixing of these two positions allows candidates to draw votes from the progressive forces (blacks and liberal whites) as well as from the more centrist forces (moderates and some conservatives). Most successful southern Democrats—Sam Nunn, Lloyd Bentsen, Howell Heflin, Fritz Hollings, Terry Sanford, Albert Gore, Jr., Charles Robb, Robert Graham, and Wyche Fowler, for example—do not run as consistent liberals or as wholehearted conservatives. Were they to do so, these politicians would risk alienating important elements of their electoral coalition. They need to sound like Democrats, but they also still need to sound like southern Democrats.

All of these factors are shaking up the southern Democratic parties. Conservative Democrats—truly conservative Democrats who make no appeal to either blacks or moderate to liberal whites—are a nearly extinct species in Democratic fights for statewide offices. A conservative Democrat might be able to make a runoff but seldom will have the votes to win a two-candidate contest against a competent opponent. In every southern state, the combination of blacks, liberal white Democrats, and moderate white Democrats constitutes more than three-fifths of the Democratic primary vote. If the elements of this broad coalition can agree on a candidate, the moderate to progressive forces have the votes to dominate the outcome of southern Democratic primaries. The recent nominations of Gantt in North Carolina, Mitchell in South Carolina, Zell Miller in Georgia, Ann Richards in Texas, Paul Hubbert in Alabama, and Lawton Chiles in Florida illustrate the triumph of centrist to progressive Democrats.[20]

20. For an interesting analysis of the increasingly progressive tendencies among southern Democrats, see Paul Luebke, *Tar Heel Politics: Myths and Realities* (Chapel Hill, 1990).

The trick is for these centrist to progressive candidates to prevail in the general election, where the core Democratic groups constitute far less than a majority of the voters. In 1988, for example, blacks, liberal white Democrats, moderate white Democrats, and liberal independents made up 39 percent of the southern presidential electorate. These calculations generally propel Democratic nominees toward more centrist positions so they can pick up the support of conservative Democrats and moderate independents. In general, virtually all the black vote plus about 40 percent of the white vote would be sufficient for victory. Democrats need to maximize the size and cohesion of their black supporters but at the same time ensure that they get the minimum amount of white support necessary. When executed with vision and finesse, this centrist campaigning has produced and will continue to produce Democratic victories. Truly liberal Democrats, those who offer nothing to conservatives and little to moderates, will find it difficult to win unless they face a badly flawed opponent.

The alternative strategy, pursued either by choice or necessity by most Republicans, is to work for a landslide majority of the white vote. Most Republicans assume that the vast majority of the vote cast by blacks will go to their opponents. To attract the huge white vote needed, they position themselves as "reasonable" or "practical" conservatives. In this way, they hope to solidify the vote from white conservatives but also to draw support from white moderates. The fundamental weakness of the GOP strategy is its reliance on landslide majorities of the white vote. In the southern politics of Cash's day, whichever candidate got the largest share of the vote cast by whites was the automatic winner. This outcome is no longer the case in the South, as many Republican candidates have discovered. Clayton Williams, David Duke, and James Broyhill differed in many respects, but they had something in common: each of these Republican candidates received well over half of the white vote in recent elections but lost to Democratic opponents who garnered virtually all of the black vote plus enough of a minority of the white vote to win. Some Republicans, such as Senator Helms, Governor Guy Hunt of Alabama, and senatorial candidate Duke in Louisiana, have used racist appeals to generate the extraordinary share of the white vote that they need to win.

Senator Helms has represented North Carolina from a consistently right-wing view for eighteen years and still operates as though blacks do not vote in large numbers. About twenty of every one hundred voters in North Carolina are black. Helms concedes these twenty black voters to his opponent, which means that he must win his fifty-one votes from the remaining eighty whites, or about 63 percent of the white vote. The only way he can get this high share of the vote is to run a negative campaign to make the opponent unacceptable and to emphasize emotional issues—racial quotas is a perfect example—in which Helms speaks for the position held by the vast majority of whites. In his hands, it still works.

Yet Helms is doing it the hard way. On the same day that Helms was fighting for his political life, Strom Thurmond of South Carolina, the Dixiecrat presidential candidate in 1948, easily won reelection to the Senate. Thurmond has never lost his ability to count and has made changes over the years in his style of representing blacks and dealing with white Democrats so that he does not face substantial opposition. Thurmond is doing it a much easier way.

In elections for the major statewide offices, governorships, and the U.S. Senate, contests between 1986 and 1990 show a continuing, sizable Democratic advantage. In the eighteen gubernatorial elections, Democrats captured eleven and Republicans only seven. The Democrats have done particularly well in Arkansas, Tennessee, and Virginia in the peripheral South, as well as Georgia, Mississippi, and Louisiana in the Deep South. The Republicans have been successful in Alabama and South Carolina. Democrats have taken over from Republicans in the region's two largest states, Texas and Florida. Florida Republicans have been plagued by incompetent one-term governors. Robert Martinez followed in the footsteps of Claude Kirk, whose one term in the 1960s set Florida Republicans back more than a decade. If Democrat Lawton Chiles can perform well in office, the Democrats might reestablish themselves in state government. The Texas campaign was not so much won by Ann Richards as lost by Williams, who pumped up too many barrels of West Texas crude.

Democrats did even better in the twenty-two Senate contests between 1986 and 1990, winning fifteen and losing seven. After the 1990 elections, the Democrats held both Senate seats in Arkansas, Tennessee, Georgia, Alabama, and Louisiana, while the Republicans monopolized the Senate seats only in Mississippi. In the remaining states—Texas, Virginia, Florida, North Carolina, and South Carolina—each party had a U.S. senator.

PRESIDENTIAL POLITICS

If the Republican strategy of polling landslide white majorities has sometimes worked in state elections, it has achieved far greater success in presidential politics. The South, once the assured base of the Democratic party, was completely solid for the Democratic presidential candidate for the last time in 1944. The Democrats carried only Texas in 1968, no southern state in 1972, all of the South except Virginia in 1976, only Georgia in 1980, and no southern state in 1984 and 1988. After the Wallace movement burned itself out in 1968, the Republicans won landslide victories in 1972, 1984, and 1988, won close victories in 1980, and lost most of the southern states only in 1976. Indeed, the South has become relatively the strongest part of the Republican party's electoral college base. When the Republicans sweep the South, they need to win only one-third of the remaining electoral college vote to control the White House. By contrast, the collapse of the Democratic presidential base in the South has meant that Democratic party candidates need to win two-thirds outside the South, a task that is not impossible but is surely improbable except under unusual conditions.

The GOP's success has rested on extraordinary strength among whites. Reagan won 61 percent of southern whites in 1980 and rose to 72 percent against Walter Mondale in 1984, and Bush captured 67 percent against Michael Dukakis in 1988. Sometimes this large share of the white vote has been generated through racial or quasi-racial appeals, such as the Willie Horton ads in the 1988 contest. Republican presidential candidates Reagan and Bush have seemed to be more sympathetic than their Democratic rivals to the racial views of the white majority in the South. The potential still exists for appealing to prejudicial feelings and calling attention to conflicts of interest between whites and blacks (the racial quota issue, for example). Yet the appeal of Republican presidential candidates for white voters in the South is by no means limited to racial matters. Republican success in the 1980s was also based, among those who voted, on a return of economic prosperity and a belief that the Republicans were better able to defend the nation's international interests than the Democrats. Recent Republican presidents have been seen by many southern whites as more likely to protect their values and advance their interests over a broad range of matters.[21]

21. For a much fuller discussion of these trends see Earl Black and Merle Black,

Only when the Democrats nominated former Georgia governor Jimmy Carter was the Republican candidate denied a victory. Carter received 47 percent of the white vote, the highest recorded for a Democratic presidential candidate since the mid-1960s. By 1980, though, Carter was not able to carry his native region against Ronald Reagan.

The Republican share of the vote—an average of 58 percent from 1972 to 1988—has fallen far short of the three-quarters of the vote that Franklin Roosevelt drew during the peak periods of the New Deal. Although it amounts to a landslide, it is not beyond a Democratic resurgence if a Republican administration were to preside over a foreign policy disaster or a severe downturn in the economy.

The South of Cash's day was the most Democratic part of the nation. The modern South presents two different political faces. In presidential politics the South has emerged as the most Republican portion of the nation. The South and West have come together again, united behind Republican presidential candidates. In elections for the Senate, the House of Representatives, and most state and local offices, however, the South persists as the most Democratic part of the nation. Whether the Republicans will continue to win the presidency, and whether the Democrats will still be able to dominate state and local offices, constitute some of the most fascinating questions of the still evolving politics of the modern South.

The Vital South: How Presidents Are Elected (Cambridge, Mass., 1992). Interesting analyses of recent presidential politics in the South are found in Laurence W. Moreland, Robert P. Steed, and Tod A. Baker, eds., *The 1984 Presidential Election in the South* (New York, 1986).

Economic Progress and the Mind of the South

GAVIN WRIGHT

The Mind of the South is not primarily concerned with economics or with the economic history of the South. It is a book about social psychology and the character of southern politics, sometimes invoking earlier economic history to trace the origins and development of that psychology but avoiding the task of explaining the region's persistent economic backwardness. It is useful just the same to consider the view of southern economic history implicit in W. J. Cash and to ask how much of that history we should rewrite today on the basis of what we have learned—and what has happened in the South and in the world—in the fifty years since publication of his book. There are some advantages to doing so; because there is no great purpose in criticizing Cash for neglecting a subject he had no interest in pursuing, we can concentrate instead on identifying the conceptions about southern economic history that were taken for granted by thoughtful, well-read southern writers of the time. Though Cash did not draw this inference explicitly, the pathological southern social psychology and politics that he portrayed so vividly have often been seen as root causes of regional economic backwardness. Thus *The Mind of the South* leads us to consider some basic issues about historical connections between economic progress and regional culture.

SOUTHERN ECONOMIC HISTORY IN
THE MIND OF THE SOUTH

Although the southerners described by Cash would seem to be poorly adapted, not just to modern times but to any times at all, it is noteworthy that in the formal structure of his analysis, he shows prevailing regional traits growing out of the material conditions of the antebellum era. The process was not exactly a rational adaptation to circumstances but something more permissive, an unvarying, easygoing environment that offered satisfaction but not challenge. Plantation slavery, he argued, froze the region in a frontier state, blocking forces that elsewhere generated complexity and social dissatisfaction. The Old South, he wrote, was "static and unchanging . . . inherently conservative" (*Mind,* 100), "a world . . . in which not a single factor operated to break up the old pattern of outdoor activity laid down on the frontier" (99). He noted the tendencies toward isolated, self-sufficient units both large and small, the sparsity of towns and cities, and the absence of foreign immigration. In such a simple world, tendencies toward sentimentality, romanticism, and unreality could flourish unchecked.

Southern attitudes were shaped not just by the environment that plantation slavery fostered but by slavery itself. Slavery offered opportunities for rapid advancement by ordinary farmers and hence strengthened the sense of racial identity among whites of all classes. Access to slave labor affected attitudes toward work and toward women, and the security requirements of a slave society called for the suppression of dissent and diversity of opinion. The moral contradictions of a slave society generated a sense of shame and guilt and a continuing need for fictions and rationalizations.

Although these traits were presented by Cash as logically derived from antebellum circumstances, the crucial step in his argument is the proposition that "the essential Southern mind and will" was left "entirely unshaken" by the catastrophic events of war, Reconstruction, and economic depression (105). The only fundamental change during these years, as he saw it, was that traditional southern tendencies came to be infused with a sense of regional identity and patriotism. Though Cash himself could hardly have been called a regional patriot, he clearly accepted the southern nationalist view that the hardships of the Reconstruction period resulted from Reconstruction, the northern policy of "ruining [the South] economically and holding it ruined" (109). Despite repeated references to the machinations of "the tariff gang," however, he attributed the subsequent deterioration of agrarian conditions during the remainder of the century, "the jungle growth of poverty and ruin" (149), primarily to an internal dynamic.

That story went something like this (148–52). The South came out of the war desperately poor and in need of money. To gain money, the region turned more intensely than ever to cotton. But because the new cotton lands were of poor quality, heavy fertilization was necessary. The need for fertilizer and food required financing, and to meet this demand, "there sprang into existence one of the worst systems ever developed: that of the supply merchants" (151). The attraction of the merchant supply business was irresistible to small, aspiring entrepreneurs, so that "by the 1880's almost every crossroad was provided with at least one such banker-merchant, and every village had from two to half a score" (151). The problem with this development was that despite their numbers, these "new masters of Southern economics" (151) charged exorbitant monopoly credit prices, and the cotton-growing South was saddled with a crushing burden of payments. To complete the tragedy, this dramatic expansion of cotton produced a "glut in the world market" (152), forcing prices steadily downward. This account is only a modest variation on interpretations that were common during the 1890s, rooted in contemporary complaints about overproduction and excessive costs of credit.[1]

Cash saw the forces behind southern industrialization in an entirely different way (175–86). He focused on cotton textiles, fully accepting the thesis of Broadus Mitchell that the campaign to "bring the mills to the cotton" was a civic and patriotic movement to improve the lot of poor southern whites.[2] To be sure, the movement was also a response to economic hardship and an act of regional patriotism, with frequent use of military metaphors harking back to the Civil War. Cash explicitly rejected the "profit motive" as a primary force (179–83). All of this was essential background for his larger contention that industrialization in the South did not represent something fundamentally new in social relations or consciousness. The cotton mills were not much more than plantations "brought bodily over" into a new economic sector (205–206).

In describing the twentieth-century South, Cash clearly felt that the region's economic progress was deeply flawed. He knew that both agriculture and industry enjoyed prosperity after 1900 and especially during the war years but believed that both farmers and cotton-mill work-

1. The "standard work" (according to C. Vann Woodward writing in 1938) is Matthew B. Hammond, *The Cotton Industry* (New York, 1897). Abundant contemporary testimony may be found in *Senate Reports,* 53rd Cong., 3rd sess., no. 986.
   2. Broadus Mitchell, *The Rise of the Cotton Mills in the South* (Baltimore, 1921).

ers had squandered their earnings recklessly, "after the romantic-hedonistic pattern fixed in the past" (281). Such statements would seem to support an essentially cultural explanation for southern poverty. But Cash also pointed to the inexorable pressure of rising rural population against available land—perhaps viewing the high fertility rate as a sign of sexual indulgence, though he did not say so explicitly. And he saw no merit in the common moralistic advice that farmers should "Live at Home," noting that the pressures of indebtedness gave the majority little real choice (282–83). So Cash seemed to blame both the victim and the oppressors, respectively.

A similar ambivalence may be found in Cash's account of the course of the cotton textile industry in the South. He argued that the region's main competitive advantage was cheap labor and that mill workers shared very little of the fruits of progress (202–205). Yet he also observed that the rapid multiplication of mills provided opportunities for career advancement for men with little technical training (262–63)—a consideration he could hardly have missed inasmuch as his father had advanced to the position of superintendent in a hosiery mill by 1923.[3] As critical as he was of traditional southern attitudes, he was even more critical of the new "cold-faced Northern slave-masters" who were sent in "to run the mills on strictly business-is-business lines" (267). He blamed the region's leadership for recruiting these outside firms, "virtually giving away the inherent resources of the section, physical and human" (267). These were rather conventional views among southern writers during the interwar period.

Cash's most strongly felt and clearly articulated opinions, however, were not so much about economics as political economy, particularly the incapacity of the mass of southerners to act politically in their own class interests. The absence of a class-based politics was the major cost of the "inertia of tradition" in the South. Implicit in this analysis is the idea that a class-based politics would have resulted in economic progress for the South as a whole. This proposition is surely debatable, but Cash did not set out the terms of such a debate with any clarity. He criticized demagogues such as Blease and Tillman for having no concrete program, but one could say the same of Cash himself, judging at

3. Bruce Clayton, "A Southern Modernist: The Mind of W. J. Cash," in *The South Is Another Land,* ed. Bruce Clayton and John A. Salmond (Westport, Conn., 1987), 171–85.

least from *The Mind of the South*. But like the economist William H. Nicholls writing twenty years later,[4] Cash clearly saw a tension between southern tradition and regional progress in some important sense of that term, and we can ask how well that analysis has characterized southern politics over that period of history.

NEW RESEARCH IN SOUTHERN ECONOMIC HISTORY

In offering a selective summary of research on the economic history of the South since 1940, I want to resist the temptation to construct (and hide behind) a barricade of technical expertise. Economists do not have secret ways of knowing things that no outsider is entitled to understand or criticize. But for a range of issues, economics does provide a systematic set of categories and a research strategy, and knowledge in some areas has advanced over the past fifty years. I propose to start with some of these, the relatively easy part, before tackling the harder conceptual issues that a work like *The Mind of the South* obliges us to consider.

The Economics of Slavery

Beginning with Alfred H. Conrad and John R. Meyer's famous 1958 essay "The Economics of Slavery" and continuing through Robert Fogel's recent *Without Consent or Contract,* slavery has been one of the most robust areas of study in economic history. It would be foolhardy for me to try to summarize all of this research and not very appropriate because Cash himself gave slavery relatively cursory attention. But it is safe to say that we now think of slavery and the antebellum southern economy as far more complex and dynamic than the "static and unchanging" world described by Cash. On many major issues there is now a fair degree of consensus: slaveownership was profitable; farms and plantations using slave labor were productive and responsive to market opportunities; the late antebellum southern economy was prosperous and growing, supported by rapidly expanding world demand for American cotton; slaveowners, even small ones, were among the wealthiest people in the country; and their behavior in the major markets of the day (slaves, land, and cotton) indicates that most of them

4. William H. Nicholls, *Southern Tradition and Regional Progress* (Chapel Hill, 1960).

were optimistic about their economic future at the time of secession. To be sure, these statements would not have surprised some earlier writers such as Lewis Cecil Gray, but they were far from clearly established in the general writing and thinking of the 1930s.[5]

There is significant disagreement in this literature on the underlying sources of slavery's economic success. Robert Fogel attributes it primarily to efficiency, by which he means the level of physical exertion expended by slaves under the gang labor system. I (and I hope a few others) argue that the performance derived instead mainly from the allocative properties of slavery, which is to say the ability of owners to transport slaves to any location where slavery was legal; to assign them to any tasks, including females to field work; and to allocate a larger fraction of the farm's resources to production for market than did slaveless farms. These factors, plus an ideal geography for cotton growing during a time of increasing world demand, are in my view the main reasons for the exceptional prosperity of slaveowners at the time of secession. But important as it is, this issue does not seem to bear directly on the matters of most concern to historians of the South.[6]

What historians have wanted is something the economist cannot deliver, a way to infer from economic behavior a psychological and cultural profile of slaveowners, specifically whether they had a capitalist mentality. There is no legitimate way to do this. A given set of choices and outcomes may derive from an infinite number of motivations and

5. Alfred H. Conrad and John R. Meyer, "The Economics of Slavery in the Antebellum South," *Journal of Political Economy,* LXVI (April, 1958), 95–130; Robert William Fogel, *Without Consent or Contract: The Rise and Fall of American Slavery* (New York, 1990).

6. Fogel's case was first presented in Robert W. Fogel and Stanley Engerman, *Time on the Cross: The Economics of American Negro Slavery* (Boston, 1974). See the critiques in Paul A. David, Herbert G. Gutman, Richard Sutch, Peter Temin, and Gavin Wright, *Reckoning with Slavery: A Critical Study in the Quantitative History of American Negro Slavery* (New York, 1976). The issues have been debated in the *American Economic Review* as follows: Robert W. Fogel and Stanley L. Engerman, "Explaining the Relative Efficiency of Slave Agriculture in the Antebellum South," LXVI (June, 1977), 275–96; Thomas L. Haskell, "Explaining the Relative Efficiency of Slave Agriculture in the Antebellum South: A Reply to Fogel-Engerman," LXIX (March, 1979), 206–207; Donald F. Schaeffer and Mark D. Schmitz, "The Relative Efficiency of Slave Agriculture: A Comment," *ibid.*, 208–12; Paul A. David and Peter Temin, "Explaining the Relative Efficiency of Slave Agriculture in the Antebellum South: Comment," *ibid.*, 213–18; Gavin Wright, "The Efficiency of Slavery: Another Interpretation," *ibid.*, 219–20; Robert W. Fogel and Stanley L. Engerman, "Explaining the Relative Efficiency of Slave Agriculture in the Antebellum South: A Reply," LXX (September, 1980), 672–90.

pressures. We know, for example, that slave markets were highly developed, and the most recent evidence suggests that their role in the slave economy was more pervasive than previously thought.[7] But this evidence does not tell us how buying or selling slaves entered into the thinking and feeling of slaveowners. Even if we knew these answers for some, they were surely not the same for everyone involved. The main problem with this long debate, however, is not with the evidence but with the question itself: how can we hope to determine whether southerners were culturally similar to northerners by examining their behavior in a market that did not and could not exist outside of the South? The economic calculations made by southerners were clearly different from those of northerners, but they had to be different because circumstances were different, primarily because of slavery. To try to define and measure an abstraction like "capitalist mentality" in a setting entirely different from the one that gave rise to the abstraction is to embark on a fool's errand. There are many interesting questions to ask about the course of southern economic development under slavery; the persistent focus on psychology (to which Cash contributed) has if anything gotten in the way of a more constructive research agenda.

If we look at structures and incentives rather than psychologies, it is not hard to show that what was happening economically in the South was quite different from events in the North. Despite its superficiality, there was an essential accuracy in Cash's description: the antebellum South was lush but primitive. In comparison with the North, settlement was more dispersed; there were fewer towns, cities, and schools; farming was unmechanized; wage labor markets were undeveloped; manufacturing activity was limited; and economic prosperity had an entirely different relationship to population growth, particularly to immigration. Life may not have been static and unchanging, and slaveowners as a class (by no means a tiny minority of the free population) were wealthy and getting wealthier. But the level of economic and cultural diversity was nowhere near that of the northern states, and the two regions were not converging. Whether we choose to call these structural differences economic backwardness depends on the reference point and on one's views about Progress (which W. J. Cash chose to spell with a capital *P*).

7. Michael Tadman, *Speculators and Slaves: Masters, Traders, and Slaves in the Old South* (Madison, 1989).

The Agrarian Transformation in the Postbellum South

Treating the antebellum era in terms of psychology served the essential function for Cash of allowing him to argue that the drastic changes that occurred after the war were not fundamental changes at all. Thus, although he accepted most of the southern nationalist indictment of Reconstruction, which was the prevalent view at the time he wrote (the redistribution of plantation land, impoverishment at the hands of corrupt governments, manipulation of "ignorant and ductile" blacks by unscrupulous carpetbaggers), he is generally grouped with those who interpret southern history as characterized by basic long-term continuities. The broad issue of continuity has long been debated, and it has its indeterminate and irresolvable elements. But in economic terms, a substantial body of research justifies the view that emancipation brought revolutionary changes to the South.

Economic change did not take the form that Cash suggested, the breakup and redistribution of plantation land. Most of the large land units seem to have remained intact, often with continuity in family ownership; the impression to the contrary arose because of the census practice of listing individual tenancies and sharecropping plots as separate farms. But whatever the size of the holding, emancipation fundamentally changed the relationship between land and labor. Perhaps the most basic new element was the mobility of labor. No matter how many times the statement has been repeated that postbellum sharecropping was no different from slavery, it was indeed different. Tenants and sharecroppers, black as well as white, moved from one plantation to another with great frequency, and they did so consistently from the 1870s to the 1930s. Because of labor mobility, work discipline and work incentives were very different, and that difference was physically represented by the change in plantation layout. The cluster of slave cabins near the owner's house, appropriate for the centralized methods of labor organization under slavery, was replaced by a dispersed pattern of housing on individual tenants' and sharecroppers' plots of land. This entire development was neglected by Cash, who gave little special attention to the plantation areas or to black southerners generally.[8]

---

8. Roger Ransom and Richard Sutch, *One Kind of Freedom: The Economic Consequences of Emancipation* (New York, 1977); Gerald David Jaynes, *Branches Without Roots: The Genesis of the Black Working Class in the American South, 1862–1882* (New York, 1986).

Decentralization of the plantation was only the beginning. As I have argued in *Old South, New South,* the abolition of slavery also caused a change in economic incentives for the planters. Their economic interests became far more locally rooted than they had been under slavery, far more directed toward squeezing the maximum potential from every acre of land. Labor was no longer a fixed cost. This alteration in property rights, in my view, is the most fundamental reason for the postbellum shift of acreage into cotton and the move away from self-sufficiency. Here again, the broad forces and incentives behind the move are easier to identify than the specific mechanisms, pressures, and decisions that individuals made. Undoubtedly the pressures of indebtedness and financial stringency were decisive in many cases; but these pressures all pointed toward cotton for the basic reason that cotton generated revenues per acre that were far higher than any alternative uses.

Why, then, did the swing into cotton not produce a more prosperous South, and why did southerners come to associate cotton with poverty, exploitation, and moral decline? Cash was right to suggest that the problem had to do with supply and demand but wrong to infer that the South had caused it by overproduction. Instead, the root of the matter was external to the South, specifically the slow growth of world demand for cotton during the last three decades of the nineteenth century. Perceptions and political rhetoric confounded the microeconomic problems of individual farmers and their costs of credit with macroeconomic forces beyond the reach of anyone in the South. It is true that a collective decision to cut back on cotton production would have forced up the price. But putting aside the problem that the South had no vehicle for taking such a step, it still would not have raised total revenue from cotton because total revenue was limited by demand.

Much of the apparent pathology of southern agriculture stems from several simple considerations: that under the limits of prescientific farming methods, much of the South was a one-cash-crop region willy-nilly because the next-best alternatives to cotton were not commercially competitive under prevailing conditions of soil, climate, and environment. The choices were cotton or production for home use, and both became less favorable over time as population grew relative to land. Contrary to the impression one gets from references to "the wholesale expropriation of the cracker and the small farmer" (161), the rise in tenancy did not reflect a decline in the number of farm owners but instead a steady increase in the number of younger farmers not yet able to purchase land. This is certainly not to suggest that all social and political developments were economically irrelevant, much less that they were shaped by aggregate economic imperatives. But the range of feasible possibilities in southern agriculture was sharply limited by aggregate constraints, though contemporaries were understandably reluctant to accept this as a fact of life. Historical explanations for southern rural poverty have to come down to explanations for the growth and persistence of the rural population in the face of such unfavorable conditions. That topic is indeed one for which cultural and political history made a big difference.

The Cotton Mill Movement and the Profit Motive

Before moving on to larger issues of regional identity, it is instructive to look at the Cash-Mitchell account of the rise of the cotton mills, in light of more recent research. It might seem an interpretation hardly worth discussing, because virtually all modern writers have regarded it as patently implausible to think that a vast regional industry composed of private profit-seeking firms could have been constructed out of purely altruistic motives of civic betterment. Without the benign motivation, however, other historians do advance interpretations that are formally similar, depicting the movement as a "revolution from above" conducted by the planter class, or an act of regional patriotism and warfare.[9] Like Cash and Mitchell, these writers are not troubled by attributing collective purposes and actions to groups of many hundreds of individuals who had no apparent means of collusion or coordination.

It is clear enough that the organizers of new cotton mills hoped to earn profits and did earn profits and that they succeeded because they had a raw material, an available technology (with outside assistance if needed), and a labor supply. A close look at the social background of mill owners and managers and the management of mill work in practice—as opposed to relying, as Mitchell did, on the extravagant boosterist rhetoric of mill promoters—should quickly dispel the idea that

---

9. Dwight B. Billings, Jr., *Planters and the Making of a "New South": Class, Politics, and Development in North Carolina, 1865–1900* (Chapel Hill, 1979); Patrick J. Hearden, *Independence and Empire: The New South's Cotton Mill Campaign, 1865–1901* (DeKalb, 1982).

these men were in business because of their close fellow feeling with their workers.[10] In the context of the national market, the advance of the southern producers did indeed derive from their low wages relative to New England. But there was also a genuine process of development, as profits were reinvested and as managers and workers gained experience and sophistication and gradually moved into finer cloth varieties and new product lines.[11]

There is more to the story than profits and progress. The rhetoric of the New South has something to teach us if we don't take it literally but ask where it was coming from. As David Carlton has argued, the cotton mill crusade can best be understood as an outgrowth of town building, and boosterism is the standard spiel of the chamber of commerce, representing the interest of the town as a collective enterprise. Though the claims are mostly thin propaganda, there is an element of truth in the underlying conception, which is that local landowners and merchants do have a common interest in the development of a local community. Workers in the area may also have an interest in opening up job opportunities, but it is evident that the most enthusiastic promoters did not picture themselves as mill workers. Indeed, it was not long before mill workers came to be seen as an alien and somewhat threatening presence by middle-class townspeople, so different were their origins and their way of life. But the broadly based character of the early support was real. Carlton and Peter Coclanis have recently argued that southern textile firms were handicapped by their obligation to numerous small subscribers, as opposed to a well-developed financial sector. Here too, however, the market for cotton mill stocks gradually broadened and matured so that twentieth-century firms could mobilize capital from much wider geographic areas.[12] The South had a lot of

10. Paul D. Escott, *Many Excellent People: Power and Privilege in North Carolina, 1850–1900* (Chapel Hill, 1985), chap. 8.

11. David Carlton, "The Revolution from Above: The National Economy and the Beginnings of Industrialization in North Carolina," *Journal of American History,* LXXVII (September, 1990), 445–75; Leonard Carlson, "Labor Supply, the Acquisition of Skills, and the Location of Southern Textile Mills, 1880–1900," *Journal of Economic History,* XLI (March, 1981), 65–71; Gavin Wright, "Cheap Labor and Southern Textiles, 1880–1930," *Quarterly Journal of Economics,* XCVI (November, 1981), 605–29.

12. David Carlton, *Mill and Town in South Carolina, 1880–1920* (Baton Rouge, 1982); Carlton and Peter Coclanis, "Capital Mobilization and Southern Industry, 1880–1905: The Case of the Carolina Piedmont," *Journal of Economic History,* XLIX (March, 1989), 73–94.

catching up to do, but from an industrial development perspective the progress was reasonably steady until the 1920s.

Were these promoters and investors a new class, or was this a new direction for the old master class? That is not a good historical question, because it forces a theoretical abstraction into a rigid empirical straitjacket. The cotton mill movement was not a centrally orchestrated class activity, because the South lacked the instruments for such collective measures. It was a decentralized social process, carried out by thousands of local investors in hundreds of locations, all pursuing their own profit interest in roughly similar circumstances. Undoubtedly, many of these investors did come from backgrounds of agrarian wealth traceable back to antebellum times, but the focus and impact of their new ventures were entirely different. As it emerged over time, the geographic locus of southern industry became highly distinct and distinctly separate from the black-majority plantation belts.[13] In short, whether or not they began as members of an old class, the process itself transformed them into a new class, with new economic and political interests. There may be many useful reasons to follow Cash in tracing threads of continuity in southern thinking back to antebellum times, but precision in the analysis of political economy is often lost in the process.

The Interwar Period

It is hardly fair to W. J. Cash, or to anyone writing in 1940, to say that he was not able to place his own era in historical perspective. Obviously, we have the advantage of knowing what came afterward. From the standpoint of economic history, however, Cash was much more aware than many later historians have been that the southern economic calamities of the 1920s and 1930s were new and qualitatively different from those of earlier times. Historians have been far too ready to attribute hard times to "backwardness" or to the persistence of "traditional" structures and behaviors, even when these allegations have a reasonably evident self-serving class origin. It is ironic, therefore, that Cash is

13. See particularly David Carlton, "Unbalanced Growth and Industrialization: The Case of South Carolina," in *Developing Dixie: Modernization in a Traditional Society*, ed. Winfred B. Moore, Jr., and Joseph F. Tripp (Westport, Conn., 1988).

known today mainly as the theoretician of pathological continuity in the South.

In agriculture, the major cause of stagnation after 1920 was the malfunctioning of the international economy as a result of the demise of the prewar gold standard and Britain's inability to reestablish itself as the world's banker. Americans think of the 1920s as a prosperous decade, and it was, for those sectors of the economy producing new products for the domestic market. The United States was unique among the major nations of the world in its relative insulation from international economic forces. But much of American agriculture had long been integrated into world markets, and virtually all sectors dependent on international demand suffered during that time. The interwar period was a two-decade interruption of the long-term trend toward globalization, a retreat behind national borders that was nearly complete by the early 1930s. Cash could not resist the gibe at southern farmers for their naïve speculation in farmland during the wartime boom (which lasted until late 1920). But the deflation of 1920–21 brought similar problems of financial maladjustment and foreclosures to farmers in all parts of the country.[14] What distinguished the South was not its psychology or the underlying economic problem, but the sheer number of people still employed in agriculture as late as the 1920s, and the boll weevil, which had its most devastating impact in many areas only after 1920.[15]

When the Depression hit in the 1930s, the political leadership of the South emphasized the broad-based suffering in the region because of the collapse of cotton prices, stressing particularly the plight of small tenant farmers. Federal farm programs of that decade, however, designed and implemented largely by major landowners and their representatives, precipitated drastic reorganization of plantations and displacement of tenants. The resulting hardships were seen by many observers as reflections of backwardness and traditional southern race relations; in fact, they were new. The apparent continuity and un-

14. Lee J. Alston, "Farm Foreclosures in the United States During the Interwar Period," *Journal of Economic History,* XLIII (December, 1983), 885–903; H. Thomas Johnson, "Postwar Optimism and the Rural Financial Crisis of the 1920s," *Explorations in Economic History,* II (Winter, 1973–74), 173–92.

15. Robert Higgs, "The Boll Weevil, the Cotton Economy, and Black Migration, 1910–1930," *Agricultural History,* L (April, 1976), 335–50.

changeability of southern agriculture on the eve of World War II was at best superficial, because key economic underpinnings of the plantation system had been removed.[16]

For the textiles industry, the interwar years were depressed even before the Great Depression, but for quite different reasons. Cash knew that the real hourly wages of southern cotton-mill workers had risen by more than 50 percent compared with prewar levels. But he suggested that these hourly rates were not actually realized by the workers because the length of the standard workweek fell (from sixty to fifty-five hours) and many were not able to get as many hours of work as they wanted, even at the new, lower level. He was right. Textile jobs were scarce in the 1920s, and prospective workers often had to go from mill to mill trying to pick up work as spare hands. The extraordinarily high turnover rates reported in that decade have often been attributed to the traits of southern workers, their shiftlessness, roving disposition, or retained links with the countryside. I think the problem was the shortage of work.

But what Cash could not see was that the high hourly wages and the scarcity of jobs were two sides of the same coin. The fact that southern textile wages stayed high while southern wages in agriculture, sawmills, and lumbering declined reflects (among other things) the influence of outside political forces on the southern labor market. In the 1920s, the plight of the southern mill worker was a major object of national reformist concern. When strikes broke out at the end of the decade, reporters, organizers, and other supporters arrived from all over the country. Where did this concern come from? It is a simplification, but not a distortion of the truth, to say that the concern was driven by the efforts of mill owners and textile workers in New England to focus attention on the South because they believed correctly that their own market position was being rapidly undercut by low-wage southern competition.

Outside pressure to raise southern textile wages became more explicit and more extensive during the 1930s, first through the National Industrial Recovery Act (in which the New England–dominated Cotton Textile Institute played a leading role), later through the Wagner

---

16. Warren Whatley, "Labor for the Picking: The New Deal in the South," *Journal of Economic History*, XLIII (December, 1983), 1191–1215; Pete Daniel, *Breaking the Land: The Transformation of Cotton, Tobacco, and Rice Cultures Since 1880* (Urbana, 1985).

Act and the Fair Labor Standards Act of 1938. Cash accurately reported that the major effect of these measures was to induce mill owners to dispense with as many workers as possible (373–74). The experience was often bewildering to the mill workers. Of course they wanted higher wages, but no one offered them an alternative combination of moderate wages and more regular work or a more moderate work pace. The exclusive emphasis on higher hourly wage rates clearly did not represent the authentic grass-roots priorities of southern mill workers as a class.[17]

Cash lamented that southern mill workers could not seem to make a sustained commitment to organized labor, attributing their problem to lack of mature class consciousness. Yet he also acknowledged that the textile strikes of 1929–34 were doomed from the start because of surplus labor conditions (354). Cash was surely right that southern mill workers lacked a firm grip on their own self-interest, either psychologically or organizationally. But in the circumstances of the interwar South, this is setting a fairly high standard for class consciousness, and Cash himself seemed to accept the naïve faith that a move toward a more class-based politics as defined in northern terms would serve the interests of the southern working class.

THE MIND OF THE SOUTH AND THE NATIONAL ECONOMY

Behind these specific research issues in southern economic history is a larger conceptual question. Can we understand or explain the history of economic development in the South without first asking whether there was a southern economy in the first place? And if so, what was it? I do not mean merely to raise the matter of economic diversity within the South, because diversity occurs in any region or any country. The question is not whether there was diversity but whether there was any real unity, any sense in which the South was a functioning entity in economic life. If there was a certain degree of cultural and psychological unity (as Cash believed and as there obviously was), did this translate into economic relationships?

One approach is to ask this question of the country as a whole. Compared with other large countries, the United States had a high level

17. James R. Hodges, *New Deal Labor Policy and the Southern Cotton Textile Industry, 1933–1941* (Knoxville, 1986), 33.

of cultural and linguistic unity, which did translate into substantial homogeneity in political and legal traditions, the South being more or less
deviant depending on the specific issue at hand. What gave the nation
its coherence as an economic entity, however, was not mere uniformity
but the high degree of integration at the national level, including integration in markets for both commodities and resources and integration
in networks of communication in business, technology, and other cultural areas. Engineers and mechanics moved freely between states, and
from the late nineteenth century, business establishments designed
products and marketing efforts on a national basis. The search for industrial fuels and raw materials was national in scope. The national
economic achievement was in significant respects a collective achievement by a national economic entity, though not a centrally managed
economic entity. Boundaries, markets, and cultural affinities were such
that the benefits to investments in education and technology were in-
ternalized within the nation.

How much of this economic unity did the South have as a proto-
nation? On some counts, such as language, transportation, and product
markets, it was part of the larger national entity. The southern states
had some common economic interests as producers of cotton and a few
other crops, but only as linked to external markets that were unreliable.
The South did have a degree of cultural unity, and as I have argued,
southern culture was linked to regional integration in the labor market,
which is to say that channels of communication and migration tended
to develop within the South. But even this limited economic unity came
at a cost, because highly educated southerners had a tendency to be
drawn into the larger national networks. Thus the preservation of regional identity and regionalism in the labor market carried with it a
built-in disincentive to invest in education and technical training. Not
being a nation, having no control of its borders and no control over
major areas of economic policy that countries normally control, the
South as a quasi-political entity had virtually no policy instruments operating at a regional level. The idea of a southern ruling class can certainly be entertained as a useful metaphor, but only if it is understood
that class power in the South was by necessity much more negative than
positive in character. Southern elites had many ways to block change
and maintain their local power, and the background of regionalism in
culture and in the labor market gave this stance a certain coherence in

national politics. But the capacity to initiate a genuinely regional development program did not exist.

It is helpful to distinguish two alternate paths to regional economic development: establishment of an independent growth center, with distinct technologies and organizations adapted to local circumstances, versus development via absorption into the larger national economy. Twentieth-century Japan is an example of the first type. The postwar American South, by and large, is an example of the second. Here and there one can point to signs of incipient "southernization" in important industries: the school of textile engineering at Georgia Tech, the early work by I. H. Hardeman on applications of air conditioning and humidity control to southern mills, resource-based research programs at various universities in the South.[18] But none of these had a distinctive association with fundamental aspects of southern culture. And when it came to the prospect of a sophisticated low-wage industrial technology in the South (*i.e.*, the path taken by Japan and other Asian followers), the concept was politically unacceptable in a national context. Hence the only feasible path to progress in the South implied a sacrifice of southern cultural distinctiveness, and that intuitive association was consistent with Cash's view of the world.

There was another dimension of the issue, however, largely implicit in Cash's thinking and in the thinking of most of his contemporaries about problems of regional economic development. The mind of the South meant the white mind, and economic progress for the South meant progress for the white South. To be sure, the problems of the region were often described in ways that seemed to include the plight of black southerners, and conversely, the plight of black southerners was often attributed to the backwardness of the region—with greater or lesser accuracy, depending on the issue. Southern blacks and whites certainly did experience labor market pressures in common, just as black and white farmers shared the vicissitudes of the market for cotton. But the question is, Did black southerners have any integral place in the process or program of southern economic development? It is questionable whether they did.

18. Raymond Arsenault, "The End of the Long Hot Summer: The Air Conditioner and Southern Culture," *Journal of Southern History*, L (1984), 597–628; Robert McMath *et al., Engineering and the New South: Georgia Tech, 1885–1985* (Athens, Ga., 1985).

There is an important strand in southern economic history, continuous from the time of Reconstruction, which may be read as the gradual convergence of the economic standards of the white population toward national norms, with the blacks left out. Cash thought that the cotton mill movement was prompted by the fear that poor southern whites would fall to the level of the former slaves (175–76). But the evidence suggests that in the late nineteenth-century South, a large segment of the white population was already at the same basic living standard as the black population. Although racial inequality, segregation, and discrimination were present at all times, before World War I there was no large gap between the wage levels of unskilled black and white workers. Black tenants and croppers were impoverished, but white tenancy rates were also growing as population growth pressed against the supply of land. Rising generations of white farmers also found themselves on small plots of poor-quality land and poorly equipped with education or experience for urban or industrial jobs. Even industries that were restricted to whites only, like textiles, paid wages that were essentially comparable with the wages available to unskilled black labor in agriculture, mining, or sawmills.[19]

Southern progressive and reform movements essentially promised liberation from these backward levels for the white population. The best-known manifestation is public education, in which wide racial gaps in expenditures and standards were implemented between 1890 and 1910. Educational reform groups such as the Southern Education Board were not necessarily hostile to blacks but always seemed to find that upgrading for white schools was more realistic financially and politically, with black schools left behind. In this way, they were accommodating both the prejudice of whites and the economic interests of the planters, who actively opposed expansion of black schooling. Even outside organizations such as the Rosenwald Fund found ways to rationalize highly unequal support for black and white educational institutions.[20]

19. These statements are documented in Gavin Wright, *Old South, New South: Revolutions in the Southern Economy Since the Civil War* (New York, 1986), 177–86; and Warren Whatley and Gavin Wright, "Black Labor in the American Economy Since Emancipation," in *The Wealth of Races,* ed. Richard F. America (Westport, Conn., 1990).

20. John W. Cell, *The Highest Stage of White Supremacy: The Origins of Segregation in South Africa and the American South* (New York, 1982); James D. Anderson, *The Education of Blacks in the South, 1860–1935* (Chapel Hill, 1988); Robert Margo, *Race and Schooling in the South, 1900–1950* (Chicago, 1990).

By the 1920s, a distinct gap had emerged between entry-level wages for black and white workers, across and within industries. When federal pressure to raise wages was felt more broadly in the 1930s, a strong component of southern opinion was all in favor. Whether intended or not, the net effect of the pressure to upgrade both wage levels and job qualifications was to push the southern industrial sector increasingly toward an all-white labor force, with blacks consigned to only the most menial, dead-end tasks. Many job opportunities that had formerly been open to blacks were lost during the interwar period.[21] From the 1920s onward, virtually all of the newly created industrial jobs in the South were reserved for whites. Increasingly, one heard that the South's reputation for backwardness was unjustified, that there were few true differences in the quality of workers between regions, and that the only reason for apparent regional differentials was the presence in the South of large numbers of poor blacks.

This interpretation of political trends in the white South should not be taken to imply that black southerners were quietly accepting the fate assigned to them, or that these were the only forces at work. James Anderson's work on black schooling makes it clear that there were many ways to resist and evade the restrictions on school curricula that the authorities thought they were imposing. The NAACP's long-term assault on educational discrimination was launched in the early 1930s, with great ultimate success. But this activity did not lead white southerners to think of southern blacks as full members of the regional community.

For present purposes, my main point is that large racial differentials in schooling, jobs, and wages were explained away and justified by appeal to southern traditions and the mind of the South. But they were not traditional; they were the outcome of political choices at a time when blacks were deprived of political representation. The appeal to tradition was mainly a way of saying that nothing could be done about it. Yet many of those who called for the South to put aside its fixation on the Negro problem and catch up to the rest of the nation were advocating a line of development in which southern blacks had no in-

---

21. On the steel industry, see Robert J. Norrell, "Caste in Steel: Jim Crow Careers in Birmingham, Alabama," *Journal of American History*, LXXIII (December, 1986), 669–94; on railroads, see William A. Sundstrom, "Half a Career: Discrimination and Railroad Internal Labor Markets," *Industrial Relations*, XXIX (Fall, 1990), 423–40; on tobacco, see Wright, *Old South, New South*, 224–25.

tegral place. It is hardly surprising that out-migration from the South
during the 1940s and 1950s was overwhelmingly black, even though
the region was growing economically much faster than the rest of the
nation. During World War I, out-migration by southern whites exceeded that of southern blacks; during World War II, in contrast, twice
as many blacks as whites departed the region,[22] and the disproportion-
ality was far greater during the 1950s.

Jack Temple Kirby has argued that the term "*Southerner* is a rather
pernicious abstraction when closely examined," a political tool more
than an authentic folk consciousness or sense of cultural identity.[23] Cash
believed that southern regional consciousness emerged in the context
of conflict with the North, but it is equally true that the sense of re-
gionhood, and in many respects the explicitly articulated regional interest, were largely defined in relationship to the submerged black population. There is no valid way to separate the issues of southern economic
development from the parallel task of defining the cultural and historical identity of the South as an economic entity, an identity that in my
view had a strong racial component. Cash saw clearly that the South
was hung up on the race issue and that this hangup had damaging social
and political implications. But his vision did not extend to seeing the
black population as full-fledged members of the southern community,
a limitation he shared with nearly all white southerners of his time.
Reconsidering *The Mind of the South* from an economic standpoint is
instructive, therefore, primarily because the exercise forces us to acknowledge that conceptions of economic progress are ultimately inseparable from the issues of group consciousness with which he was
concerned.

22. Gavin Wright, "The Economic Revolution in the American South," *Journal of Economic Perspectives,* I (Summer, 1987), 174.
23. Jack Temple Kirby, *Rural Worlds Lost: The American South, 1920–1960* (Baton Rouge, 1987), 223.

Passion and Discontinuities: A Semicycle of *Mind*, 1941–1991

JACK TEMPLE KIRBY

The year W. J. Cash's *Mind of the South* appeared, 1941, approximates a turning point in the American South's history that arguably was more profound than 1865. World War II—a journey through chaos, as one journalist put it—accelerated vast demographic and economic changes already under way. In a short time, mules and sharecroppers nearly disappeared; southerners abruptly became an urban and manufacturing people. The "bulldozer revolution" (C. Vann Woodward's memorable expression) had begun. The civil rights revolution is rooted in the 1940s, too, and with it the Solid South virtually dissolved. Black political power became permanent. And a white Georgian, liberal on race and other social issues, served a term as president of the United States and failed because (among other reasons) he presumed to instruct Yankees in moral historical consciousness.[1] Much of the world known to Wilbur Joseph Cash, it would seem, has turned upside down.

In the historiography of the South, Cash's great book represented a turning point, too. Or was it—like the notorious description of the European revolutions of 1848—a turning point at which history did not turn? Cash's book belongs to him and his time, culminating certain complex intellectual trends. It also seemed to be a great departure,

---

1. George Brown Tindall first summarized the enormous impact of World War II on the region in *The Emergence of the New South, 1913–1945* (Baton Rouge, 1967), esp. 700–703. See also C. Vann Woodward, *The Burden of Southern History* (Rev. ed.; Baton Rouge, 1968), 6, 10; David R. Goldfield, *Promised Land: The South Since 1945* (Arlington Heights, Ill., 1987); and (for the countryside) Pete Daniel, *Breaking the Land: The Transformation of Cotton, Tobacco, and Rice Cultures Since 1880* (Urbana, 1985), 155–84, 239–55, and *passim*.

instructing professional learning for more than a quarter-century. Through the 1930s historians of the region were in the main preoccupied with the Old South and the Civil War. Cash devoted hardly a quarter of *The Mind of the South* to the antebellum experience. He was obsessed with the so-called New South, a subject that until 1941 had been addressed by few scholars, mostly economists. Yet in his brief treatment of the Old South, Cash introduced two of the three conceptual principles of his book. First, the "man at the center" was the white yeoman, the core and soul of southern culture. Here Cash echoed and anticipated the Vanderbilt Agrarian Frank L. Owsley and his postwar historical school, as well as a current preoccupation of professional scholars. The second was the "Proto-Dorian bond" of white racial solidarity, which submerged class differences and conflict. In this Cash affirmed Ulrich Bonnell Phillips and anticipated George Fredrickson's recent elaboration of *Herrenvolk* democracy.[2] Overall, Cash's contempt for antebellum mythology of a Cavalier civilization steeped in manners and intellectuality approached the revolutionary, coming as it did from close to the heart of Dixie.

With the New South, Cash introduced his third concept, the "savage ideal." Defeated and thrown back economically, politically, and educationally, white southerners clung tenaciously to their sense of folk and to their God. The latter became more and more tribal, a grim Calvinized Jehovah who tested his chosen people beyond any ancient folk. "In the end," wrote Cash, "almost the only pleasures which might be practiced openly and without moral obloquy were those of orgiastic religion and those of violence" (*Mind,* 136). So was "established what I have called the savage ideal as it had not been established in any Western people since the decay of medieval feudalism, and almost as truly as it is established today in Fascist Italy, in Nazi Germany, in Soviet Russia—and so paralyzed Southern culture at the root" (137). Synthesizing, in effect, the man at the center and the Proto-Dorian bond, Cash's

---

2. See George M. Fredrickson, *The Black Image in the White Mind: The Debate on Afro-American Character and Destiny, 1817–1914* (New York, 1971); and Fredrickson, *White Supremacy: A Comparative Study in American and South African History* (New York, 1981), esp. 154–55, 221–34. See also Ulrich Bonnell Phillips, "The Central Theme of Southern History," *American Historical Review,* XXXIV (October, 1928), 30–43; and Pierre L. van den Berghe, *Race and Racism* (New York, 1967). Among those noticing the similarity of *Herrenvolk* democracy to Cash's savage ideal is Bertram Wyatt-Brown, in *Yankee Saints and Southern Sinners* (Baton Rouge, 1985), 153.

savage ideal summed up the New South to 1940 and demonstrated a doleful continuity from the Old. Thus though Cash shared a perception of New South origins in the Old with such scholars as U. B. Phillips and Broadus Mitchell, Cash's dismissal of Old South/Lost Cause hagiography and his merciless pillorying of the mindless New South worship of progress and industrialism were a most refreshing departure, a significant and enduring contribution.[3]

With the exception of certain Agrarians offended by Cash's irreverence for heroes and for religion, reviewers were pleased with *The Mind of the South*. The book sold about fourteen hundred copies during February and March, 1941, and Alfred Knopf ordered another printing. Cash went to Mexico and to his pathetic death. For the next nineteen years, several thousand cloth-bound copies of the book circulated from college and public libraries and were admiringly perused in the private hands of scholars, journalists, and students. *Mind* was, wrote Dewey Grantham on its twentieth anniversary, "perhaps the most brilliant essay ever written on the Southern character," a work deserving (as it indeed was) to be "studied in classrooms and book groups throughout the country." Much later Joel Williamson grasped, I think, the essence of *Mind*'s lengthy tenure. "The Cashian view of the cultural history of the South gained high credibility, in part, because *there was no one to challenge it,*" he wrote. "After 1941 if one needed to say something, almost anything, about the Southern ethos, one simply cited Cash and moved confidently and comfortably on."[4]

Cash's posthumous influence was hugely magnified in February, 1960, when Knopf reissued *Mind* in paper—an important event of the "paperback revolution" in so-called "quality" books just beginning. A second printing followed in August. Knopf's timing could hardly have been more propitious. The most confrontational and engrossing phase of the civil rights movement was about to begin, and journalistic as well as scholarly craving for insights into the region reached the obsessive. *Mind* became the essential guide, the "veritable Baedeker to the boon-

---

3. In addition to Cash himself, on his debunking of southern mythology and its significance see Richard H. King, *A Southern Renaissance: The Cultural Awakening of the American South, 1930–1955* (New York, 1980), 146–72, esp. 152.

4. Dewey W. Grantham, "Mr. Cash Writes a Book," *Progressive,* XXV (1961), 40–42; King, *Southern Renaissance,* 40; Joel Williamson, *The Crucible of Race: Black-White Relations in the American South Since Reconstruction* (New York, 1984), 3 (emphasis added).

docks," as David Hackett Fischer put it in 1970. C. Vann Woodward
had already observed Cash's magic among readers—his "bold simplifi-
cations, the memorable formulas, the striking symbols, and the felici-
tous phraseology" had earned "unstinted praise [that] would gratify the
vanity of any author." Woodward ventured "to guess that no other
book on Southern history rivals Cash's in influence among laymen and
few among professional historians."[5]

Many of the professionals assigned the new paperback to undergraduate students, deepening Cash's entrenchment. Then in 1965, as
the civil rights movement reached its apogee in Montgomery, professionals created an influential historiographical anthology called *Writing
Southern History,* which virtually enshrined *The Mind of the South.* There
are nine citations of Cash in the text, most with enthusiastic approba-
tion. James C. Bonner reaffirmed the Proto-Dorian bond. Herbert J.
Doherty thought Clement Eaton's intellectual history exceeded Cash's
only in depth of research and credibility, for Eaton also perceived white
southerners' guilt over slavery at the center of antebellum thinking and
behavior. Horace H. Cunningham praised Cash's treatment of the New
South "mind" with but mild reservation. George Tindall suggested
Mind as a model for "folk history." And Dewey Grantham again celebrated "Wilbur J. Cash's brilliant essay on the southern character."[6]

So the Cash paradigm towered tallest just before the barrages that
brought it down—if I may follow Gene Wise (who followed Thomas
Kuhn) on the unmaking of historical interpretations. At least two shots
had already been fired. In the middle of his 1961 essay Dewey Grantham inserted portentous criticism between the accolades. Cash's "major thesis," Grantham wrote, "is the continuity of the Southern mind."

5. David Hackett Fischer, *Historians' Fallacies: Toward a Logic of Historical Thought*
(New York, 1970), 220; C. Vann Woodward, "The Elusive Mind of the South," in
Woodward, *American Counterpoint: Slavery and Racism in the North-South Dialogue* (Bos-
ton, 1971), 263.

6. Richard King recalls reading Cash as an undergraduate at Chapel Hill during
the 1960s in *Southern Renaissance,* viii. (I read *Mind* first as an undergraduate in 1961,
again as a graduate student in 1963.) In *Writing Southern History: Essays in Historiography
in Honor of Fletcher M. Green,* ed. Arthur S. Link and Rembert W. Patrick (Baton Rouge,
1965), see James C. Bonner, "Plantation and Farm: The Agricultural South," 147–84
(esp. 150); Herbert J. Doherty, "The Mind of the Antebellum South," 198–223 (esp.
201); George B. Tindall, "Southern Negroes Since Reconstruction," 337–66 (esp. 359);
Horace H. Cunningham, "The Southern Mind Since the Civil War," 383–409 (esp.
384); and Dewey W. Grantham, "The Twentieth Century South," 410–44 (esp. 442).
(The index to *Writing Southern History* offers eight citations of Cash; I counted nine.)

This was "undoubtedly a valuable corrective to the popular stereotype that draws a sharp distinction between the Old and the New South, and to the professional historians' habit of dividing the past into well-defined periods." Yet Grantham thought Cash committed serious errors of selection and emphasis in order to support continuity. "The result is that a certain unreality attaches itself to his treatment of such historical developments as Populism and to the social and economic implications of industrialism. For it can be argued with greater logic, perhaps, that these developments are evidence of class conflict, of political dissent, and of a society racked by profound internal disagreement." Grantham did not specify the scholarly sources of his doubts about Cash's central theme, but he almost certainly had in mind Vann Woodward's first book, a biography of the Populist Tom Watson published three years before *Mind;* Vernon Wharton's and George Tindall's postwar works on blacks and race relations in Mississippi and South Carolina; Woodward's great books of the 1950s on the 1877 Compromise, the New South's origins, and the history of Jim Crow—and probably Grantham's own recent work on the late nineteenth-century South.[7] All this scholarship revealed considerable conflict and discontinuity in southern history.

A second shot was Allen J. Going's curt dismissal in 1965—unaccompanied by praise—which was the great exception to the Cashfest in *Writing Southern History*. "W. J. Cash's famous work on the continuity of the southern mind rejects the concept of a dichotomy within the New South and its sharp break with the Old," wrote Going, who had no patience with Cash's subordination of southern Populism within a vague national farmers' protest against the East. Going recommended instead Woodward's *Origins of the New South* as "provid[ing] the clearest understanding and most significant interpretation of the agrarian revolt."[8]

---

7. Gene Wise, *American Historical Explanations: A Strategy for Grounded Inquiry* (Homewood, Ill., 1973), esp. 179–359; Grantham, "Mr. Cash Writes a Book," 41. See also Vernon Lane Wharton, *The Negro in Mississippi, 1865–1890* (Chapel Hill, 1947); George Brown Tindall, *South Carolina Negroes, 1877–1900* (Columbia, S.C., 1952); C. Vann Woodward, *Reunion and Reaction: The Compromise of 1877 and the End of Reconstruction* (Boston, 1951); Woodward, *Origins of the New South, 1877–1913* (Baton Rouge, 1951); Woodward, *The Strange Career of Jim Crow* (New York, 1957); Dewey W. Grantham, *Hoke Smith and the Politics of the New South* (Baton Rouge, 1958).

8. Allen J. Going, "The Agrarian Revolt," in *Writing Southern History*, ed. Link and Patrick, 375.

When Vann Woodward himself at last leveled big guns at Cash in 1967, 1969, and 1971 (and yet again in 1986 and 1989), paradigm degradation hastened to rubble. Writing first in the *New Republic,* then the *New York Times Magazine,* and expanding somewhat in his essay collection *American Counterpoint,* Woodward fired on broad fronts: Cash's southern "mind" was narrowly parochial and manifestly anti-intellectual. He entitled a book *Mind* whose thesis was "no mind." Woodward suggested instead "The Temperament of the South," "The Feelings of the South," and "The Mindlessness of the South" as more descriptive of Cash's contents. (Too bad that *mentalité* was not yet *au courant* in the United States, but this might have confused the attack.) Jefferson, Madison, and Calhoun barely appear in Cash—William Byrd II, John Taylor of Caroline, John Randolph of Roanoke, John Marshall, George Fitzhugh, Edmund Ruffin, Hugh Legaré, and Alexander H. Stephens not at all. There is no late eighteenth-century Enlightenment, no mid-nineteenth-century "Reactionary Enlightenment" (Louis Hartz's term), exemplified by Fitzhugh. No wonder that recently Michael O'Brien—who has begun to rescue and redefine nineteenth-century southern intellectual history—declared that "*The Mind of the South* has immeasurably inhibited the study of the mind of the South."[9]

Woodward's exposure of *Mind*'s mindlessness perhaps overshadowed at the time his more important criticism of Cash, which appeared in the last dozen pages of *American Counterpoint*. This concerned what Woodward termed "the warp and woof" of Cash's book—"*the thesis of unity* and *the thesis of continuity*—the fundamental unity of the Southern mind and people, a spiritually solid South, and the continuity of Southern history." *Mind*'s very "integrity" depended upon "the soundness of these two theses," Woodward argued. Allowing first that there is no history of any people at all without coherence—or continuity and unity—Woodward wisely exonerated Cash from "anticipating the consensus school of American history by more than a decade": unlike Daniel Boorstin and other writers of the 1950s, Cash had "genuine insight

9. C. Vann Woodward, "White Man, White Mind," *New Republic,* CLVII (December, 1967), 28–30; Woodward, "American History (White Man's Version) Needs an Infusion of Soul," *New York Times Magazine,* April 20, 1969, pp. 32–33, 108–14 (reprinted as "Clio with Soul," *Journal of American History,* LVI [June, 1969], 5–20); Woodward, "The Elusive Mind of the South," 264–65; Michael O'Brien, "A Private Passion: W. J. Cash," in O'Brien, *Rethinking the South: Essays in Intellectual History* (Baltimore, 1988), 179.

into class relationships." Cash's great fallacy was locked into his greatest contribution, the Proto-Dorian white consensus, which frustrated economic interests by class. Cash erred through emphasis and selection (as Grantham had posited in 1961). Woodward suggested a contextural explanation for Cash's themes of unity and continuity. "Perhaps it was because Cash wrote toward the end of the longest and most stable of successive [southern] orders," he wrote, "the one that lasted from 1877 to the 1950s, that he acquired his conviction." But to Woodward and other historians who had survived the 1960s, the region's past "would seem to be characterized more by *dis*continuity, one trait that helps account for the distinctiveness of the South and its history." In a collection of essays published in 1989, Woodward's contexturalism became an operative imperative for historians: "With the unprecedented acceleration of the rate of change resulting from [the] Second World War, and with terrifying innovations and discontinuities tumbling one over another," he declared, "historians of any awareness of how much was being replaced are *obliged* to shift their emphasis from continuities to discontinuities."[10]

Context, indeed—in this case one of often violent change—would appear to explain this belated discovery of Cash's fallacies. First, an age of black revolt could not support a "white mind" merely haunted by African-southerners. In 1956—the year of the Montgomery Improvement Association's bus boycott—Kenneth M. Stampp published *The Peculiar Institution,* a long, neoabolitionist treatment of slavery emphasizing brutality and rebellion and based on Stampp's liberal assumption "that innately Negroes *are,* after all, only white men with black skins, nothing more, nothing less." Only three years later appeared Stanley M. Elkins' brilliantly wrong *Slavery: A Problem in American Institutional and Intellectual Life,* which proposed by "extended metaphor" that American slaves behaved as docile children because, like Nazi concentration camps, slavery was a "closed system," institutionally and psychologically. African-Americans were offended, and by the time Stokeley Carmichael raised the cry of "Black Power" in 1966, a few white scholars, too, were beginning to accept the notion and the substance of African-American cultural identity. The unhappily coincidental publication of William Styron's historical novel *The Confessions*

10. Woodward, "The Elusive Mind of the South," 271, 273, 275–76; last quotation from Woodward, *The Future of History* (New York, 1989), 73 (emphasis added).

of Nat Turner—and its award of the Pulitzer Prize for fiction in 1967—provoked a furious reaction from black intellectuals. Styron, a white native of Virginia, had arrogantly assumed a black rebel's voice and soul. Styron erred historically, critics declared, and demeaned a famous figure.[11]

Out of the turmoil over Stampp's naïveté, Elkins' challenging hypotheses, the Styron novel, and the cultural renaissance associated with Black Power, however, there evolved during the 1970s a sophisticated new black history. It was a conceptual world most whites had not imagined in Cash's time, the high age of Jim Crow. For a while black history probably represented the best of the American new social history. Black scholars such as John Blassingame, Leslie Howard Owens, Nathan Irvin Huggins, Nell Irvin Painter, Albert Raboteau, and Thomas Holt pursued it—as did such white historians as Woodward, Lawrence Levine, and especially Eugene D. Genovese, who by 1970 had emerged as the preeminent historian of the Old South and of slavery.[12]

Genovese's first book, *The Political Economy of Slavery* (1965), created a sensation. The young Marxist insisted that a relatively small number of planters—self-consciously and determinedly antibourgeois—maintained hegemony over the Old South, finally carrying most of the slave country to fatal confrontation with the Yankees. Genovese's slave-based economy (much like U. B. Phillips') was hopelessly inefficient and uneconomic. Cash's man at the center, the yeoman, was merely a

11. Kenneth M. Stampp, *The Peculiar Institution: Slavery in the Ante-Bellum South* (New York, 1956), vii; Stanley M. Elkins, *Slavery: A Problem in American Institutional and Intellectual Life* (New York, 1959); William Styron, *The Confessions of Nat Turner: A Novel* (New York, 1966); John Henrik Clarke, ed., *William Styron's Nat Turner: Ten Black Writers Respond* (Boston, 1968). I have written at greater length about the Styron-Turner controversy in *Media-Made Dixie: The South in the American Imagination* (Baton Rouge, 1978), 124–30.

12. See John W. Blassingame, *The Slave Community: Plantation Life in the Antebellum South* (New York, 1972; rev. ed. 1979); Leslie Howard Owens, *This Species of Property: Slave Life and Culture in the Old South* (New York, 1976); Nathan Irvin Huggins, *Harlem Renaissance* (New York, 1971); Nell Irvin Painter, *The Exodusters: Black Migration to Kansas After Reconstruction* (New York, 1977); Albert J. Raboteau, *Slave Religion: The "Invisible Institution" in the Antebellum South* (New York, 1978); Thomas Holt, *Black over White: Negro Political Leadership in South Carolina During Reconstruction* (Urbana, 1977). Woodward heralded, in effect, black history, in the "Clio with Soul" article cited above. See also Lawrence Levine, *Black Culture and Black Consciousness* (New York, 1977). Genovese's relevant works are cited below.

pawn and ally to the planter, marginal in Genovese's scheme. Curiously, Cash is not mentioned, save incidentally and favorably in a note.[13] If Genovese, like Woodward, had not yet grasped the chasm between his own work and Cash's main themes, he was not long in the reckoning. In *The World the Slaveholders Made* (1969), Genovese leveled artillery of his own, seemingly in concert with Woodward's bombardment, in a war over more than the honor of a dead writer. How shall American (not merely southern) history be characterized and periodized? How does change occur? "Cash's *Mind of the South*," Genovese wrote, "has probably done more than any other [work] to set the historical profession against the interpretation of the Old South as other than bourgeois." Genovese thought there was "a small irony here, for Cash's argument will serve nicely to refute Cash on this very point"—meaning that Cash's crude frontier could be harnessed to the premodern wagon rather handily. Equally important to Genovese was Cash's identity with more recent liberal presentist scholars who maintained that the southern white mind was racked with guilt over slavery. This Genovese derisively dubbed "guiltomania": "W. J. Cash bears heavy responsibility for the spread of guiltomania; at least his name is the one most often invoked by the patients." Genovese's world of slaveholders was premodern, psychologically unconflicted, and decidedly illiberal.[14]

In his magnum opus, *Roll, Jordan, Roll: The World the Slaves Made* (1974), Genovese combined the best of the newer black history with the analytical tools of Antonio Gramsci to produce a monumental and still-satisfying history of slaves and slavery. The slaves' world may have been created initially by masters, but daily life and labor were shaped and reshaped by a dialectical relationship between paternalistic masters on one hand and slaves, living within a distinctive "black nation" based largely on black Christianity, on the other. Slaves generally accepted paternalism's obligations and exploited them, often beyond white-conceived limits, all the while enriching their "black national culture."

13. Eugene D. Genovese, *The Political Economy of Slavery: Studies in the Economy and Society of the Slave South* (New York, 1965), 128, 146, and *passim*.

14. Eugene D. Genovese, *The World the Slaveholders Made: Two Essays in Interpretation* (New York, 1969), 137, 144. Other than Cash, patients of "guiltomania" include Clement Eaton, Kenneth Stampp, and Charles Sellers, among many others. An excellent recent discussion of the phenomenon is Gaines M. Foster, "Guilt over Slavery: A Historiographical Analysis," *Journal of Southern History,* LVI (November, 1990), 665–94.

Cash had been utterly innocent of such a culture. Stampp had perhaps an inkling. Elkins was undone.[15]

Eugene Genovese also played a central role in another elemental development in the historiography of slavery. This was the emergence of the comparative approach, which, among American scholars, began with anthropologist Frank Tannenbaum's *Slave and Citizen* in 1946, then quickened after Stanley Elkins suggested further institutional differences between slavery in Latin-Catholic and Anglo-Protestant countries. The first of David Brion Davis' magisterial *Problem of Slavery* volumes appeared in 1966, and soon Genovese, Woodward, and others were reading French, Spanish, Portuguese, and Dutch works. The appearance in 1969 of Philip D. Curtin's *Atlantic Slave Trade: A Census* expedited comparative labors with credible data on live African immigrants to the Western Hemisphere, by country, and censuses of African-Americans at emancipations. Genovese devised the first sensible scheme for evaluating the treatment of slaves in different countries, and Woodward exploited Curtin's data brilliantly, finding that in every Latin-Catholic country, Africans' population growth rate was negative over the course of slavery. In North America the rate was not only positive, but Africans multiplied ten times over in little more than two centuries, an essential for creation of the black nation-within-a-nation.[16]

Among historians of the African-American South—then of many other subjects—it was Eugene Genovese who was principally responsible for introducing Antonio Gramsci's conceptual vocabulary of class rule— "hegemony," including hegemonic ideology, which renders underclasses "marginal" (*i marginali*). By the 1970s (but especially in the 1980s), as Genovese and others rewrote the history of slaves, expanding and vastly complicating southern and all other historical studies, the Gramscian vocabulary came to guide many historians' discourse and

15. Eugene D. Genovese, *Roll, Jordan, Roll: The World the Slaves Made* (New York, 1974), esp. xv–xvii, 2–7, 280–84, and 661–65.

16. Frank Tannenbaum, *Slave and Citizen: The Negro and the Americas* (New York, 1946); David Brion Davis, *The Problem of Slavery in Western Culture* (Ithaca, 1966); Eugene D. Genovese, "The Treatment of Slaves in Different Countries: Problems in the Applications of the Comparative Method," in *Slavery in the New World: A Reader in Comparative History,* ed. Genovese and Laura Foner (Englewood Cliffs, N.J., 1969), 202–10; Woodward, *American Counterpoint,* 47–77 and esp. 78–106. Woodward's interest in the comparative approach exceeded the limits of the South and slavery; see Woodward, *The Future of the Past* (New York, 1989), 53–74, 131–44.

their research. Other racial and ethnic minorities—the unenslaved working classes everywhere—and homosexuals all were marginal and deserved attention on their own terms. Then suddenly women, of all colors and classes, became *marginale,* and a new scholarly enterprise was under way. Cash's world had been masculine as well as white, with pedestalized white women serving mainly as abstractions and fantasies, earthy black women as workers and whores. Cash's Freudianism, indeed, must be yet another significant dimension of his paradigm's demise; for the founder of psychoanalysis, who never could figure females, was about to meet his own demise in the renewed international feminism.[17]

Anne Firor Scott published a pioneering small work on the southern white "lady" in 1970, just at the flood of the new feminism in the United States but before the women's studies phenomenon materialized. Following pathbreaking studies of women and social relations in northern cities, during the 1980s women's history came south in earnest. Among the notable resulting works were Jean E. Friedman's history of white women and nineteenth-century church communities (1985), Jacqueline Jones's ambitious book on black women in slavery and freedom (1985), Suzanne Lebsock's study of the white and black free women of Petersburg, Virginia (1984), and Elizabeth Fox-Genovese's theoretically ambitious and controversial work on black and white women in antebellum plantation households (1988).[18]

Such gendering of historical studies led at last to critical appraisals of masculine culture—as opposed to unconscious assumption making,

17. On Gramsci (whose *Prison Notebooks* was not yet translated into English in the late 1960s) and Genovese, see Eugene D. Genovese, *In Red and Black: Marxian Explorations in Southern and Afro-American History* (1971; rpr. Knoxville, 1984), esp. 391–421 (the essay in these pages was first published in a small magazine in 1967). Genovese has not been so much concerned with marginals as have his many admirers. An excellent example of Gramsci-inspired southern history, focusing on marginals and their culture, is Jacquelyn Dowd Hall, James Leloudis, Robert Korstad, Mary Murphy, Lu Ann Jones, and Christopher B. Daily, *Like a Family: The Making of a Southern Cotton Mill World* (Chapel Hill, 1987). On Cash's Freudianism see King, *Southern Renaissance,* esp. 160 (although feminists' hostility to Freud is not pertinent to King's discussion).

18. Jean E. Friedman, *The Enclosed Garden: Women and Community in the Evangelical South, 1830–1900* (Chapel Hill, 1985); Jacqueline Jones, *Labor of Love, Labor of Sorrow: Black Women, Work, and the Family from Slavery to the Present* (New York, 1985); Suzanne Lebsock, *The Free Women of Petersburg: Status and Culture in a Southern Town, 1784–1860* (New York, 1984); Elizabeth Fox-Genovese, *Within the Plantation Household: Black and White Women of the Old South* (Chapel Hill, 1988).

as in Cash's day and long afterward. In 1985 Elliott J. Gorn, a historian
of sport—a subject appropriate to gendered history—examined men's
carousing and informal fighting customs on the southern frontier.
More recently, Ted Ownby has assayed masculine recreations and evangelicals' struggle against them from the Civil War to the 1920s. Ownby
confronted W. J. Cash directly, disputing Cash's assertion that hedonism and religiosity coexisted in the southern psyche. In Ownby's
South the two were at war increasingly from the 1880s or so, until the
evangelicals restricted and controlled men's boozy, sanguinary fun early
in this century.[19] Cash's hedonist/evangelical men may have actually existed, following Ownby's chronology, in the interwar years of Cash's
personal observation, when evangelical reform had forced men to confront previously separate and irreconcilable traditions.

Ownby's southern white men are not the near-anarchical individ-
ualists Cash (and many others) described, but rather are conformist
creatures not yet socialized to modern conventions. Ownby built upon
Bertram Wyatt-Brown's and Edward Ayers' incorporation of insights
from European historiography and anthropological theory in their
works on honor, modernization, and behavior. Premodern men derive
status from the opinions of their fellows; they are outer-directed. Modern (bourgeois) men and women derive dignity (not honor) from abstract codes of behavior such as religion.[20] Cash more or less had things
backward, with little understanding of the complex and often paradoxical modernizing roles of evangelical religion. The study of southern
religious culture remains a historiographical frontier, however.[21]

In the historiographical groves, meanwhile, from the mid-1970s
through most of the 1980s, a *Kulturkampf* of another sort raged among
southernists. At stake were not so much race or gender as a renewed

19. Elliott J. Gorn, "'Gouge and Bite, Pull Hair and Scratch': The Social Significance of Fighting in the Southern Backcountry," *American Historical Review,* XC (February, 1985), 18–43; Ted Ownby, *Subduing Satan: Religion, Recreation, and Manhood in
the Rural South, 1865–1920* (Chapel Hill, 1990).

20. See Bertram Wyatt-Brown, *Southern Honor: Ethics and Behavior in the Old South*
(New York, 1982); and Edward L. Ayers, *Vengeance and Justice: Crime and Punishment
in the 19th-Century South* (New York, 1984), esp. 9–33.

21. On the newness and incompleteness of religious cultural studies, see John B.
Boles, "The Discovery of Southern Religious History," in *Interpreting Southern History:
Historiographical Essays in Honor of Sanford W. Higginbotham,* ed. Boles and Evelyn
Thomas Nolen (Baton Rouge, 1987), 510–48.

dispute about class, along with interlocking and elemental disagreements over the significance of the Civil War to southern history—was it much of a turning point, after all?—the nature of antebellum culture and its postbellum persistence or nonpersistence, and the identity of the New South leadership. Eventually the sides were tagged Cash versus Woodward (and sometimes Genovese)—or Continuitarians versus Discontinuitarians. By the mid-1980s James C. Cobb exclaimed that "the planter-industrialist dichotomy established by Cash and Woodward has itself become a first-rate specimen of continuity. So powerful is its spell that other historians whose findings fall between the two extremes have found themselves either forced to take sides or simply assigned by reviewers to the Woodward or the Cash camp."[22]

In this curious strife no one spoke for the Continuitarians. They never cohered or, insofar as one may gauge motivations, wanted to cohere, for there was no ideological or demographic common denominator—only research-driven or speculative attachments to Cash's themes of unity and continuity. They were—if I may pursue the martial metaphor one further step—a poor army, a North American version of Afghan rebels, *sans* Pentagon aid. As such, how great a threat did they pose? Anticipating the Soviet withdrawal from Kabul, Woodward himself named and finally spoke for the Continuitarians. The tactics were excellent, but the master seemed as perplexed as he was alarmed by the opposing host.

"The main thrust of criticism [of his theses] in the 1970s and 1980s," wrote Woodward in 1986, "embraced representatives of points across the whole political spectrum." There were young Marxists, conservatives of youthful and middling age, and older liberals. Woodward singled out especially George Tindall, Carl Degler, James Tice Moore, Jonathan M. Wiener, Dwight B. Billings, Jr., and Grady McWhiney. Tindall—on whose early work the theme of discontinuity was partly based—published a collection of essays in 1975 called *The Persistent Tradition in New South Politics,* whose title expressed its thesis. Degler—previously a historian of southern dissent (among other subjects)—offered in 1977 a little book called *Place over Time: The Continuity of Southern Distinctiveness,* which proceeded upon the premise that

22. James C. Cobb, "Beyond Planters and Industrialists: A New Perspective on the New South," *Journal of Southern History,* LIV (February, 1988), 45–68 (quotation 46). (The article is a revision of a paper read late in 1985.)

if the South remained different from the rest of the nation, there must be continuity. Moore wrote an influential historiographical essay on the late nineteenth century which appeared in the August, 1978, number of the *Journal of Southern History*. Surveying political historical scholarship at local, state, regional, and national levels, Moore concluded that the weight of evidence lent "further support to the notion of continuity between Old and New Souths. All things had not changed with Appomattox, much less with the Compromise of 1877." Wiener and Billings published controversial books in 1978 and 1979 on planter-landlord persistence and the industrial movements in Alabama and North Carolina, respectively. Both challenged Woodward directly. Wiener never mentioned Cash, but Billings proclaimed his legitimacy: "My discovery that members of North Carolina's small landed class led in rebuilding and expanding the textile industry gives new credence to W. J. Cash's argument in *The Mind of the South*," he wrote. Cash's "central thesis of the continuity of southern institutions," Billings concluded, was "right on target." McWhiney—writing in 1981 in a conservative journal called, of all things, *Continuity*—persisted in his (and collaborator Forrest McDonald's) pursuit of the timelessness of Celtic ways, from ancient battles to the streets of Dallas, where McWhiney himself jaywalked.[23]

Woodward apparently took no notice of Numan V. Bartley's *Creation of Modern Georgia* (1983), which is the most satisfying state history I have ever read and perhaps the most convincing of Continuitarian-leaning historical works of recent date. During the 1970s, Bartley, a quantifier (who sometimes collaborated with Hugh Davis Graham), wrote political analyses of the tumultuous post–World War II South that revealed considerable persistence of Cash-era white behavior. In the Georgia history, Bartley quoted both Cash and Woodward with admiration; nowhere are there brash paradigmatic announcements. In a brief preface Bartley acknowledged the influence of Wiener and Bil-

---

23. C. Vann Woodward, *Thinking Back: The Perils of Writing History* (Baton Rouge, 1986), 69–70; George B. Tindall, *The Persistent Tradition in New South Politics* (Baton Rouge, 1986); Carl Degler, *Place over Time: The Continuity of Southern Distinctiveness* (Baton Rouge, 1977); James Tice Moore, "Redeemers Reconsidered: Change and Continuity in the Democratic South, 1870–1900," *Journal of Southern History*, XLIV (August, 1978), 357–78 (quotation 378); Jonathan M. Wiener, *Social Origins of the New South: Alabama, 1860–1885* (Baton Rouge, 1978); Billings, *Planters and the Making of a "New South,"* 102, 217; Grady McWhiney, "Continuity in Celtic Warfare," *Continuity: A Journal of History*, I (Spring, 1981), 1–17.

lings but named them in a distant endnote. The text measures change aplenty, sometimes near-chaos, in Georgia's transit from colonial times past those of Martin Luther King, Jr., and Jimmy Carter. In his second chapter, however—a brief masterpiece called "The Cotton Kingdom"—Bartley covers the entire nineteenth century, relegating the Civil War and emancipation to a large blip in the state's continuity of agricultural staple production with a powerless labor force. A chapter on Reconstruction records planters' loss of national political influence but ends with their persistence in power at home. Indeed, Georgia's county seat moguls held sway well past World War II.[24]

With or without Bartley, the Continuitarians' sudden appearance, without collaboration or conventional political identity, demanded explanation. Woodward took the historian's route, where smoking-gun evidence is lacking: it was the times. The lot of Continuitarians represented "in some degree," he wrote, "a common return to the old pre-1950 orthodox ideology of continuity." Following the civil rights and anti–Vietnam War movements there was a relative calm, "something like social stability," so "the chorus of continuity took up where it had left off a generation before." From the mid-1980s, the interregnum of Discontinuitarian history seemed merely "*continuity interuptus.*"[25] The explanation from context may be correct, yet it seems to me to impute a species of primal psychological insecurity to the Continuitarians: honest scholars' interpretations become like a fetal position, assumed for reassurance and oblivion in boring times.

Woodward took comfort nonetheless in the persistence of discontinuity as the theme in many recent and meritorious works—some with origins beyond New Haven. Economist Gavin Wright's *Political Economy of the Cotton South* (1978) termed the changes of the 1860s "massive" and "sudden." Michael Wayne's study of the late antebellum and postbellum Natchez District (1983) and David Carlton's work on industrialization in South Carolina (1983) described profound structural change, even as superficial continuities remained, especially in the Natchez area. Barbara Fields also chose an ante/postbellum chronology

---

24. Numan V. Bartley, *The Creation of Modern Georgia* (Athens, Ga., 1983), *passim*, esp. vii, 16–74, and 127–46. On the Bartley-Graham political histories, see Hugh Davis Graham, "Southern Politics Since World War II," in *Interpreting Southern History,* ed. Boles and Nolen, 401. They "found more Wilbur Cash than Woodward and [V. O.] Key" in their data.

25. Woodward, *Thinking Back,* 70.

in *Slavery and Freedom on the Middle Ground* (1985), establishing dramatic discontinuity in the nineteenth-century history of Maryland.[26] There were many others, notably two more Yale dissertations-cum-monographs, Edward Ayers' *Vengeance and Justice* (1984), a brilliantly executed study of changing definitions of crime and punishment from the late antebellum period to the 1890s, and Steven Hahn's acclaimed history of the Georgia up-country, *The Roots of Southern Populism* (1984).[27] The Civil War and the 1890s mean almost everything in these works, as in Woodward's theses, albeit often in ways no Discontinuitarian had imagined before.

By the time Woodward's imposition of order among Continuitarians found print in 1986, the historiographical civil war seemed to have fizzled. The Discontinuitarians, I think, had won, though not unconditionally. Boredom can end such strife, too, and there has been some peacemaking. Evidence of the former is to be found in John Boles and Evelyn Nolen's collection of historiographical essays, *Interpreting Southern History* (1987), the successor to *Writing Southern History.* Cash appears but three times, briefly and incidentally, never directing discussion of an issue.[28] Bertram Wyatt-Brown appeared as peacemaker—he was never bored with Cash, much less Woodward, his former mentor. In a 1985 essay in *Yankee Saints and Southern Sinners,* Wyatt-Brown suggested a novel placement of Cash's work within the history of historical writing. Woodward, in his intellectual autobiography, *Thinking Back,* located *Mind* at the climax of the Continuitarian New South School. Wyatt-Brown considered *Mind* a model for a future school, the American Studies national character movement, whose heyday was about 1945 to about 1965. This insight enlarges understanding of the sources of attacks on Cash beginning in 1967, for as Wyatt-Brown observed, this "entire mode of writing . . . [*i.e.,* Ameri-

---

26. Gavin Wright, *The Political Economy of the Cotton South: Households, Markets, and Wealth in the Nineteenth Century* (New York, 1978); Michael Wayne, *The Reshaping of Plantation Society: The Natchez District, 1860–1880* (Baton Rouge, 1983); David Carlton, *Mill and Town in South Carolina, 1880–1920* (Baton Rouge, 1982); Barbara Fields, *Slavery and Freedom on the Middle Ground: Maryland During the Nineteenth Century* (New Haven, 1985).

27. Steven Hahn, *The Roots of Southern Populism: Yeoman Farmers and the Transformation of the Georgia Upcountry, 1850–1890* (New York, 1983).

28. Boles and Nolen, eds., *Interpreting Southern History,* 53–54 and n. 8, 260 and n. 10, 401.

can Studies] had come into question. Cash's book had been one of the earliest examples of the genre." Now "Cash and American Studies were out, Marx and Malcolm X were in."[29]

Michael O'Brien is a peacemaker of another sort. Though dismissive of Cash in his own pursuit of nineteenth-century southern intellectual life, O'Brien, like Wyatt-Brown and Richard King, takes seriously Cash's mind in his own time. Cash had failings as a historian, O'Brien wrote in 1989—"an irritating fuzziness, especially of chronology. One is constantly shown change and then told it amounts to little." And, like Woodward and David Hackett Fischer, O'Brien thought "Cash wrote an ingenious book about the development of Southern identity, while he thought he was writing a book about the South." Yet in Cash, O'Brien discovers a fellow Hegelian, "a philosophical Idealist, not only in the crude sense of believing that ideas can be forces in the historical process but also in a more specific dialectical sense. There is the movement of thesis-antithesis-synthesis in the book"—those being, in order, antebellum rural society and landscape, the antislavery movement and Yankee attack, finally the savage ideal and self-conscious nationhood.[30]

James C. Cobb, whose career as a historian of southern industrialization began late in the Cash-Woodward war, has always maintained a principled neutrality. Reviewing the literature from Broadus Mitchell and Cash through Woodward, Wiener, and Billings in 1982 (in his first book), Cobb conceded to the Continuitarians "the durability of the . . . 'conservative modernization' pattern." Yet *conservative* seemed to Cobb not a conclusive term at all, for the South had not only an "agrarian heritage but" also "an 'industrial tradition' approaching centenary status."[31] Two years later, in his synthesis, *Industrialization and Southern Society,* Cobb once more straddled, but sensibly: nineteenth-century modes of economic and political behavior persisted oppressively until the 1940s. Much of the region's industry remained extractive, even into the 1980s. The region's middle class was for a long while

29. Wyatt-Brown, *Yankee Saints and Southern Sinners,* 145–46. Wyatt-Brown's accommodation of Cash began earlier, in a somewhat different version of this essay, "W. J. Cash and Southern Culture," in *From the Old South to the New: Essays on the Transitional South,* ed. Walter J. Fraser, Jr., and Winfred B. Moore, Jr. (Westport, Conn., 1981), 195–214. See also Woodward, *Thinking Back,* 27.

30. O'Brien, "A Private Passion," 182–83, 180.

31. James C. Cobb, *The Selling of the South: The Southern Crusade for Industrial Development, 1936–1980* (Baton Rouge, 1982), 266–67.

small and weak, more a collection of branch office managers and corporate salesmen than entrepreneurs. Factories were often located in rural areas. Consequently, the late twentieth-century industrial South did not become another Northeast or Middle West.[32] Cobb's South is sharply distinct from the North, then, but in this 1984 work and in a later essay Cobb began, I think, to sort out distinctiveness from continuity, a confusion that had muddled issues in the historiographical wars for years. Continuity, discontinuity, and distinctiveness might coexist peaceably—and, more important, empirically.

Finally, two recent essays of surpassing breadth and learning by David Carlton and Steven Hahn—both young Discontinuitarians—expanded understanding and stilled waters. In an early 1990 article, Hahn addressed the subject of rural elites in postemancipation societies, beginning within the framework of the old debate posing premodern landed elites against bourgeois modernizers and seeming at first to attempt an undoing of James Tice Moore's Continuitarian 1978 article. But finally Hahn agreed that postbellum planters—like their counterparts in Prussia, Brazil, and elsewhere—succeeded in cementing alliances with business and persisting in power in virtually all southern states—rather as Moore had argued. But, Hahn continued, unlike Junkers and *fazendeiros,* southern planters almost utterly lost power and influence at the national level. The war and emancipation cost them far more than the value of slaves, and they never recovered.[33]

Carlton, writing later in 1990, addressed issues Wiener and Billings had raised during the late 1970s—the persistence of planters in the New South and, especially in North Carolina, planter leadership of the industrial movement. Carlton acknowledged considerable "continuity in personnel" during the late nineteenth century but argued that Continuitarian scholars had assumed the "proposition, that the enduring

32. James C. Cobb, *Industrialization and Southern Society, 1877–1984* (Lexington, Ky., 1984), 1–3, 136–64, and *passim*. See also Cobb, "Beyond Planters and Industrialists."

33. Steven Hahn, "Class and State in Postemancipation Societies: Southern Planters in Comparative Perspective," *American Historical Review,* XCV (February, 1990), 75–98. Hahn's scope does not include the twentieth century, but large-scale southern agriculturists regained enormous national power (in league especially with western ranchers) during the 1920s and particularly during the 1930s and afterward. See Grant McConnell, *The Decline of Agrarian Democracy* (Berkeley, 1953); and Jack Temple Kirby, *Rural Worlds Lost: The American South, 1920–1960* (Baton Rouge, 1987), esp. 51–79, 334–60.

distinctiveness of the region stems from a fundamental continuity in its social structure." Perceptively concluding (one would certainly hope) Cobb's start at disentangling distinctiveness from continuity, Carlton insisted that planter persistence did not equal "class identity." Leopards may, indeed, change their spots, and planters become bourgeois. Nor, Carlton continued, was the plantation the industrialists' model for factories; rather, the North was that model. Unfortunately for North Carolina, the industrialists built an unbalanced economy that became an unprosperous adjunct of the national market. The New South, in other words, did not become the North. Its modern history is both distinct and discontinuous.

Equally important was Carlton's crediting of W. J. Cash and his followers in broader issues of southern history. "The 'continuitarian' approach," Carlton posited, "has had a salutary impact on our historical understanding, because it has forced us to rethink the distinctions between the Old South and the New, and to recognize the sometimes surprising ways in which the past has shaped modern life."[34]

So has concluded, for the moment, a semicycle of *The Mind of the South*'s strange and fascinating career. From minor *succès d'estime,* Bible, and Baedeker to the boondocks, to insidious influence and impediment to understanding, *Mind* has become at last both a troublesome work of genius and a conduit to enlightenment. This seems to me very appropriate. Cash loved paradox so well. Experience the amphetamine spin of so many of his conclusions, sentences that began "And yet—and yet . . ."

34. David Carlton, "The Revolution from Above: The National Market and the Beginnings of Industrialization in North Carolina," *Journal of American History,* LXXVII (September, 1990), 445–75 (quotations 446).

Mind and Countermind: A Personal Perspective on W. J. Cash's *Mind of the South*

C. ERIC LINCOLN

> A mind is a terrible thing to waste.
> —Slogan of the United Negro College Fund

The South, according to W. J. Cash, is that area of America "roughly delineated by the boundaries of the former Confederate States . . . shading over into some . . . border states . . . [and exhibiting] a fairly definite mental pattern, associated with a fairly definite social pattern [and] a complex of established relationships and habits of thought, sentiments, prejudices, standards and values" (*Mind,* viii). Hence the South, as Cash understands it, is a state of mind geographically defined: a kind of regional *Weltanschauung* that could not exist in the absence of any of its principals. The definition is clear enough, but its utility is seriously emasculated when the principals, as Cash perceives them, are so delimited as to exclude for all practical purposes the one component that makes sense of all the others. Cash's mind of the South is a mind strictly limited by race. It is a *white* mind, in Cash's terms, a "superior mind" of the "best people" to which has been ceded custody, care, and articulation of whatever sentiments and values the lower-class whites may once have claimed for themselves. Black southerners were, of course, "out of mind" altogether, and because they were, the limitations of Cash's excursus begin at the beginning and persist throughout the book.

The South *was* and *is* about Negroes—African-Americans. They figure with implacable pervasiveness in every identifiable interest by

226

which the region is defined: economics, law, jurisprudence, politics, religion, sex, social relations—the list is endless. Take away the black component and the whole notion of "the South" collapses. It becomes unimaginable, like Lawrence of Arabia with no Arabs. The argument will be made, of course, that Cash's "mind of the South" has no black component, not because there were no black people there but because in the prevailing order the black mind (if any) had no voice and was in consequence inconsequential. This is a specious argument: however suppressed and however subliminal it may have been, there was a black mentality, and though privately denied and publicly ignored, it seeped into the ruling white mind extolled by Cash and left an understated impress there for future reference. Cash's decision to go with convention and the alleged "ancient docility" of the African in America left him vulnerable to the questions of a larger, less indulgent reality than the one he wrote about.

I know something about the mind of the South. I was in the South and of the South the same time W. J. Cash was there participating in that "mind" on which he would later unshutter the windows of the big house and give the world a qualified look. Cash was writing about the South projected by the "best white men," by the ruling hegemony. I was part of the South, Cash's South, but by Cash's definition, I was not a part of the southern mind. Nor could I ever be. But I was a part of what that mind-set was all about, and being a Negro, I was the definitive focus of that mind, its *raison d'être*. Leave me out, and the South itself did not, does not, will not exist, and W. J. Cash's daring and intriguing sociological apology self-destructs for want of substance, for want of reason, for want of opportunity. It is mere sound and fury, significant, perhaps, of nothing more serious than "the Southern fondness for rhetoric" (53) to which he laid claim as his heritage. Still, it must be recognized that the most engaging rhetorical romance is not necessarily reliable sociology. No commentary on Yoknapatawpa could be seriously considered which excluded Negroes as a prime ingredient of ambience, and W. J. Cash's more ambitious excursus is no exception. The black presence is indeed a part of an unstated premise by which his book is informed, but it is so subdued by "color" as to render that presence an innocuous, colorful human tapestry restricted to "singing . . . sad songs in the cotton" (viii).

I grew up in Alabama, and if that does not entitle me to membership or participation in the mind of the South, it at least gives reasonable certification to my credentials for commenting on that mind. I am, in Langston Hughes's words, the "darker brother," but to borrow a different imagery from T. S. Eliot, I am also, in W. J. Cash's conceptualization, "form without substance, paralyzed force."[1] But I *do* exist, and with some possible violence to Cartesian logic it is probable that I also think. I concede in advance that mere thinking is not necessarily to think relevantly; perhaps more important in the present instance, nor is it necessarily relevant to those thinking of others about thinking in the challenge to define a relevant mind-set for a way of life perceived to be both significant and unique.

The year *The Mind of the South* was published was the year I dated my emancipation from that mind. I left Alabama in 1941 and headed north to Chicago. I wrote on the lid of the shoe box I carried stuffed with fried chicken, soda biscuits, and my grandma's prayers the feelings that tortured *my* mind:

> Thou are my native state
> But am I proud?
> My being seethes with hate
> And like a cloud
> Cruel scenes flock back to me
> Of greed and death
> Of fear and misery
> Here's to your health.[2]

I was leaving Alabama, I was leaving the South. But how could I have known that I was not necessarily leaving *the mind* of the South? Having come out of the South a little earlier, Cash had already discovered what I was hardly prepared to learn—that the mind of the South "proceeds from the *common* American heritage, and many of its elements are readily recognizable as simply being variations on the primary American theme" (viii, emphasis added). I had judged Alabama in the fitful flare of a miner's lamp struggling against the stygian darkness of that nether world that was "the South" for anyone of African descent. When I had seen a whole lot more of America and my native

---

1. Adapted from T. S. Eliot, "The Hollow Men," in Eliot, *The Complete Poems and Plays* (1930; rpr. New York, 1952), 56.

2. "Toast to My Native State" (Unpublished manuscript in the possession of the author).

state came to encompass that larger universe, I would call back that earlier judgment for modification in the light of a broadened experience.

EXPERIENCING "THE MIND"

I know experientially what Cash was writing about. I know about "black men singing . . . sad songs in the cotton." I know because I was there in the cotton, and I was black. And if I never sang sad songs on such occasions, I heard those who did and cursed them for their resignation. And if I didn't know that the "po' crackers" and the "white trash" Cash refers to as that "vague race lumped together indiscriminately" sprang "for the most part from the convict servants, redemptioners, and debtors" (ix), I did know instinctively to stay away from them. Whatever their origins, po' white trash meant trouble—lots of trouble. And to many a black man that trouble proved terminal. Growing up in the South, I learned about that about the same time I learned my name. But so dread were the consequences of *not* knowing, that instinct was constantly reinforced by precept and by inculcation—every day. Long before I reached puberty my grandma was constant and insistent: "Son, when you have to go in town, go on directly about your business. *Don't have nothing to do with that trash hanging around the courthouse yard.* Don't fight with them redneck boys, and don't even look at them po' white gals. Just do your business and get on back home directly." It was a reasonably effective prescription for survival.

Even the Yankee principal of the missionary school I attended sensed our peril and prayed about it. Once or twice a year she assembled in her office those teenaged boys whose voices had begun to rumble and whose upper lips were beginning to smudge, and after an extended session of fervent prayer and earnest admonition, she would dismiss us with the blessings of God in exchange for faithful promises that whenever we "went abroad," that is, whenever we encountered white folks in general and white women in particular, we would "avert the eyes lest they compromise the soul." It was the same clear warning couched in Yankee religious jargon: Don't give the rednecks, the crackers, the po' white trash any pretext to hang you from a tree or roast you on some lonesome creek bank.

I was in the South. I was one of those boys with a sprinkling of hair on his lip and a voice that alternately rumbled and quavered. And if my life circumstances required that I venture with regularity into the forbidden valley among forbidding people, then my survival depended on how innocuously invisible I could make myself until my fateful foray could be accomplished. Yes, I knew the po' white trash had an unabated lust for my discomfiture and for my blood, that they represented an unrelenting commitment to my nonbeing. At the time, I didn't understand why. It didn't make sense to me. Nor did I know for sure that behind the so-called rednecks, who so readily laid down their Bibles, quit their revivals, and leaped from their pulpits to go "coon huntin'," was all the time the stealthy hand of the "quality white folks," who taught us to hate the "trash" in the first place. Mr. Cash calls these "the best people," and it was not until he laid bare the controlling mind of the South in contrast to the reactive impulses of his "common man" that the vision of "quality" so carefully nurtured in the big house and its derivative institutions began to fade and drip.

I worked for "quality folk" for 50¢ a week and my breakfast, leaving home at three in the morning to be "milk boy" for a small diary. I washed the steel crates of thick, heavy glass bottles and delivered the milk and cream to the front porches of the sleeping gentry until eight in the morning, every morning. My grandpa milked eighteen cows twice a day, every day. For that the "best people" paid him $3.50 a week and praised him for his industry. My grandma washed and ironed for the same family of five white folks of the very best quality, including two elderly spinster ladies whose crinolines and ruffles and shirtwaists kept her busy "rubbing" in a tin tub on our back porch and "pressing" with a pair of sadirons heated in the fireplace from Monday to Saturday every week, winter and summer. For this the "best people" paid her $1.25 and called her "Aunt Mattie" with that peculiar affection and respect quality white folks reserve for their favorite black retainers.

That $5.25 we managed to eke out together, augmented by an additional 35¢ I got in the summertime for watering the flowers and mowing the lawn for another quality family, meant survival. It was also the wages of accommodation to a system that taught us to work without stinting, hate the cracker, be suspicious of the Jew, and maintain a developed sense of contingency to a recognized family of the ruling class. This was the understanding that put bread and salt pork on the tables of the "good," that is, the accommodated Negroes; insured them against "trouble with the law"; kept the po' white trash at bay; sent the white doctor to see them when they were down sick; and brought the white folks they worked for to their funerals when they could work no more.

Despite the official posture of hostility and perceived sacred mission to keep the nigger in his place, there were elements of Cash's "common whites," including the po' white trash, which on occasion (covert though it had to be) carried on relationships with black people, which except for the cultural stigma against such a thing would have been called "friendships." They fished and hunted with blacks, drank rotgut whiskey with blacks, and not infrequently ate and slept with blacks. I was there, and I knew such people and such relationships. Black midwives often "pulled their young uns," and if the color was in conflict with the cause, some black mama took on another child to raise as her own.

SOURCES OF COUNTERMIND

I know about the schools for Negroes Cash talks about. I know first-hand about the South's tardy takeover of the schools for the primary reason of ousting the Yankee schoolmarms from their lairs of black contamination. North Carolina's Charles Brantley Aycock's perception of "Yankee money and Yankee teachers . . . pouring down" and "plainly determined" on educating the Negroes (178) was not without substance. In 1866 the American Missionary Association built a school for freedmen in Limestone County, north Alabama. It was promptly burned by the Ku Kluxers, but the Yankee zeal to "bring enlightenment" to the hapless victims of the South's "peculiar institution" was not to be trampled or discouraged by such arrant intimidation. They built it back. I am glad they did, for if they had not, there would have been no possibility of a high school education for me in my hometown of Athens when I was ready for that venture three-quarters of a century later. High schools were there for the white children but no public schools beyond the sixth grade for blacks in my town and county until 1942, a year after *The Mind of the South* was published.

In a very curious way, I was benefited by that remission. In Athens, at Trinity School, while I was safely in the hands of the Yankee intruders from Boston, New London, New Haven, and other citadels of

Yankee determination, my friends and counterparts "out in the county" were treated by the state of Alabama to five to seven months of "schooling" each school year in one-room shacks with cardboard blackboards, no electricity, and outdoor "closets." In the winter these schools were heated by wood brought by the students and the teacher (who was privileged to work for $30 a month), and when cotton-chopping time arrived in late March and cotton-picking time extended from August into late October or early November, the schools were closed and the black children sent to the fields.

But at Trinity I was fortunate enough to receive the best education available in the area, provided by dedicated New England spinsters who did not teach for money but who bargained their lives and their comfort out of a sense of *ought* the "best people" of the South were unable to entertain, the enlightened fulminations of their own J. L. M. Curry notwithstanding. Even Henry Grady's arguments about white self-interest, which prescribed limited training for the Negro that would "rigidly veto the idea of academic schools for him" (178), but would provide him the elementals of useful labor and inure him against the rape of white women, failed to garner any enthusiasm.

Nevertheless, there clearly was a problem, and it had to be dealt with, and soon. The misguided errantry of the ever-meddlesome Yankees had already loosed upon the South a potentially dangerous horde of benighted Africans, who, deprived of the benign but resolute guidance of their God-appointed "masters," were already slopping noisily at the trough of exported Yankee education, a prospect patently unacceptable to the distressed convolutions of the prevailing southern mentality. The effective answer to so ignominious a threat seemed implicit in the arguments of North Carolina's Charles Brantley Aycock, who reasoned that the best way to defang the Yankee education of Negroes was for the South itself to do the educating. Eventually, Aycock's logic was so compelling that in the face of nothing better it found implementation of a sort. But Aycock's covert hope of truly meaningful education for Negroes was never implemented, of course, for it was never a serious agendum on the southern mind.

Neither, of course, was the African-American mind even an incipient possibility that could ever be a factor of consequence in the determination of southern destiny. Nevertheless, the African mind *was* there and functioning, despite all constraints. I was a case in point. At Trinity I read everything the library could afford and everything my surprised and delighted Yankee schoolmarms could import for me—Walter Scott, Shakespeare, Dryden, Pope, Goethe, Ovid, Pushkin, Plutarch, Milton, Plato, Aesop, Washington Irving, and the Transcendentalists. I also read the entire Bible at least three times. And in one of the barrels of clothing, books, and other reusables sent down from the North to be distributed at the school, I found the works of Karl Marx, Lenin, and Adam Smith and read them *inter alia* with H. G. Wells, Kafka, Victor Hugo, Dostoyevski, Tolstoy, John Dewey, Richard Wright, and all of the poets of the Harlem Renaissance. Twice a week (and any other time I could cadge the key to the school music room) I sat enraptured in another world listening to the music that poured out of the wind-up Victrola that stood gleaming majestically in mahogany and brass, waiting to share the wondrous works of Wagner, Beethoven, Schubert, Verdi, Bach, Strauss, Brahms, Rachmaninoff, and the Fisk Jubilee Singers. Certainly my opportunities were not typical, for none of this would have been possible in any school or academic program the South provided for black children. Nevertheless, thinking was going on among black people at whatever levels of opportunity and experience circumstances happened to permit, and that thinking was inevitably destined to become a countermind to the mind Cash recognized as the only significant expression of the southern perception of reality, past, present, and to come.

In 1942, a year after I quit Alabama for Chicago, the South's takeover program for Yankee-based Negro schools finally took over Trinity, and Camelot ceased to exist in north Alabama, just as it was being choked to death all across the South. The last Yankee principal at Trinity was sent packing; the venerable old New England teachers, who had come out of Mount Holyoke eons before with the gleam of the challenge of enlightenment in their eyes and the dream of Christian service in their hearts, went back at last to limp out their remaining days among their ancestral Yankee roots.

All left save one, a Miss Mildred, who was not a Yankee but a scion of one of Alabama's most prominent cotton-rich families, who as a young woman had offered herself as a teacher at Trinity. She was accepted, although with much fear and trembling for all concerned, and she was promptly disinherited by her family, who thereafter refused all communication with her. The price she paid for her commitment to Christian service or whatever her private motivations may have been can only be guessed at. Nobody heard of her after the dream ended and the denouement began. But the seeds of an alternative worldview of what the South was and what the South should become had already been sown, and not just by the Yankees. The South has always had an independent black mind, and the best evidence of its quality was its prudence of expression in the face of a consummate self-defeating futility. But time harbors a certain benevolence for patience and restraint.

In the places of the Yankee schoolmarms came "colored" teachers, native-born and educated in the ways and wiles of the South. At their head at Trinity there was placed as principal a reliable colored preacher, adept at divining the mind of the South and putting that mind at ease. But the handwriting of things to come was even then on the wall, and in scarcely more than a decade the South's plans for Negro education would experience the most implausible, the most *impossible* surprise. But *Brown* v. *Board of Education* had long been in the making in that *other* mind of the South that had neither been recognized nor explored. And now that mind was in the courts, challenging the settled dogma and bent on reformulating the mind of the South forever. If a mind is a "terrible thing to waste," it can also be a perilous thing to discount or overlook.

COMMUNISM

The southern preoccupation with communism was an aspect of the mind of the South that I rarely encountered while growing up in Alabama. My stumbling upon Marx and Lenin in the charity barrel at Trinity was fortuitous and not a part, I am sure, of any dark Machiavellian attempt at secret Yankee indoctrination. Certainly there was never any discussion or even any mention of communism by any of my teachers. I read communist ideology with the same innocence of intellectual inquisitiveness as I read Thomas Jefferson and Cotton Mather. The cotton mills in my town had been closed, I guess, before I was born. They were still standing there in stark brick surrounded by iron fences, but they were closed, and the whites who lived in the old mill houses were not likely to offer any explanations, even if they had any. The quality white folks were no more forthcoming, at least in my presence, so there was only the vague and shadowy legend that the mills were somehow connected with "Jews" who didn't live in Athens. The whole matter fell into the forbidden category of "white folks' business," which meant that black folks were to "let it alone."

About the only time I heard the word *communist* in Athens was in connection with the Scottsboro Boys. Scottsboro was only thirty or forty miles from where I grew up, so the Scottsboro case was much on the minds and in the covert conversation of black people I knew. The stately old mansion of the venerable Judge James E. Horton, who tried the case, was on my milk route, and I passed through his yard every day. The official wisdom dribbled down from the "white folks," which is to say the responsible ruling class, was that the white girls allegedly raped on a freight train near Scottsboro were "trash" and that "the colored boys who allegedly did it were put up to it by communists down here trying to stir up trouble." These "communists" were usually linked to the "N-Double-A-C-P," which was contemptuously dismissed as a "nigger front for Communist Jews" and which had no known membership in Limestone County, where I lived.

Oddly enough, it was not until I left Alabama in 1941 that I met any real communists, but when I did, there turned out to be a prospective southern connection. On my first job in Chicago at a large North Side hospital, I was almost immediately surrounded by new "white friends," who invited me to their parties, took me to rallies to "free Earl Browder," introduced me to Elizabeth Gurley Flynn, and proposed a free college education for me in Russia if I would join the Young Communist League and agree to "return to Alabama and work for the Party" after my Russian education was completed. When I shared the news of this amazing opportunity with my erstwhile Yankee principal (now expatriated from Alabama, as was I, but still in touch), his response was immediate if not altogether reassuring. The universities they had in Chicago, he said, were better than anything they had in Leningrad, and if I graduated from one of them, I would be under no obligation to go to Alabama or anywhere else to pay for my education. In the meantime, he thought he could obtain a scholarship for me at one of the black colleges in the South. He did, and I went. But even in college in the South, I never did encounter anybody who had any known connections with or advocacy of communism.

Cash's reading of the black response to the issue of communism is essentially correct. First, it was an ism, an ideology. Black people have learned by bitter experience that ideology and its realization are two different things, and even if the ends of ideology are accomplished, they have a way of vanishing or watering down long before the black estate is benefited. The African-American's cold response to communism was not so much a matter of insufficient resentment against things as they were as it was the instinctive realization that it was an ism designed by and for whites, whose primary concern, despite their protestations to the contrary, was their own peculiar interests. Their promise to erase the centuries-old color line and their eager demonstrations to prove their sincerity flew in the face of experience and ran counter to the instincts of survival. Moreover, critical to the black sense of survival was God, who in the black experience had proven Himself more powerful than any ideology and more reliable than any ideologue. Cash calls the communist dream of black involvement "foolish" and "fatuous" in the supposition "that white men of the lower orders could be persuaded to join with [blacks] against their ruling kin" (325). How much more foolish and fatuous must have been the expectation that blacks, whose whole history of past survival and whose expectations for future relief in America were anchored in their faith in God, His justice, and His grace, were going to switch loyalties on the specious lure of social acceptance. Hence if the mind of the South seriously entertained the fear of communist-based Negro equality (362), then the southern claim to "know the Negro" (a convention that never had much credibility) had completely disgraced itself. Black communism was never a threat to the South, or the North, or anywhere else in America. Like other possibilities in a situation so critical that no possibility could be ignored, it was embraced by a few, a *very* few, but it was never the great hope of the black masses. Nor could it ever be. God got there first.[3]

THE MIND OF RELIGION

This brings us inevitably to the question of religion and derivative concepts in the official mind Cash writes about. His ruminations on this subject are disconcerting to say the least, and pursued to their logical conclusions (if indeed there be any logic lurking undetected in their allegations), they raise dire questions that are troublesome about the locus of moral responsibility in the mind of the South.

According to Cash, the southern mentality is informed by two conflicting, compelling interests—puritanism and hedonism. But curiously, these "incompatible tendencies . . . [never] come into open and

---

3. See, however, Robin D. G. Kelly, *Hammer and Hoe: Alabama Communists During the Great Depression* (Chapel Hill, 1990).

decisive contention" and are "without conscious imposture" (60). More curious still is Cash's categorical denial of "hypocrisy." "Far from it," he avers. Perhaps "a sort of social schizophrenia," he admits with measured reluctance, but "more simply and more safely . . . it was all part and parcel of that naïve capacity for unreality which was characteristic of him" (60), that is, the southerner. If Cash is right, then the unfortunate southerner of whatever class is to be more pitied than blamed, for he is a mere creature of the characteristic unrealities through which he views the world and no less the subject of his unrestrained passions than the savage African he charged himself, as the left hand of God, to tame and civilize. How abysmally tragic that is, if true; but Gunnar Myrdal, who wrote on the American mentality about the same time as Cash, was considerably less accepting. Myrdal thought the incongruity between religious precept and moral performance to be so disturbing that he labeled it a national dilemma characteristic of American behavior, the South not excepted. If Myrdal is creditable, then Cash walks the narrow rim of casuistry. History is still assessing the effects (if not the culpability) of the South's prolonged commitment to what appears to be an inordinate self-indulgence protected by some miraculous, immanent immunity lodged securely in its private imaginings. Above the noisome debate it has engendered, the burden of that commitment still falls where it always did—on the unfortunates who, if they were ever aware that it was taking place, were seldom permitted to address it.

In the long run, however, the ultimate impairment must lie in the redefinition of the religion that was once thought by many to be the common worldview undergirding the Republic without reference to race or region (and by the grace of God), to be clearly within the capabilities of all Americans of reasonable understanding. After so many centuries of sober acceptance it is disquieting to be suddenly challenged with the possibility that those Americans most avid and most demonstrable in their religious commitment were, alas, by some irreversible tragic flaw, barred from the realization of their spiritual efforts and blind to the realities of their own delinquency.

Could this be the burden of Cash's apologetic? I do not think so. The disarming candor with which he approaches even the most intimate foibles of the southern mind suggest an earnestness and sincerity that must not be discredited on this troublesome issue of moral schizophrenia, critical as it is to the understanding of a pattern of behavior with such awesome consequences for so many millions of people for so many hundreds of years. Yet if Cash's assessment of the southerner's moral naïvete is taken at face value, then his whole appraisal of the mind of the South seems a gratuitous exercise. It cannot mean anything, because the people he writes about are rendered puppets to forces over which they have no control, involved in the pursuit of a spectrum of manifest behavior that can have no moral consequences (84). Hence the roasting of a nigger and the roasting of a shoat are alike experiences in the same spectrum of plausibility. And blaming the Yankee for making the South hate Negroes (116–17) is acceptable logic in a world-view of such distressed realities. The strange psychological gymnastics (so troublesome to contemporary apologists) that "explain" how a Christian "master" could beget children by the black women he owned and controlled, declare them surplus, and sell them for money suddenly clicks into focus when seen through W. J. Cash's prism of the mind of the South. And the taboo that forbids to this day any recognition of kinship between the millions of blacks and whites who continue to share the southern region a hundred years or more after the last African-American innocent of "Col. Bascombe's" meanderings was born there underscores the intensity with which the mind of the South remains successfully battened down against the obvious and remains contemptuous of any "logic" not its own. But sooner or later logic has a way of managing its own manifestation. There is an Ashanti proverb that reminds us

> If you sow wild peppers to the wind
> they will sprout around your feet.

THE RULING MIND

Despite his courage in the effort to offer a plausible analysis of his own cultural roots, W. J. Cash was fettered by the very conventions and perceptions he labored to explain. He was a creature of his own times and of his own class, and he was sacked in the same spiritual haircloth that afflicted the people he wrote about. In consequence, his commitment to the illusion that the ruling mind is the only mind of moment is instinctive, but the lessons of history, ancient, recent, and contemporary, must not be permitted to stand for nothing.

> Nations and empires rise and decline
> Princes and prelates rule for a day[4]

The ruling mind is not invulnerable to the vagaries of change; and even when change appears to be precipitous and without reasonable cause, in the province of human affairs the evidences of previously unrecognized cerebral ferment will likely surface in the afterbirth. There is no smoke until the gun is fired.

At the very time that Cash was being hailed for his disclosure of the traditional establishment mind of the South, a countermind that was destined to change the South forever was taking on definition in the form of a civil rights revolution. It was a different mind-set that ere long would augur a somber reappraisal of that "ancient and docile" Negro the white South contended it knew "through and through" (326). A new and unanticipated reality was looming on the horizon, and the Negro the ruling mind knew so well stood up in graceless betrayal of that dogma. Suddenly a mind admitted to exist only in the embryonic craftiness extolled in the homilies of old Uncle Remus was about to break through the carefully crafted iron mesh of three centuries of political and cultural restraint in a public demonstration of maturity and independence, and the stubborn calculatedness with which the ruling mind of the South dismissed lesser minds would be painfully ruptured. The cultivated obliviousness of the Nat Turners, David Walkers, Frederick Douglasses, Harriet Tubmans, Richard Allens, and Henry Turners in favor of a more comforting vision of darkies in the cotton singing away their miseries proved shortsighted in the long run and left the South ill-prepared to confront and worse prepared to understand the sudden arrival of the future on the heels of World War II.

The truth is that the future symbolized by *Brown* v. *Board of Education,* which seemed to fall on Dixie like an intruding comet in 1954 trailing fire and ice all across America, was not a cataclysmic arrival at all. There had always been that *other* mind. There had always been that muted *countermind,* denied expression, but there nonetheless. There is such a mind in every repressive society, building its venires, weighing its options, waiting to be heard. Such is the lesson implicit in the disintegration of the Soviet empire and the dismantling of South Africa, where the ruling minds ran to communism and apartheid while the

---

4. "Return O Lord," in C. Eric Lincoln, *This Road Since Freedom* (Durham, 1990), 59.

counterminds were bent on freedom. The time must come for the people to be heard, "or the very stones will cry out" (Luke 19:40).

It has been fifty years, a scant half-century, since Cash's southern exposure titillated the literati, baffled the historians, and outraged the folks back home. He probably convinced no one, least of all those missing from his assessment of what mattered and who made that determination.

America has changed a lot since then. The industries that brought progress to the South are now taking that progress to Japan and Korea. The cotton mills that damned the unions, exploited the poor whites, and disdained the Negroes have gone to Hong Kong and Taiwan. The communism the South fretted about is in serious decline all over the world and has long been a dead horse and a dead issue in the catalog of black political aspiration. The Ku Klux Klan, that alleged "authentic folk movement" (346), is authentic no longer. It remains nonetheless a public shrine for the rallying of a diverse collectivity of unrepentant ankle biters unwilling to accept any part of the painfully wrought, still emergent new dispensation history has decreed for any world we may know tomorrow. This new dispensation is symbolized in America by the transition of those same muted black voices singing in the cotton yesterday, who are found increasingly in more respected environments today, sharing with their erstwhile "keepers" the delicate decisions determining the welfare of a common constituency. This is true progress. This is as it should be.

The mind of the South that Cash wrote about, the mind that imagined itself to be the projection of the Virginia aristocracy or of origins equally distinctive, would be hard put to explain the leadership of Virginia today, because the old distinctions between the "best people," "the common people," and the "trash" are increasingly blurred. The opportunities for education at all levels are vastly improved, though the South remains at the low end of the national average. A less restrictive mobility renders the old conventional social typologies and classifications increasingly hazardous and unreliable, even despite a still formidably resistant color line.

Rub the carefully cultivated, relaxed patina of the southern professional or businessman, and as likely as not you will find a transplanted Yankee. The "good ol' boys" who used to be dismissed as trash have modified their image and their style. Once they draw the curtains of the voting booth, they are as likely to vote Republican as they are to hew the line that once made the South solid in politics and sentiment. The

Solid South has gone the way of the bustle. It exists only in the eye of the most nostalgic beholder. Among the remaining critical symbols of Cash's mind of the South, the cult of white womanhood, though still sacred to the sensitivities that guard the heroic image of the southern white male, has been grievously threatened and confused, not by the lust of the savage African but by the determination of the southern white woman herself. She has dared to trade in her romantic pedestal for the level ground of the office, the courtroom, the pulpit, the marketplace, the halls of academe, and wherever else the appreciation of her mind (rather than of her symbol) will take her. It was her decision to make, and she made it. If there is any attendant trauma, it does not seem to be hers.

Racial intermarriage, that most improbable, impossible renunciation of the most critical underpinnings of the mind of the South, has not been a salient feature of the new order of things in the South. Such decisions remain essentially a matter of private judgment and personal decision, but the people who have made that decision do not appear to be of the trashier classes of either race, as was the universal presumption in times past. Today's statistical profiles suggest quite the contrary. Times change if minds do not.

BLACK CHURCH

Finally, in the fifty years since Cash, the decline of religion and of the church as the principal arbiter of social behavior and social acceptability is perhaps the most critical index of a region in the throes of change. That the whole nation has taken a serious turn toward secularity is one thing, but the notion that the South could be a part of that same spiritual erosion is another. The South has always counted itself God's special preserve, and upon that notion rested the principal foundation stones of that region's call to trial and suffering, its oblique reading of righteousness and providential trust, and its expectation of a triumphant Armageddon in the end. Under the leadership of a class of pontifical preachers who obligingly capped the free will and individual responsibility of Methodism with the fixed destiny of Calvinism, the hedonism the South could not abandon and the puritanism it could not escape were forced to live together in the same house, but it could find in that arrangement a divine sanction for an otherwise improbable reading of Christian responsibility and spiritual health. So emerged a tribal deity safely unsusceptible to the childish complaints of the heathen Africans or to the raucous yowlings of the Yankees and all others not bona fide supplicants at the shrine of southern destiny.

It was the fixity of divine decree that established the proper place for everyone who was a participant in God's scheme of things. Critical to this arrangement and its maintenance was the preacher, the vicegerent of the tribal deity charged with the ordering of the society through the ordering of the faith in accordance with the order of the preferences and responsibilities mutually understood and agreed upon. It was the preacher who could stave off God's wrath or bring on God's blessings. It was the preacher who could invoke an eternity of hellfire and damnation upon spiritual sluggards, evil-minded Yankees, the black sons of Ham, and all others who implicitly or explicitly challenged the Way of the Chosen as interpreted by those called to that task.

But change was not on the side of the cloth. Ecumenism in the form of denominational mergers transcending the demographics of politics and personal preferences weakened the absolutism of the local preachers and forced the recognition (if not the consideration) of ideas and ideologies that were sometimes alien to the southern temper. Southern and northern Baptists, Methodists, and Presbyterians who went their separate ways a hundred years earlier over "unreconcilable" issues of the Civil War did find reconciliation after all (*mutatis mutandis,* of course). And even the blacks who were the root cause of the century-old schisms found new arrangements of sorts for their accommodation in the reconstituted churches, should they choose to accept them. The vast majority did not, of course, opting overwhelmingly in favor of the black denominations, which found little recognition and less consideration in the official mind of the South. But the black church had a mind of its own. It was the genesis, the womb, the sustainer, and the projector of the countermind that would eventually challenge the ruling mind of the South and would ultimately humanize its determinations in the interest of a new southern temper W. J. Cash just might find to be both liberating and refreshing if he were to undertake a new assessment of the mind of the South today.

Afterword

PAUL D. ESCOTT

The essays in this volume raise many of the issues that enlivened the symposium convened by "Jack" Cash's *alma mater,* Wake Forest University. Despite the high quality of these essays, however, they did not exhaust the agenda of discussion, nor could they represent the spectrum of fertile minds that assembled to reconsider *The Mind of the South.* A variety of scholars and journalists, speaking from the podium and the floor, made other notable contributions that struck sparks among the large and attentive audience.[1] Ideas about the South, and about the particular entity that might be called Cash's South, multiplied as this gathering of academics and citizens developed its own momentum. This essay summarizes a few of the principal themes that emerged from five days of vigorous discussion.

Both the amateur and the professional students of the South who assembled in Winston-Salem quickly realized that the size and character of the conference demanded an explanation. Why had so many people come together to devote an entire weekend to discussing one book? Admittedly, *The Mind of the South* has been recognized for decades as an unusually influential book, but the large turnout at every session surprised most participants nonetheless. They wanted to know why everyone, presenters and members of the audience alike, had such intense

---

1. Other scholars who appeared on the program were Thadious Davis, Samuel Hill, Pete Daniel, C. Vann Woodward, George Tindall, and Dan Carter. Journalists making presentations included Ed Williams, Frye Gaillard, Marilyn Milloy, Hodding Carter III, Howell Raines, Michael Riley, Claude Sitton, and Edwin Yoder. Former Governor Gerald Baliles of Virginia also spoke as did six Conference Fellows, younger scholars and journalists whose work shows significant early achievement and great promise: Pamela Grundy, Bradley Bond, Terence Finnegan, Claudia Smith Brinson, Colin Campbell, and Jason DeParle.

interest in W. J. Cash and his sweeping but outdated interpretation. What was it about the South or the themes of Cash's book that could evoke such a strong response?

C. Vann Woodward noted that professional historians, whose faces were familiar to him, accounted for only a minority of the large audience. The presence of so many other people, he declared, constituted a "cultural phenomenon."[2] Historian Larry Tise, a native of North Carolina who now works in Pennsylvania, suggested a name for that phenomenon. "I was at a *happening*," Tise observed, "in the 1960's sense of that word." Like the 1960s "happenings," this event seemed to have its greatest attraction for a particular audience. Along with "a great number of like-minded people," Tise had come "to commune and contemplate" the mind of the South, yet he found that friends and associates back in Pennsylvania did not understand his passion. "Try as I might," reported Tise, "I was not able to explain satisfactorily to any non-southerner why" attendance at such an event was important.[3]

In an attempt to understand this phenomenon, participants offered a number of explanations. "The turnout here," commented George Tindall, "is a testimony to the continuing power of Cash to provoke both approval and disapproval in different ways and the continuing power of the book to draw both praise and blame." The numerous debates of the conference had demonstrated beyond any question, Tindall observed, that "Cash was a provocative writer." Jack Cash intended to provoke his readers, but surely even he never imagined that his impact would be so enduring.

To Woodward, however, there was more to the explanation "than a fifty-year-old book," even a book that Woodward has admitted has no rivals "in influence among laymen and few among professional historians."[4] "I think it's the subject that brings them together," he commented. "It is an original phenomenon. It's a historical urge and interest in the South that explains this outpouring of interest." Two factors were at work: the influence of Cash's ideas and a compelling concern for the South.

2. This quotation and subsequent quotations from participants at the symposium, unless otherwise noted, have been transcribed from audio recordings of the proceedings.

3. Larry Tise published his reactions in the Winston-Salem *Journal* on February 23, 1991. These quotations are taken from his article.

4. C. Vann Woodward, "The Elusive Mind of the South," in Woodward, *American Counterpoint: Slavery and Racism in the North-South Dialogue* (New York, 1983), 263.

As the scholars talked more specifically about their reactions to *The Mind of the South,* the reasons for its appeal became more clear. W. J. Cash had touched people's minds and hearts, in part, because he gave of himself profoundly. "It's my belief," said George Tindall, "that W. J. Cash wrote out of his inner consciousness. . . . It's a personal book." Others agreed that the personal dimension of Cash's writing gave it a special and memorable quality. They agreed with Richard King's judgment that Cash succeeded "where most academic historians fail: he conveys something of the joy and agony of telling a story that . . . he cared deeply about. . . . The urgency that breaks through . . . makes *The Mind of the South* still count for something, even today."[5] The passion in Cash's writing enables it to speak to people across fifty years of history.

Much of what Cash cared about, despite his shortcomings when judged by contemporary standards, involved race. It was not accidental that his continuing relevance to a large audience in 1991 also concerned the troubled issue of race. W. J. Cash lived in and was shaped by a racist culture, yet he had enough humanity to struggle against that culture's influence. Bertram Wyatt-Brown noted the importance for today's readers of that inner struggle. "The book," he commented, "is a working-out of his own sense of who he is in relationship to the culture from which he comes. . . . There's something very southern—essential southernness—about Cash himself, so he could look within and find that. I think that's the key to his genius and why we still read him. Because . . . many of us, at least many whites, can understand those very conflicts he's trying to deal with about race and prejudice."

To Dan Carter the experience of first reading *The Mind of the South* in the 1960s came back vividly. He remembered most strongly "the sense of burning injustice that drove Cash through all his many mistaken and paradoxical statements. As we have learned, his history was shaky. He was biased by his race, his class, his sex, even the subregion of the South in which he lived. But his persistent love for the region and his anger towards its imperfections drew me into the book in 1961 and still draws me to the spirit of Jack Cash." The legacy of slavery and the evil of racism were at the heart of the South's imperfections, and Carter sensed that W. J. Cash "was a moralist" who "sought to understand the source of evil in the South, which he loved."

A similar quest brought many members of the audience to Wake

---

5. These words appear in the closing lines of King's essay in this volume.

Forest. Larry Tise offered "my own experience and purpose as a case in point. I was born only a mile from the spot where we met. I grew up as a seventh- or eighth-generation southerner in that very place and lived through the rise of the civil rights movement. I was so troubled with the history of racism and repression in my community and in the South that I became a professional historian basically hoping to understand the roots of this racism and somehow to help cleanse my society of these insidious blemishes." The conference, he thought, happened "at just the right moment in time" to permit "all of us—even those of us who are spending entire careers on the subject—to seek again that very personal understanding of the historic mind of the South."

Throughout the conference members of the audience revealed this deep concern about race. Their personal histories in relation to the race issue were broadly similar to Tise's. Most were native southerners (if voluntary comments were representative), white, and over forty. They were old enough to have experienced the civil rights movement as a colossal change in southern society, and its influence on them was indelible. They seemed moved by a desire to see, at long last, a satisfactory resolution of the South's history of racial oppression. Perhaps, like Jack Cash, they had loved the South but been troubled by the evil that lay within southern culture. Cash's book, written when segregation still dominated a nearly monolithic, intolerant South, spoke to their concerns. His book was one of the first to attempt, from the inside, to analyze the morbid racism of southern life, and his "assault on superstition and entrenched prejudice"[6] struck a chord with a generation of white southern liberals. Their presence at a reconsideration of *The Mind of the South* explained much of the "cultural phenomenon" that Woodward identified.

Most probably agreed with Frye Gaillard of the Charlotte *Observer,* who defined white southerners as "recovering racists." Like alcoholics, recovering racists know that they never entirely escape their problem. To have any hope of recovering, they must acknowledge racism's continuing power and resist it consciously and continuously. Journalists Ed Williams, Marilyn Milloy, and Frye Gaillard agreed from their differing vantage points on the South that racism is still alive and may be gathering power just below the surface of daily events. This diagnosis un-

6. Gerald W. Johnson, *The Battle of Ideas* (Winston-Salem, N.C., 1975), 1–12.

derscored the relevance of Cash's message to the generation that heard his early, muted protest of racism.

The contribution of racism to the South's identity proved to be another much-debated issue. In *The Crucible of Race* Joel Williamson has argued that the connection between white racism and southernness was intimate and profound. "Southern white identity at any given time," he asserted, "was intimately bound up with the Southern white image of the Negro. . . . To let that image go, to see black people as people, was a precarious and exceedingly dangerous venture that exposed the individual to alienation from his natal culture and to the loss of his sense of self. . . . A very large part of the race problem in the South resolves itself into the question of how one takes the racism . . . out of the Southern mind without killing the Southerner."[7] His query found an echo in the passionately argued thoughts of Hodding Carter III.

To Carter the essence of the South, in Cash's time and throughout its earlier history, was white racism. That racism, or "racial bonding" among whites, formed the basis of southern identity. "I am aware," Hodding Carter acknowledged, "that there is a thesis which says that race is not central to the South's sense of itself, to the definition of an enduring South; that deeper and more important cultural matters inform our southernness." But, he declared, "I will tell you as sure as I stand here that, without the bonding of race, this conference is not going to be thinkable fifty years hence. Without that enduring reality bonding this region, you will be able to say many things of it, but not that it [is] the South of the preceding three hundred years."

Racism, Carter stressed, "still binds us down as a nation," but no longer can it be seen as "a southern dilemma." In fact, "that bonding, as a southern phenomenon, is dead, *dead*." The civil rights movement and economic development transformed the traditional South and brought multiple dimensions of change to southern life. In politics, observed Hodding Carter, "Douglas Wilder got more white votes [in Virginia in 1990] than any black candidate running north of the Mason-Dixon Line for a statewide office has ever gotten in any election, any time." In the distribution of population there has been so much migration that by "1988 roughly 50 percent of everyone who voted in

7. Joel Williamson, *The Crucible of Race: Black-White Relations in the American South Since Reconstruction* (New York, 1984), 499.

the South in the presidential election was born outside the South." As for southerners' vaunted sense of place, said Carter, "We were once the region in which people moved less than anywhere else. We are now, according to the census, the region in which people move more than anywhere else."

These changes have had their inevitable destructive effects on traditional, race-based southern culture, insisted Hodding Carter. "You, like me," he told the audience, "grew up suffused, immersed either with the results of the Old South, if you were black, or the mystique and myth of the Old South, if you were white." Today's southern students, by contrast, "know more about MTV than they know about the Lost Cause or the Old South." Carter challenged his listeners to quiz "any select group of southern white students on their understanding of their past—not the past of Thomas Dixon, not even the past proclaimed by Wilbur J. Cash; no, just the past that history might tell them about the South. And I'll tell you: They don't know, they don't care, they're not interested, they don't have a clue. . . . They are as one with their nation."

Southern distinctiveness, according to Hodding Carter, had always meant a society shaped by, and a culture bound by, white racism. That South, a region described by Cash, long endured, but today "it is the dying South; it is the South of backwater and bywater." By contrast, "I cannot tell you about an enduring South in the growing South." To Carter, both southern race relations and southern character are becoming one with the nation. Change in racial matters means the end of southern distinctiveness. Nevertheless, he acknowledged that "if, in fact, the South is dead, you can't prove it by a lot of southerners."

There was no agreement about the South's recent death or continued vitality among the experts assembled in Winston-Salem. Probably the dimensions of change in the modern era have guaranteed that any judgment must be problematic and disputed. "The South today," as Pete Daniel observed, "is vastly different from that of 1941, so different, in fact, that there is a minor industry devoted to determining if there still is 'a South,' and if so, how long it might endure and what form it may take." Among the experts present, opinion seemed to divide along occupational lines.

Journalists, whose work requires them to focus an attentive eye on the changing present, tended to agree with their colleague Hodding Carter that southern distinctiveness was gone. Claude Sitton, who asserted that "there has never been one South . . . there are and always have been many Souths," also affirmed that "the South as we have known it will *not* endure. What John Egerton called 'the Americanization of Dixie' is a *fact*." The region's peculiar political, economic, and social characteristics, he argued, "are fading fast away. Even the myths that kept old Dixie alive are being lost in that mindless electronic fog of ignorance with which television blankets our nation." The South is losing its folkways, said Sitton, because "folkways cannot compete against television, the jet plane, and the interstate highway in our mobile society." Edwin Yoder was not willing to go that far, but he declared himself frankly pessimistic about the South's survival and predicted that "Dixie has a future only if it can be 'Dixified' again," that is, if it can keep reinventing itself. Mike Riley, alone among a panel of journalists discussing the South's future, was willing to declare that "the South still stands as a land apart." Yet he conceded that change had produced "stark dualities" and rendered the region "schizophrenic."

Historians, by contrast, tended to be optimistic about the survival of southern distinctiveness. "Hodding Carter's speech on the vanishing South," George Tindall reminded the audience, "stands in one of the oldest traditions of the South." Many examples of such predictions could be cited, he observed, including the statement of a Freedmen's Bureau official in Greenville, South Carolina, in the 1860s, who expected that the "peculiar people" who surrounded him would "soon lose its peculiarity." C. Vann Woodward likewise told the Winston-Salem *Journal,* "I resist this idea of the homogenized South." Good minds are attracted to the study of southern history, he argued, because of the South's peculiarity, uniqueness, and "continued distinctiveness." Although many scholarly arguments revolve around the nature of that distinctiveness, it nonetheless is real. Woodward pointed to one delightful manifestation of it when, at lunch, he listened to a string band "playing blues, hillbilly and country music. It was wonderful. That doesn't happen in Connecticut or Minnesota."[8]

Yet the contribution that white racism made to southern distinctiveness was great, as Hodding Carter contended. Indeed, the dominant role of racism in much of southern history was one of the things that those drawn to the symposium were seeking to understand. Con-

8. "Scholar Sees Regional Differences as Enriching," Winston-Salem *Journal,* February 12, 1991, p. 8.

sequently, the racial progress of the last fifty years forces change in our definitions of southernness. The South and southern identity no longer mean what they did through most of the region's past, and new generations are growing up without the poisonous burden of white racism or "racial bonding." For this reason, Hodding Carter was right to predict that *The Mind of the South* will have an entirely different significance to readers in 2041. Historical change, one hopes, will have turned W. J. Cash's passion into a historical artifact. As the reality of Cash's savage and intolerant South ceases to be a shared and deeply felt experience, the grip of Cash's message on white southerners also will cease.

The Mind of the South has little power to grip black southerners today. That fact was apparent at the symposium, whose audience contained only a modest number of black people, despite the presence on the program of prominent African-American scholars. No questionnaires were administered and no scientific data exist to explain the comparative absence of blacks, but obviously the white racism that Cash explored never had the same intriguing character for them that it did for those whites who had absorbed racism yet wanted to break free of it. Probably black southerners never were as interested in the origins or nature of white racism as were the South's white critics. Black people had to endure the effects of racism, and they simply wanted it to end. For this reason, Cash's criticism of his natal culture could not be as interesting to African-Americans or as much of an achievement in their eyes as it seemed to white southerners.

This same important difference of experience and perspective produced the pointed criticism of Wilbur Cash by C. Eric Lincoln and Nell Irvin Painter. Because Lincoln's paper recognized valuable insights in Cash's work as well as its shortcomings, most debate centered around Nell Painter's uncompromising criticism of Cash, and particularly her judgment of him as a racist and a sexist. David Hackett Fischer, more than anyone else, stepped forward to challenge Nell Painter and argue for a different assessment of Cash.

Agreeing with Dan Carter, Fischer insisted that Cash "really did have an idea of racial justice." Moreover, "on the question of race in Cash," Fischer said, "I think it's important to render, and I think we are capable of rendering, a kind of double judgment on this man—to judge him against the standards of his time and also against those of ours. And I think it's a great mistake to judge him by only one. It's worth remembering when we judge him by his own time, that in that world he was a liberal. He spoke out against the Ku Klux Klan, against lynching, when it was not merely unpopular but dangerous to do so." Fischer admitted that "this liberalism may pale when we measure it against our standards," but he insisted that "it was very real nonetheless."

Nell Painter gave no ground in responding to these points. She returned to the unflattering descriptive language and stereotypical images of black southerners that abound in *The Mind of the South*. The language, she declared, "is really filthy, and you don't have to be a black reader to see this. You don't have to be a woman to see the patronizing language that Cash uses on women." Blanche Knopf may not have been offended by Cash's words, Painter admitted, but her own grandparents would have been offended, even in 1929, by such "racist talk." Moreover, "There were people in Cash's world who were black and white who really stood for the things he mouthed. . . . There were other people actually doing things," Painter argued, to combat the racism that Cash merely analyzed.

David Hackett Fischer granted "many things you say" but nonetheless contended that "it is possible to work out a larger and more balanced set of judgments about Cash on race and also about gender." In fact, he said, "on gender I would disagree quite head-on. There's not a lot in this book that's explicitly about gender. But if we look at what is, I should have thought you would be on Cash's side when he [analyzes] that cult of gyneolatry. That, I thought, was a step toward . . . a world where people of all races and genders are recognized as entitled to what J. R. Pole calls 'equality of esteem.' And although Cash's conversion to that idea was incomplete, and its incompleteness is part of the judgment that I suppose we render upon him, I think we still have to see the progress he was making in that direction."

Later in the conference, Fischer's perspective received some support from George Brown Tindall, both on the issue of language and on Cash's historical treatment of black southerners. "Critics of the book," Tindall remarked, "should keep in mind that parts of the book were written ironically. In many parts of the book Cash is not speaking for himself. He is speaking as the mouthpiece, the surrogate for the southern mind-set." (On this point Bruce Clayton also argued that Cash never intended many of his words to be taken as his personal opinions on southern issues.) Moreover, speaking as a pioneer in the scholarly study of southern blacks, Tindall commented: "At the time Cash wrote there wasn't much history that depicted blacks as anything other than the static image of people who were part of the background, who were acted upon, who were not actors themselves. Cash at least was vaguely aware of . . . W. E. B. Du Bois and James Weldon Johnson." By modern standards, Cash's grasp of black aspirations and initiative is sorely deficient, but Tindall saw progress compared with most writers of his day.

Drawing on his personal experiences as a southerner, Tindall also offered a defense of the overall picture presented in *The Mind of the South*. "[Cash and I] did grow up in similar milieus twenty-one years apart and I guess approximately one hundred miles apart," said Tindall, who thus had an experiential basis for assessing Cash's portrait of the piedmont. "What [Cash] had learned in growing up, what he picked up leaning back against that courthouse wall in Shelby, is the same sort of thing that I picked up hanging around the family hardware store in Greenville, South Carolina." The society Cash tried to represent or speak for is not a pretty sight, but Tindall warned, "Don't shoot the messenger who brings us a picture of the South of that time."

If Cash's language created problems for the conference's participants, they admitted to having problems of their own with language. Nell Painter's attack on Cash, and a complaint from the audience that white females were not represented among the speakers, raised issues that many people cared about but felt unable to discuss comfortably. "White males," reported one newspaper, "found themselves unexpectedly on the defensive,"[9] and most people—whether male or female, black or white—were hesitant to address questions of sexism and racism publicly. Jason DeParle of the New York *Times* broke the silence in a closing session by acknowledging that "I heard white males say they wanted to respond to [Nell Painter] but didn't know how. They were afraid that if they stood up and said certain things, they'd say them wrong. They'd be accused of being racist or defending the indefensible. There's a clog in dialogue on that issue."

So clogged were the channels of discourse, in fact, that there was no dialogue. Amid whispered private comments about gender issues, only Dan Carter had the temerity to express a concern openly, and he prefaced his remark by admitting that "I'm the wrong one to say this: a white man." Nevertheless, he asked, "If we have embraced a new ideal in which men and women, black and white, particularly those who have suffered the sting of oppression, are encouraged to embrace their sepa-

9. Raleigh *News and Observer*, February 17, 1991.

rate group identity, must we also abandon, in our history and in our common life, the search for common ground?" What troubled Carter—a feeling of "fragmentation and division"—was something that many participants in the conference desired to overcome. That desire had helped bring them, as it brought Larry Tise, to Winston-Salem, but few saw any way to talk about what mattered.

It was as difficult to discuss race as it was to examine gender. C. Vann Woodward criticized "racial chauvinism" and said that the word "racism . . . has become a cliché . . . that can go in countless directions." Later, away from the audience, he explained to a reporter that he disapproved of "this business of the black origins of everything. And this 'multicultural' business. I deplore it. It's nonsense. We have, with all our differences, a common culture."[10] Mike Riley had the frankness to declare that "there's a subtle racism at work for both blacks and whites" in today's South. "Blacks sometimes cry racism when it's not there," he remarked, and "whites too often are insensitive and too impatient." Others undoubtedly agreed with him and would have liked to make his comments the starting point for discussion, but the issues were too explosive and the potential for misunderstanding too great. "Both sides," Riley accurately observed, "are paralyzed by confusion."

American society today, commented Jason DeParle, lacks the means to talk about sensitive issues of race, gender, and poverty. "As a society we're looking for an ideology and a vocabulary for how to address these problems," especially problems of persistent poverty. "We are caught up in our own complicated emotions and mythology toward these problems," DeParle argued, just as "in similar ways the South was caught up in its mythology" in Cash's day. In America of the 1990s there is a "tremendous need for someone to do the same thing" for social welfare issues that Cash did for race and intolerance in the South. "What Cash did provide, imperfectly and incompletely," concluded DeParle, "was a language of dissent, and a way of breaking free of myths, and a way of beginning to address an injustice in society."

Few southern journalists today are following Cash's lead, lamented Colin Campbell of the Atlanta *Journal* and the Atlanta *Constitution*. "I find it sad that modern southern journalism . . . seems [to have] so little room and talent for Cash's brand of regional criticism, for his passion,

10. *Ibid.* For a fuller exposition of Woodward's views, see his review of *Illiberal Education* by Dinesh D'Souza in the *New York Review of Books*, July 18, 1991, pp. 32–37.

his mockery, satire, anger, desire to demythologize." Cash's editors forbade him to write about Charlotte, and Campbell noted that the same thing happens today. A lengthy, serious, critical piece on the South by a southern journalist has become "a rarity." "I certainly don't see much of it in Georgia," said Campbell, who concluded that the reasons for this dearth of critical writing lie not "in Cashian habits of mind [but] in the homogenization and centralization of the news media, not to mention their mediocrity and boosterism."

Southern journalism also needs to rise to the challenge of full and unslanted reporting, said Claudia Smith Brinson of the *State* in Columbia, South Carolina. "As a journalist I have decided that when I look back into the past and how we covered the South, I cannot find the truth." Her retrospective investigations of South Carolina in the 1960s revealed that many voices of dissent and many initiatives against the status quo were never reported. "Events were covered only from the end result and were covered only by the white male spokesmen. . . . We as journalists are told that we write the first draft of history. What does that mean for history if we have left out all those voices?" To uncover a more complete record of events, Brinson found that she had to become "a detective. . . . But if those voices are missing, do we have history? I think not."

As a journalist and as a writer, W. J. Cash helped direct southerners' attention to realities that many preferred to ignore. Perhaps in Cash's creative criticism of society everyone can still appreciate his contribution to understanding the South. Otherwise, opinion differed on whether his analysis of southern culture retains any modern applicability. Claude Sitton judged that Cash had admirably described the region's politics in an earlier era, an era of "outrageous" politicians such as Eugene Talmadge, who manipulated the "rural rustics." Talmadge knew that his voters were "gut-driven, susceptible to emotional appeals, ready to be gulled by political irrationality." Despite the accuracy of the portrait, however, Sitton declared, "that politics has passed into history."

Not so, at least not in Alabama, was the contrary judgment of Howell Raines. "In the twenty-seven years I've been a reporter," Raines told the audience, "one of the enduring paradoxes of New South politics has been the tendency of southerners to vote against their own financial and social interests." "My native Alabama," he said, "has been operated as an economic colony of the Northeast since 1900," with modern paper companies replacing U.S. Steel as the state's "principal absentee landlords." Corporations enjoy "the region's lowest property taxes" while the state "has Third World infant mortality rates" and a school system "starved for money. Yet last fall—and here we're coming to the paradox that I think Cash can help us penetrate—Alabama re-elected a governor who has pledged to preserve the tax breaks of the paper companies that are now using the state as one vast tree farm." Cash's analysis, Raines concluded, was still on target. It laid bare the historical roots of "a habit of political servitude, a habit of obedience that is deeply rooted in our psyche, and is influencing the political choices of voters up to this day."

Most of the historians and journalists seemed to agree, however, that the South described by W. J. Cash was now part of history. The avalanche of social, economic, and political change that has swept over the South since 1941 created a different country. W. J. Cash had a part in that transformation. *The Mind of the South* helped launch a process of change that was to assume dimensions Cash himself could not have imagined. But he saw and described the first cracks in the structure of orthodoxy and intolerance, and his writing inspired a generation or more of like-minded southerners to respond critically to the mores of their native region.

That writing, for all its faults, won the admiration of most partici-pants in the conference. Conceived and expressed in passion, *The Mind of the South* was not dull or academic writing. It was written "with energy, sometimes with brilliance," in the words of Tom Howard of the Richmond *Times-Dispatch*.[11] George Tindall suggested that we should not judge Cash "by the historical standards of another day. He be-longed to a higher calling—that of a journalist and writer. I see *The Mind of the South* as a work of the imagination."

Imaginative it was, and audacious. The audacity of Cash's title, "*the* mind of *the* South," noted Ray Jenkins of the Baltimore *Sun,* "is in itself a little breathtaking."[12] It also is not likely to be seen again because all of us know full well that today's South is no longer of one mind. The change that Cash helped to bring has allowed diverse voices to flourish and the rich variety in southern culture to express itself. "Cash's masterpiece," said Sam Hill, "is linear and arrowlike. The South's his-

11. Richmond *Times-Dispatch,* February 17, 1991.
12. Baltimore *Sun,* February 17, 1991.

tory, by contrast, is 'thick' and textured." Predicted Dan Carter: "We will never again in our lifetime, we'll *never* again, see the kind of 'linear, arrowlike' work of W. J. Cash . . . because we so clearly see now those many voices . . . the complexity of voices. No one would be foolish enough to attempt that kind of analysis of southern culture, for we see that the search for a single mind . . . is an illusion."

Surely Dan Carter is right, at least about the complexity of southern minds and voices. Yet Cash's achievement still stands as a challenge to future writers and scholars. *The Mind of the South,* as Hill reminded the audience, is "not history in the usual academic sense. This is an essay in interpretation." And what Cash wrought with his passion and imagination, what he produced in his personal interpretation, Hill concluded, "is a phenomenon. I once heard Talcott Parsons say of Emile Durkheim and *The Elementary Forms of the Religious Life,* 'He wrote only one book on religion, but what a book!' Cash too wrote only one, but what a book."

Contributors

MERLE BLACK is Asa G. Candler Professor of Politics and Government at Emory University. With Earl Black he authored *Politics and Society in the South* (Cambridge, Mass., 1987).

BRUCE CLAYTON is Harry A. Logan, Sr., Professor of American History at Allegheny College and the author of *W. J. Cash: A Life* (Baton Rouge, 1991).

DAVID HACKETT FISCHER, Professor of History at Brandeis University, is known for several works, including *Albion's Seed: Four British Folkways in America* (New York, 1989).

RAYMOND GAVINS is Professor of History at Duke University. His publications include *The Perils and Prospects of Southern Black Leadership: Gordon Blaine Hancock, 1884–1970* (Durham, 1977).

ELIZABETH JACOWAY has taught at the University of Florida and the University of Arkansas. She has published *Yankee Missionaries in the South: The Penn School Experiment* (Baton Rouge, 1980) and contributed to and coedited *Southern Businessmen and Desegregation* (Baton Rouge, 1982).

RICHARD KING is Reader in American Studies at the University of Nottingham, England. He is the author of *A Southern Renaissance: The Cultural Awakening of the American South, 1930–1955* (New York, 1980).

JACK TEMPLE KIRBY, the W. E. Smith Professor of History at Miami University, most recently published *Rural Worlds Lost: The American South, 1930–1960* (Baton Rouge, 1987).

C. ERIC LINCOLN is Professor of Religion and Culture at Duke University. The most recent of his many books is *The Black Church in the African American Experience* (Durham, 1990).

NELL IRVIN PAINTER, the Edwards Professor of History at Princeton University, is the author of *The Narrative of Hosea Hudson: His Life as a Negro Communist in the South* (Cambridge, Mass., 1979) and other works. She is currently writing a biography of the feminist abolitionist Sojourner Truth.

GAVIN WRIGHT, Professor of Economics at Stanford University, has written *The Political Economy of the Cotton South* (New York, 1978) and *Old South, New South: Revolutions in the Southern Economy Since the Civil War* (New York, 1986).

BERTRAM WYATT-BROWN is Milbauer Professor of History at the University of Florida. Among his many publications are *Yankee Saints and Southern Sinners* (Baton Rouge, 1985) and *Southern Honor: Ethics and Behavior in the Old South* (New York, 1982).

Index